CRIMINAL ESCAPADES

A GENERAL HISTORY OF THE MOST NOTORIOUS GANGSTERS

BY

SETH FERRANTI

Copyright © 2021 Seth Ferranti

All rights reserved. This book or any portion thereof may not be reproduced or used in any manner whatsoever without the express written permission by the publisher except for the use of brief quotations for a book review.

Gorilla Convict Publications (St. Louis)
www.gorillaconvict.com

Book design by trashpandia.art

ISBN 978-0-98897-604-7

TABLE OF CONTENTS

CHAPTER 1 CARMINE "THE SNAKE" PERSICO
A BOSS BEHIND BARS

Persico was a gangster's gangster—a stone-cold killer who maintained his position as boss of NYC's Colombo Crime Family despite being sentenced to 139 years in prison in the 1980's.

CHAPTER 2 JOE "PEG LEG" MORGAN
THE WHITE MEXICAN MAFIA LEADER

By the time Joe 'Peg Leg' Morgan joined the Mexican Mafia, he was already a jailhouse legend. Because of his reputation, which included murder, bank robberies and jail escapes, he became the unofficial godfather of *El Eme*.

CHAPTER 3 NATE "BOONE" CRAFT
EVOLUTION OF A HITMAN

Boone was a legendary hitman in blood drenched Detroit, eventually confessing to roughly 30 murders as part of a plea agreement that saw him spend 20 years in the witness protection program.

CHAPTER 4 GRISELDA "BLACK WIDOW" BLANCO
THE GODMOTHER OF COCAINE

In the 1970's and 80's, Griselda Blanco was at the forefront of the Medellin Cartel's move into the US's burgeoning cocaine market.

CHAPTER 5 EUGENE "NICK THE BLADE" GEUSALE
A REAL LIFE *GOODFELLA*

"Nick the Blade" Gesuale was a notorious capo in the Genovese crime family who was the infamous "Pittsburgh Connect" in the movie *Goodfellas*.

CHAPTER 6 DAWOOD IBRAHIM
THE BOMBAY DON WHO BECAME A TERRORIST

The Italian Mafia gets all the props in the chronicles of gangster lore, but Dawood Ibrahim and D-Company have ruled India's criminal underworld for decades.

CHAPTER 7 JOSÉ MIGUEL BATTLE, "EL PADRINO"
THE CORPORATION'S CUBAN GODFATHER

When people think about Cuban gangsters, Scarface immediately pops to mind, but José Miguel Battle, the godfather of the Cuban Mafia, made Tony Montana look tame in comparison.

CHAPTER 8 THE ARYAN BROTHERHOOD
SHAMROCKS AND SHOTCALLERS

The history of America's most notorious prison gang is rife with murders, mostly of their own members, and race wars, mostly with the DC Blacks prison gang, and several infamous prison guard killings.

CHAPTER 9 KENNETH "SUPREME" MCGRIFF
THE SUPREME TEAM DEFINE THE CRACK ERA

The Supreme Team took over the streets and became hip-hop legends. In the chronicles of gangsta rap's lyrical lore one drug crew stands above the rest in infamy due to their notorious status on the streets.

CHAPTER 10 "LITTLE VIC" AMUSO & "GASPIPE" CASSO
THE CREW THAT TRIED TO WHACK JERSEY

The story behind the New Jersey/New York mafia war between factions of the Lucchese crime family. When tensions flare and betrayals occur, the order goes out: kill them all!

CHAPTER 11   WILLIE FALCON & SAL MAGLUTA
MIAMI'S O.G. COCAINE COWBOYS

Willie Falcon and his partner Sal Magluta were the biggest cocaine kingpins in Miami when Colombian cartels were making it snow in the sunshine state.

CHAPTER 12   PAVLE "PUNCH" STAMIROVIC
LEGACY OF THE PINK PANTHERS

Operating from London to Tokyo, the Pink Panthers' exploits are reminiscent of Hollywood films like *Oceans 11* and *Reservoir Dogs*, but no one knows the group originated in America.

CHAPTER 13   CASH MONEY BROTHERS
EVEN MIKE TYSON WAS FAIR GAME

Brooklyn was a brutal breeding ground for gangsters and the lessons learned were passed down from generation to generation. The landscape and players changed, but the mentality stayed the same.

CHAPTER 14   THE KANSAS CITY MOB
THE CASINO SKIM THAT MADE MILLIONS

The movie *Casino* showed the glitz and glamour of Las Vegas and how the mob controlled the casino skim, but it didn't show the back story about who was pulling the strings—the Kansas City Mafia.

CHAPTER 15   *VORY V ZAKONE* "THIEVES-IN-LAW"
RUSSIAN GANGS OF NEW YORK

From the gulags of Siberia to the streets of New York City, the *Vory v Zakone* have made the Russian Mafia a force in the criminal underworld.

CHAPTER 16   RICHARD "THE ICEMAN" KUKLINSKI
THE PSYCHO MAFIA HITMAN

Kuklinski, immortalized in the Hollywood film *The Iceman* starring Michael Shannon, was a bonafide Mafia hitman and borderline serial killer who not only murdered people for money, but for his own enjoyment.

CHAPTER 17   BAC GUAI
CHINATOWN'S WHITE DEVIL

John Willis grew up in the working class neighborhood of Dorchester, Massachusetts playing hockey like the rest of the Catholic kids, before transcending race and becoming one of the most notorious gangsters in Boston's Chinatown.

CHAPTER 18   WHITEY BULGER
HE PLAYED THE FEDS ... AND LOST

From convict to Irish crime boss, Bulger was an enigma in Boston during his reign and became a legend when he eluded the feds for multiple decades.

CHAPTER 19   PETER "BIG PETE" JAMES
THE GODFATHER OF THE OUTLAWS

Outlaw motorcycle clubs don't subscribe to the Mafia hierarchy, but one man in Chicago became the godfather of the Outlaws.

CHAPTER 20   POP CULTURE
HOW POP CULTURE WHACKED THE MOB

Mob bosses like John Gotti, Lucky Luciano, and Al Capone have become household names and criminal celebrities in a pop culture that has hastened the Mafia's demise.

CARMINE "THE SNAKE" PERSICO
A BOSS BEHIND BARS

Carmine "The Snake" Persico's status in the American Mafia was something of an anomaly. He wasn't a rat and was even powerful enough during his multiple decade reign to call shots from prison after being convicted in the infamous Commission Trial. The Brooklyn don has become possibly one of the most polarizing mob figures of the last fifty years, both in the underworld and in mainstream pop culture. He was the last real mob boss of our time—a certified old-school OG, who some have labeled "The Immortal."

But others argue with equal passion that Persico was only ever out for one person—himself—and that persona led to him being called, "The Snake." Persico was a vicious and cunning mobster that betrayed his comrades to get ahead. His immortal legacy echoes throughout the universe of American mob bosses, criminal underworld, and beyond. To be able to keep power that long from inside prison speaks to the respect he and his family commanded on the street. When Persico died so did the real American Mafia.

JUST A KID FROM BROOKLYN

"His rise in the criminal underworld had a very atypical origin," said Christian Cipollini, the author of *Murder Inc.: Mysteries of the Mob's Most Deadly Hit Squad*. "Persico's family had it pretty good. His youth didn't bear the earmarks of poverty. That said, Persico grew up in an era when legit business folks had nothing on the 'respect' that a lot of Brooklyn kids may have sought and found in the wise-guys who basically ran the show, so to speak."

Persico, like many other kids from New York in the mid-twentieth century, looked at the mob guys with a gleam in their eyes. To the Brooklyn kids, the mobsters were the rock stars of their neighborhood. They represented a way of life that defied the law and did things their own way. Persico came up through the streets at a young age. He was a hot-headed, tough little guy who dropped out of school and joined a local gang, the Garfield Boys, where he made his mark while still just a teenager. The youngster upped the ante when he allegedly killed a rival during a brawl.

"In 1950, Carmine's Garfield Boys had a rumble with the Tigers in front of the boathouse in Prospect Park, a fight over a girl just like in *West Side Story*," said Michael Benson, the co-author of *Carmine the Snake: Carmine Persico and His Murderous Mafia Family*. "When it was over, one Tiger was dead with bullets in his guts and another writhed on the ground clutching stab wounds. No one remembers a time when Carmine wasn't a gangster. In grade school he shook down students for their lunch money. He was the kid who, for a price, promised to watch the car for you so nothing bad could happen to it while you were away."

The street brawl incident earned Persico major street credibility, particularly piquing the interest of a Profaci family capo. From there on he moved up the ranks as a good earner and, when needed, a guy who could bring the muscle. By the time he turned twenty, he'd already been arrested for murder twice. When he got old enough, he started working his way into the Profaci family, who were already controlling the Red Hook area of Brooklyn. With a reputation as a tough guy, Persico found that his talents were in high demand.

"That's how he got started. Him and his brother, Allie Boy, started moving up the ladder," explains Frank Dimatteo, who co-wrote *Carmine the Snake: Carmine Persico and His Murderous Mafia Family* and was a Mafia associate himself during the era. Persico was a gangster's gangster. A man whose life served as the inspiration for not only *West Side Story*, but *The Godfather* too. "He was cocky and blunt, an immovable object, the guy who was in charge—his every word and gesture designed to enhance his own wealth and control," Benson says. "Persico acquired power the way other men breathe."

MAKING HIS BONES

A gangster on the rise, Carmine "The Snake" Persico elevated his reputation in a stunning manner. In 1957, he participated in one of the most infamous hits ever with the brazen assassination of Murder Inc's head honcho, Albert Anastasia. It was his most defining mob moment. Allegedly, Persico and cohort Larry Gallo took credit for the shooting. Some accounts state Persico "made his bones" that day and he became a "made man" because of it. "It wouldn't be Carmine Persico if he didn't make his bones in spectacular fashion," Michael Benson said. "Young Carmine fulfilled the last of his requirements for getting his button when he became one of the barbershop quartet."

Bumping off Albert Anastasia as he was being shaved on Park Avenue, changed the course of mob history. Persico became a made man at twenty-four, the youngest in family history. Him, Joey Gallo, Larry Gallo, and Joe Jelly allegedly got the orders to go kill Albert. Jelly, the Gallo Brothers, and Persico went and killed him. Two gunmen went in, Joe Jelly and Joey Gallo. "That's who allegedly did the actual shooting. Larry and Persico were back up," Frank Dimatteo says. But the hit made Persico's career and marked him as an up-and-coming gangster in New York City at an early age.

THE COLOMBO WARS AND PRISON TIME

"Persico's rep for being merciless in his mob affairs goes all the way back to the first Colombo Family War of the 1960's where he earned his alternate nickname, 'The Snake', for his treachery," relates Scott Burnstein, the author of *Mafia Prince: Inside America's Most Violent Crime Family and the Bloody Fall of La Cosa Nostra*. "His heavy lifting on the front lines in that conflict got him bumped to a capo post, which put him in position to take the boss chair in the years to come."

Historically, Carmine and Crazy Joe Gallo, came up in the streets together. They were very close and in the same crew at one time. What happened was that Gallo and his brothers wanted to pull away from the Profaci's because they didn't like the leadership. They didn't think Joe Profaci was a good boss. They accused Profaci of stiffing the rank and file from a fair share of the family profits. The Gallo brothers were renegades and when they were plotting and trying to get the other captains to go on their side to make this move to break away, Persico was with them.

"At one point, Profaci got to Carmine and offered him something lucrative," Dimatteo said. "Persico invited Larry Gallo to a meeting and Larry, not knowing that Carmine already went back with Joe Profaci, went to see him. When he arrived Persico tried to kill Larry. That's when the first war started and it started getting hotter and hotter after that." Carmine's old running partner Larry would have been dead that day in 1961 at the Sahara Lounge in Brooklyn if a beat cop hadn't wandered in, wondering why the door was open on a Sunday morning. The attempted bar room hit became fodder for a scene in *The Godfather*.

After the attempted hit Persico was dubbed "The Snake" for switching sides during the internal mob war, which came to be known as the first Colombo War. This was the first of many times that Persico used deception and double-crossing to make his move and climb the ladder. In the Mafia, treachery is rewarded, friends kill friends to become the top dog. Frank "Punchy" Illiano, a Genovese capo was the one who gave Persico his infamous moniker. Carmine was going to court with his guys as Punchy was coming out. They had a confrontation and Punchy told Persico, "You're a fucking snake."

"That's how it stuck," Dimatteo said. "The Gallos always referred to Carmine as 'The Snake'. That's how it started from the Gallo crew doing it. After Profaci, Joe Colombo took over. He made peace in 1964 with the Gallo brothers. At the time, Persico was in jail for another short bid. Joe Colombo was the boss between 1964 and 1972 and Carmine Persico was a skipper. His crew was very strong. They ran all of one side of South Brooklyn and even intermingled with the Gallos at the time. The Gallos were part of the Profaci family, which then turned into Colombos."

Even after the war the crews weren't separated. They were shylocking in the same neighborhood. These guys, before the shooting started, had clubs together. Then in between the war, they had to hide because they were shooting at each other because of the beef. Then after it was all over, they had to figure out what to do. Who's taking the club? Who's not taking the club? Who's taking the numbers? That's why it was a big headache. It wasn't just one gang fighting another gang—it was an internal battle! After the shooting stopped, everybody had to go back together again.

"The dudes that shot each other, were hiding from each other," Dimatteo said. "It was a very difficult situation. Carmine had a strong crew. He had Hugh McIntosh, Gerry Lang, he had Scarpa. You get a deadly crew around you, it makes you look good. They all earned. When Joe Colombo got shot, Carmine was the front runner. He was in line to take over. That's why he became acting boss, at the time, until the Commission okayed it. That's how Carmine got that position. He was in jail and had to leave Joseph 'Joe Yac' Yacovelli, who was under him, in charge."

Crazy Joe Gallo was doing his own bid and when he got out in 1971, Persico put an open hit order on him, igniting the second Colombo War. A Gallo member was ultimately blamed for the Joe Colombo shooting but an open hit is an open hit. It means anybody can take the shot. There was no love loss. When Joey was executed, the Persicos became kings of the Colombo hill. Carmine was acting boss at the time because Joe Colombo was a vegetable. Carmine was in jail again but Yacovelli was running things for him in the streets.

"When there was a challenge to his leadership with the Colombos, all-out war broke out," Benson says. "Carmine loved wartime. He was always on the winning side, even when The Snake had to stab his so-called friends in the back to do it."

THE COMMISSION TRIAL

"The Persicos were a large family, with an ominous presence within the Colombos," says Larry McShane, author of *Chin: The Life and Crimes of Mafia Boss Vincent Gigante*. "Carmine's brothers Alphonse and Theodore joined the Profaci-led family while young, and a second generation followed. The Persicos took over following Joe Colombo's shooting. The Snake's son, Little Allie Boy, became his voice in the family, and another son, Michael, became a powerful figure." But that power didn't stop the law from continuing to convict Persico of crimes relating to his mafia leadership.

In 1986, the Mafia Commission Trial began. Five mob chieftains were indicted as the federal government, with lead prosecutor Rudy Giuliani, tried to take down the mob's hierarchy by convicting the bosses who resided on the commission. Big Paul Castellano, Fat

Tony Salerno, Tony Ducks Corallo, Rusty Rastelli, and Persico were all facing time for being the heads of New York's five families. At the trial Persico decided to represent himself. He had been through so many cases that he thought he was the best person to defend himself against the charges. It would prove to be a big mistake.

"He's an intelligent guy," Dimatteo explains. "He's the one that looks for the money. Hundreds of thousands of dollars for attorneys. He thought he was smart enough to do it himself. A lot of guys wouldn't do that. Carmine just had the balls to do it. He really thought they had nothing on him. He really felt that it was all hearsay and bullshit. He thought he was gonna win that. He put a good argument up, which even the judge complimented him on. But you ain't gonna win against the feds."

Rudy Giuliani's war on the mob stirred such a panic across New York's five families that a meeting of the bosses was called, wherein the suggestion of having the zealot prosecutor whacked came up. "Three of the five bosses gave the idea a thumbs down," said Cipollini. "But two others, John Gotti—who came into power after killing Castellano—and Carmine Persico, argued for killing Giuliani. However, majority ruled and Rudy's life was spared."

Giuliani hated the mafia and Persico in particular with a passion. He wasn't pulling any punches and was on a mission to throw the book at Persico and the other mafia leaders. Persico knew it was part of the game, but has often reflected on Giuliani. In prison he told Robert Rosso, a convicted meth dealer doing life, "I've been in prison almost thirty years and I'm still married. I talk to my wife every night, she comes and sees me, and I have kids that I love and adore whom I'm close to. Giuliani's been married three times and his kids hate him so much they won't even talk to him. Who's the dog?"

MAINTAINING POWER

"His brother 'Allie Boy,' his son 'Little Allie Boy,' and his cousin 'Mush' Russo have all been acting bosses for Junior," Burnstein said. "Mush Russo has kept the family dynasty going more recently. Little Allie Boy was convicted in the 1999 murder of underboss 'Wild Bill' Cutolo, the last true threat to Persico's mob regime." Persico wanted to do just one thing with his life: be the leader of a gang. His dream came true as a teenager as boss of the Garfield Boys, the toughest and deadliest gang out there. And his dream came true again years later when he became the boss of the Colombo crime family.

"The reason Carmine stayed in power for as long as he did, was because he was smart," Benson relates. "Gangsters wanted him in charge even if he was behind bars. Carmine fucked up less than the rest of them, by a lot. After going away for good, he used his most trusted men, guys he'd known since the days of the Garfield Boys, to courier information to and from his federal penitentiary." Alphonse "Little Allie Boy" Persico was eventually his successor. The Snake could deal directly with his son rather than using back channels.

"He knew the best way to keep power from behind bars was by creating a blood family dynasty that ensured loyalty," said Burnstein. "Empower close relatives, a son, brothers, nephews, and cousins to run the show on your behalf. The Snake's as crafty and resourceful as any American mob boss of his era. Persico is a rare blend of intelligence, charisma, and lethality—the perfect combination of racketeer and monster. It served him very well in terms of being able to keep his mob empire intact without having been on the street in three and a half decades." But there were always challenges to his authority and this led to the Third Colombo War.

"This is the point where things went a bit haywire," McShane said. "While the Snake was locked up, control of the family went to Little Vic Orena, a highly regarded guy who became involved with the family as a teen. He had two sons in the Colombos and they were all tight with the Persico's. Orena took his seat with bosses John Gotti and Chin Gigante. But the Snake predictably turned on Orena. The biggest and bloodiest war followed as bodies piled up and turncoat rats came out. The family was decimated by bullets, defections, and trials, with close to sixty members imprisoned. The Colombo clan never recovered from the mess."

Persico was able to maintain power for so long from behind bars because the same guys that spent their teen years terrorizing every neighborhood from Brooklyn Heights to Canarsie with him became the nucleus of his crew. "Some of those boys hanging out with Carmine as kids, taking joy rides, and stealing hubcaps, were still with him, loyal and true blue, right up until the time the RICO laws nabbed them all," explains Benson. "As the years passed, his control slipped. One by one his couriers went away and he became a largely spiritual leader for what was left of the Colombos after the RICO trials."

PRISON LIFE FOR THE MAFIA DON

"Whoever of Persico's crew that wasn't locked up took care of him," Dimatteo says. "With the boss away, his guys were loyal and did what they were supposed to do. They followed the rules. They kept him in power. Then he put his son in charge. Little Allie Boy is doing a life bid now. He was in the street. He took care of it for years. That's why he's doing one-hundred years now. Allie Persico Jr. was the boss. His father turned it over to him. He's the one that's doing the life bid now and The Snake is doing one hundred thirty-nine years."

In prison, the staff treated Carmine with respect because that's the way he treated them. Everyday, he woke up around nine in the morning and read the *New York Post*. In the afternoons, he would go to the yard and play bocce ball. On Tuesdays, Thursdays, and Sunday he cooked meals—the best linguini and white clam sauce in the Bureau of Prisons. He was a legendary gangster while still a teenager, and boss of a New York crime family longer than anyone. When he faced the music for his crimes, he stayed true to his vow, kept his mouth shut, and spent the last four decades of his life in prison.

"Carmine was a total gentleman," recalls Rosso, who did time with the gangster. "I have been in prison twenty-one years, I've been around scores of mobsters, and never have I met nor been around anyone as classy as Carmine. Far from some *mafioso* who act like they're above everyone else, Carmine treats people with respect, hates to be referred to as a 'mob boss' or 'old man,' and is really a pleasure to be around."

Many inmates were star-struck around him and they either wanted his autograph or wanted to hear John Gotti-style war stories. But that wasn't Carmine. To those inmates, he was polite, but he had nothing for them. What Rosso misses most about the legendary mob boss were the long conversations they used to have. "We talked about history, politics, you name it. I remember a family member of his sent him a bunch of photos that were taken way back when Carmine was a kid. To see Brooklyn with dirt roads, horses, and vegetable gardens in the neighborhood was incredible."

Rosso remembers Persico getting a lot of visits from his wife, children, and grandchildren. "He called his wife every night for ten minutes and when the Corrlinks email system came online for prisoners, I taught him how to email. Once he got the hang of it he loved it. He really enjoyed emailing his grandkids and keeping in touch with his family. The guy is almost a hundred years old. I think that Carmine's probably one of the last old school, real tough guys left. I really do."

THE COLOMBO CRIME FAMILY

CARMINE PERSICO
"Junior, The Snake, The Immortal"
Boss
Imprisoned (1986)
Deceased (2019)

ALPHONSE PERSICO
"Allie Boy"
Acting Boss
Imprisoned (2000)
Deceased (1989)

THOMAS FARESE
"Tom Mix"
Consigliere
Acquitted (2012)

JOHN FRANZESE
"Sonny"
Underboss
Imprisoned (1967, 2011)
Deceased (2020)

BENJAMIN CASTELLAZZO
"The Claw"
Acting Underboss
Imprisoned (2013)
Released (2015)

ANDREW RUSSO
"Andy Mush"
Street Boss
Imprisoned (1986, 1999, 2013)

DENNIS DELUCIA
"Fat Dennis"
Capo
Imprisoned (2014)

DOMINIC MONTEMARANO
"Donnie Shacks"
Capo
Imprisoned (1984, 2003)
Deceased (2021)

JAMES CLEMENZA
"Jimmy Green Eyes"
Capo
Imprisoned (2013)
Deceased (2021)

JOSEPH BAUDANZA
Capo
Imprisoned (2007)
Released (2011)

MICHAEL UVINO
Capo
Imprisoned (2009)

RALPH LAMBARDO
"Ralphie"
Capo
Imprisoned (1986, 1999, 2013)

THEODORE PERSICO
"Teddy"
Capo
Imprisoned (1986)
Deceased (2017)

THOMAS GIOELI
"Tommy Shots"
Capo
Imprisoned (2014)

WILLIAM RUSSO
"Billy"
Capo
Free

ANTHONY RUSSO
"Chuckie"
Soldier
Free

CHARLES PANARELLA
"Moose"
Soldier
House Arrest (2008)
Deceased (2017)

DINO SARACINO
"Little Dino"
Soldier
Imprisoned (2009)

MICHAEL CATAPANO
Soldier
Imprisoned (2010)
Released (2016)

RALPH F. DELEO
Soldier
Imprisoned (2012)

THEODORE N. PERSICO, JR.
"Teddy Boy"
Soldier
Imprisoned (2013)
Released (2015)

VINCENT DEMARTINO
"Chickie"
Soldier
Imprisoned (2007)

VINCENT LANGELLA
Soldier
Imprisoned (2003)
Deceased (2015)

VINCENZO ALOI
"Vinny"
Soldier
Imprisoned (1973)
Released (1985)

LAWRENCE PERSICO
Associate
Imprisoned (2005)
Released (2005)

SEAN PERSICO
Associate
Free

THE DON'S NICKNAMES

His friends and associates called Persico, "Junior." His detractors, the Gallo Brothers, called him, "The Snake." And lastly, his followers have dubbed him, "The Immortal."

JUNIOR

Persico's fans, friends, and associates called him "Junior". His real name was Carmine Persico, Jr., so the name fits. It was an easy shorthand in criminal circles so as not to identify him by his real name.

THE SNAKE

The uncomplimentary nickname of "The Snake" came from crazy Joey Gallo and his brothers, who went to war twice with the family hierarchy. First they took on Joe Profaci, then his successor Joe Colombo, who was famously whacked at a rally in Columbus Circle after Joey was released from prison. The second war ended with Joey's murder in Umberto's Clam House in Little Italy.

THE IMMORTAL

Over the years of his storied mafia career Persico has become on the of the last old school guys. He's never snitched on his comrades or betrayed the code of *omertà*. Persico is a certified O.G. who carried it like the old-time *mafioso*.

2

JOE "PEG LEG" MORGAN
A WHITE MEXICAN MAFIA LEADER

There's a scene in the movie *American Me* where actor William Forsythe, who plays J.D., the character based on the legendary Mexican Mafia godfather, Joe "Peg Leg" Morgan, hits the yard at Deuel Vocational Institution as a newbie and is immediately confronted by white prisoners. The whites quickly realize that J.D. isn't the typical "peckerwood" when he responds to them in Spanish and a group of Mexican-American gangsters roll up glaring at "the woods", embracing J.D. as one of their own.

The scene goes even more in depth when one of the Mexican-Americans questions the shot caller Santana about J.D. being white and rolling with them. Santana kills the issue by letting his homeboy know that J.D. was down with the clique. He was a young man with heart, courage, and discipline who would become a top shot caller in the vicious prison gang known as *La Eme*—an ever present and dangerous entity in California's Department of Corrections.

"Joe Morgan was a nails-tough Croatian who grew up in a Hispanic neighborhood in East LA," explains Scott Burnstein, who runs *gangsterreport.com*. "Morgan was incarcerated for forty years for crimes ranging from bank robbery to murder. He escaped jail twice, committed murders like he had a license, developed Mexican cartel connections, and ties to the Italian Mafia."

Morgan became the unofficial leader of *La Eme*—the godfather of the baddest prison gang to ever do it. Some would even say he was the brain and drive behind the Mexican Mafia's rise to power in the criminal underworld. In the chronicles of gangster lore, he was the equivalent to a John Gotti or Pablo Escobar-type figure—an infamous gangster known for cold bloodedness, ruthless ways, intelligence, and charm.

HE BECAME A PRISON CELEBRITY

"Although Slavic culturally, he adopted Mexican ways and spoke Spanish perfectly," says Richard Valdemar, a retired Los Angeles Sheriff's Department veteran gang investigator for thirty-three years. "As a kid, he joined one of the Maravilla gangs in East Los Angeles. He's unusual because he's a white boy who grew up in the projects. If you met him and hung out with him for just a few moments, you'd forget that he was white. Joe didn't fake it. He spoke regular English unless he was speaking in Spanish and then he had a beautiful accent." Although he was a *guero,* Morgan understood what it was like to be a part of LA's "vato loco" underworld.

Joseph P. Morgan was born April 10, 1929 in East Los Angeles. He might have been white on the outside, but on the inside, he was brown. Raised in the barrios of East LA, Morgan was a Chicano at heart, who identified as Mexican-American, and also happened to be one of the baddest motherfuckers around. A big kid for his age, well over six feet, it wasn't long before he got in trouble over an older woman. Elvira Rojo seduced and bedded the teenager, offering him one thousand dollars to kill her husband. In the early morning of September 16, 1945, Morgan walked into the husband's room and busted open his skull with a rubber hammer.

"At just sixteen, Joe Morgan murdered his 32-year-old girlfriend's husband and buried his body," says Chris Kasparoza, the author of *For Blood And Loyalty.* "Then, while awaiting trial in the LA County Jail, Morgan keyed in on William Westbrook, another 16-year-old who was being transferred to a country forestry camp. Morgan posed as his cellmate and escaped from jail, making it no shock that he went on to become a leader in what the government has alleged is the most dangerous prison gang ever."

Morgan became cellmates with Westbrook, studied his mannerisms, practiced his signature, and then threatened Westbrook's life if he didn't go along with Morgan's ruse. The next day Morgan impersonated Westbrook when guards came to transfer him to the camp. After forging his signature on a booking slip, Morgan got into a car with a probation officer, sans handcuffs.

At San Fernando Boulevard and Colorado Street in Glendale, Morgan jumped from the car, took off, and escaped. The Sheriff's Department didn't realize a homicide suspect had escaped until hours later. The young criminal was a fugitive, a wanted man, and he made page two of the *LA Times* with his ballsy escape. He was a daring outlaw of epic proportions, but Morgan wouldn't be free for very long.

"He got captured a couple weeks later on March 8th," says Christian Cipollini, who runs *ganglandlegend.com*. "The cops got a tip on his whereabouts and when they showed up, Morgan took off running. The officers shot the fugitive in the leg, shattering the bone, and stopping Morgan in his tracks. Due to complications his leg was amputated just below the knee. This led to authorities and the media dubbing the young criminal 'Peg Leg,' although prison lore holds that no one ever dared call him that to his face."

After getting convicted of second degree murder and sentenced to five years to life, Morgan was sent to Folsom State Prison due to what the judge called "criminal sophistication." Despite being the youngest inmate to ever hit the yard, Morgan got mad props at the prison. With his story and Elvira's photo in the papers everyday, Morgan became a jailhouse celebrity. To his fellow prisoners having sex with an attractive woman twice his age was a grand caper indeed. Morgan adjusted well and served nine years at Folsom.

"In July of 1955, Morgan was paroled, but he wasn't in the world for long," Burnstein says. "On November 30, 1955 he robbed a West Covina bank of seventeen thousand dollars with a machine gun. He was arrested by the FBI at a bar in Long Beach one week later. Barely 26-years-old, Morgan was sent back to state prison, a convicted murderer, bank robber, and escape risk. During the four decades he spent locked up in the toughest prisons in California, Morgan earned the respect of all prisoners and staff by conducting himself as a gentleman, but you could never forget that he was a gangster."

NO ONE DARED CALL HIM A "WHITE BOY"

In February 1956 *The LA Times* headline read, "Hammer Slayer Held in $17,000 Bank Hold Up." Referenced in the article as the man who went to prison for the hammer slaying of his sweetheart's husband, Morgan was slowly building up his criminal resume. He was known as the kind of guy who wasn't afraid to kill another with his bare hands or do what needed to be done to get the job done. At meals, Morgan sat with the Hispanic prisoners and started to form ties with the young Chicanos that would form the core of the Mexican Mafia. Morgan became a mentor of sorts to a lot of the young *Eme*— teaching them how to do their time in San Quentin.

"Joe had a reputation long before because his homeboys in Maravilla were probably the largest segment of incarcerated gang members," Valdemar says. "If someone called him a white boy he would have killed him. He knew what his genes were, but his heart was Chicano." Morgan was also known as one of the better handball players on the yard, despite his peg leg. His leadership skills were undeniable and he became a visionary for the budding organization.

"Morgan became first counselor and then business guru to the new gang," explains Al Profit, the director of the *American Dope* series. "Morgan studied Aztec history and formed solid relationships with carnals like Mike 'Hachet' Ison and Ruben 'Rube' Soto. In the netherworld of corruption and violence that existed inside California prisons at the time, prisoners used to settle their disputes with their fists. But when *La Eme* came along they started making and hiding weapons in strategic places on the yard, so they could grab them when things jumped off."

On February 24, 1961 after being subpoenaed to act as a character witness in a murder trial, Morgan masterminded an even man escape from LA County after a jail lock was picked and prisoners crawled through a pipe with the aid of tools, such as lock picks and hack saws, that he had hidden in his artificial leg. The jail break made the front page of the *LA Times* and was called the institution's largest escape ever. Morgan's criminal notoriety was growing.

"This guy used his own prosthetic leg to conceal tools which were used in a brazen jail break. Talk about street cred and cleverness!" Cipollini says. "When he was captured and walked back onto the yard in San Quentin in 1961, he was a California prison legend who had escaped multiple times and served fourteen years, mostly at Folsom. He learned the Aztec language and taught others so they could communicate in code. Morgan was a master negotiator, an expert on doing time, and had connections with all the racial groups."

IN THE PEN BOYS FIGHT AND MEN KILL

"*La Eme* formed in 1957 at D.V.I. (Deuel Vocational Institution), a youth prison in California that housed the state's most heinous, irredeemable, and violent teenage inmates," Kasparoza says. "Legend has it that it was the brainchild of a then 16-year-old Luis 'Huero Buff' Flores who brought together the toughest, smartest, most dangerous, and ruthless members of various Mexican street gangs at D.V.I., mostly from the barrios of East Los Angeles, uniting them. They were the 'special forces' of teenaged Mexican California gang members who ruled their youth prison yard." However, from D.V.I. *Eme soldados* were transferred to maximum security adult prisons like San Quentin where even more ruthless and murderous Mexican inmates joined their ranks.

"The Mexican Mafia did not materialize in the streets, it formed within prison confines, probably out of necessity. Like virtually any other prison gang, these guys needed to stick together to survive and thrive," Cipollini says. "The idea soon morphed into creating not just a gang, but a super-gang. Eventually that evolution created vast outside connections and reach, but of course that kind of expansion also produced enemies."

In 1969, at the age of forty, Morgan was sponsored by his friend "Hachet" Ison and joined *La Eme*, becoming the first white guy to join the organization. He was given the Aztec name "*Cocoliso*" and was immediately accepted into the inner circle, whom he had been working with in an advisory role up until that point. Morgan talked the talk, walked the walk, and embraced his role as a Mexican Mafia soldier.

"*La Eme* was founded on the principle that every man is equal and the gang operated on a one man, one vote, majority rules system," Profit says. "Leaving their rivalries in the street, the top gangsters merged into one crew. Joining required a formal sponsorship. A made member had to speak up for the individual being considered for membership and take responsibility for them. *La Eme* was recruiting gangsters with serious criminal resumés who weren't afraid to use violence as an intimidation tool."

Morgan was fearless, aggressive, intelligent, and had a willingness to kill when and wherever for the organization. In the pen they say, "boys fight and men kill" and *La Eme* had a reputation for killing with reckless abandon, it was on and popping, "on-site" as they say. Morgan was all about being the best gangster he could be and pushed his brothers to read books like Machiavelli's *The Prince* and Sun Tzu's *The Art of War*. Other books in Morgan's repertoire included *Grey's Anatomy*, books on martial arts and weapons. *La Eme* wanted to identify the most vulnerable spots to attack their enemies with prison shanks and strike the killing blow.

"For a long time there'd been a close association between the Aryan Brotherhood and the Mexican Mafia because they have the same enemy, the Black Guerrilla Family," Cipollini says. "It was the Mexican Mafia who first challenged the BGF. Since they had the same enemy they were naturally allies. But *La Eme's* sworn enemy was *Nuestra Familia*. About the same time that Morgan came on the scene the BGF and NF formed an alliance. The lines were drawn in the sand."

In 1972, there was a bloodbath in the California system. Thirty-six prisoners were killed that year and gang experts believe the Mexican Mafia was responsible for thirty of the killings. Race riots raged at Folsom and San Quentin creating major conflicts between black and brown. It jumped off after *La Eme* hit a BGF soldier at San Quentin. In Chris Blatchford's *The Black Hand*, Rene "Boxer" Enriquez says that Morgan was good for at least a dozen murders on his own and had engineered dozens more.

"*La Eme* seized control of the flow of narcotics into San Quentin and as members were transferred out they did the same thing at other prisons," explains Niko Voroybov, the author of *Dopeworld*. "Morgan had *La Eme* getting protection money from incarcerated Italian Mafia members, running all the prison hustles, and more importantly he started laying the foundation for the organization on the outside." The gang seized control of several community action groups and programs that provided jobs and income fronts for members of the gang that were paroled back to the world—ready to do the gang's bidding.

"All the members were expected to put in work," Valdemar says. "They call it 'putting in work' or 'wetting your steel'. If you hesitated, then you fell from grace. Every one of them put in work and they were reluctant to pass on work to anyone else. When I say work, I mean murder. The gang was basically a bunch of prolific murderers. Prisoners like Morgan knew the system. He lets the overt, which is me, run the system, but he runs the covert system. Overtly, they're cooperative and they know we control the walls, but inwardly, they're operating covertly and they control the inside."

A LOYAL MEMBER OF THE MEXICAN MAFIA

"He was in custody in the LA County jail when I worked there, around 1972-73. He was in my module, the high power module, where all the big people from the AB, BGF, and Mexican Mafia and some political guys like Black Panthers were," recalls Valdemar. "I had direct contact with him on a regular basis. I also ran the law library which inmates are allowed to attend. He was very polite. He would greet me in Spanish. Mindful of cultural things, but a lot of these guys at the top don't have that gangster image that's portrayed nowadays. They had the smooth, know-how-to-do-time kind of attitude, but they were dangerous."

Over the years, as Valdemar's career in law enforcement progressed, Morgan's name kept popping up in various investigations, but most of the time he was in custody. It showed the reach that Morgan and *La Eme* had.

Valdemar remembers the close relationship Morgan had with the Aryan Brotherhood. "He was a liaison, but the AB had a close relationship with all the Mexican Mafia members," Valdemar says. "I would say that he's one of those people that commanded your attention. If he was in the military, he would have been a leader. He wasn't loud. He wasn't boisterous. He didn't try to inflict himself on anyone else. He just quietly took command."

The Mexican Mafia has no real hierarchy, but members rise to de facto leadership according to what's needed at that time and who's in power. It was law enforcement that labeled Morgan a "godfather." But actually, he was just a loyal member of the Mexican Mafia who took charge for the betterment of the organization with the help of several equally powerful members who backed him. It's not like you get elected president for life or king, like the Latin Kings. Nothing like that. It's de facto control. Morgan was a leader type of guy, so he took on that leadership role. He knew he was in charge. He didn't have to prove it to anyone.

"If he rose to the pinnacle of *La Eme*, as a *guero* no less, he must have been one smart, devious, bad motherfucker," Kasparoza says. "But also a loyal, charismatic one, with a code of honor. There was a reason why so many alpha male murderers deferred to him, and even the cops tasked with locking him were impressed. Morgan could get people to calm down. He was a diplomat in a certain sense." But as his power grew Morgan developed enemies and detractors within the ranks of *La Eme*.

"Two O.G.'s, Reymundo "Bevito" Alvarez, who murdered a BGF shot caller, and Ernesto "Kilroy" Royal schemed against the rising *soldado*," Cipollini says. "They insisted that no one should be in *La Eme* who wasn't Latino. They didn't like Morgan, but Morgan had too much clout. Morgan was paroled from Folsom in 1971 and when he hit the streets there were dozens of *Eme* members on the outside as well. Morgan set about trying to organize the brothers into a criminal enterprise."

Morgan wanted to "spread the *Eme* gospel" and along with Cadena, one of *La Eme's* founders, implemented a strategy of leveraging the organization's power inside prison to control territory on the street. "The 'if you own the inside, you can own outside' philosophy grew *La Eme* to epic heights," Burnstein says. "Morgan's contributions to *La Eme's* expansion were invaluable. Not only did his connections to narcotics suppliers catapult the Mexican Mafia into being instant major players in the dope game, his skills as a gangland politician paid dividends in the form of alliances and business relationships with other criminal factions like the Italian Mafia, the Aryan Brotherhood, and outlaw biker gangs."

Morgan came to the conclusion that a lot of the gang's members were obsessed with settling old scores when they hit the street instead of making progress for the organization as a whole. He envisioned the gang getting into more profitable endeavors. He wanted the gang to become a successful criminal enterprise. Morgan knew murder had its place, but he wanted to use violence to further *La Eme*'s ends instead of settling scores. But if a brother called, he had to back their play. As early as 1973, newspapers were identifying Morgan as the leader of the Mexican Mafia. He couldn't stay out of prison though, he was always going back on parole violations.

"His main allies were Ramon 'Mundo' Mendoza, Robert 'Robot' Salas, Alfredo 'Alfie' Sosa, and Edward 'Sailor Boy' Gonzales," says Profit. "With these hard core brothers he implemented *La Eme*'s decrees on the streets, which led to more power inside the prison system. During this part of the 1970's, the Mexican Mafia would become well known all over California. All the Mexican street gangs paid tribute to *La Eme*. The organization's name spread fear and law enforcement was getting hip to the gang and who their leaders were, in and out of prison."

AFTER HIS ARREST IN 1978 MORGAN WOULD NEVER SEE THE STREETS AGAIN

"Morgan and *La Eme* were part of a new generation of drug lords that didn't answer to the Italian Mafia," Vorobyov says. "They made their own connects, getting heroin straight from the source. Before, the main smack track to the states ran through the Italians, who got it from French refineries and the Middle East. But as that route started drying up, it was time to look south of the border. Poppy's been grown in the hills of Sinaloa in Mexico since the 19th century, and the connections that Morgan put together in prison allowed *La Eme* and their street affiliates to start moving Mexican black tar heroin in the 70's."

Morgan had a lot of heroin connections. He was known as the guy who could get weight. He did business with the Italians and the Aryan Brotherhood, but Harry Buckley Gamboa, a childhood friend raised in the streets of Maravilla who was hiding out in Mexico, introduced Morgan to Jesus "Chuy" Araujo, the head of the Araujo drug cartel. Shortly after, Chuy became Morgan's main supplier of heroin. He let everyone in southern California's criminal underworld know that if they were in the dope business they had to sell Mexican Mafia dope. Refuse and you were hit—murdered.

"Morgan considered the mafia's financial condition the most important aspect, but other brothers didn't share his opinion," Burnstein says. "With made members in every major southern city in California, Morgan knew that *La Eme* was sitting on a gold mine. Morgan envisioned *La Eme* being like the Italian Mafia. He wanted the leaders of the mafia to insulate themselves from committing violence and minimize those risks." He thought of himself as a Carlo Gambino or Lucky Luciano type, counting the money all the way to the bank while calling the shots as the soldiers did the dirty work.

In the late 1970's, prominent Mafia killer Ramon "Mundo" Mendoza became a government informant. Morgan had no idea that one of his trusted confidants was actively working against him and playing ball with law enforcement. Mundo testified that Morgan was responsible for ordering multiple murders both inside the belly of the beast and out on the street. He implicated Morgan in the murder of Robert Mrazek, an *Eme* associate, who was shot to death in 1977. Mrazek's wife Helen had allegedly asked Morgan to kill her husband. After his arrest in May of 1978, Morgan would never see the streets again.

"I was housed on the same tier with Joe Morgan at Folsom in the SHU II during the mid nineteen eighties," remembers Serious Steve, a prisoner who did time in the California system. "What immediately struck me was how the guards treated him with a civility and deference I had not encountered before in the CDC. Morgan had him some presence. He was a strongly built person, a head taller than most of the rest of the *carnals* and was cat-quick on the handball court. He was fluent in like four languages and could speak intelligently on most any subject. He was a charismatic, charming individual—very intense to say the least. When Joe Morgan spoke everyone listened and I never heard anyone refer to him as 'Peg Leg.'"

EVEN IN DEATH MORGAN STAYED TRUE TO CHARACTER AND DISMISSED THE PRIEST

In 1992, the Edward James Olmos film *American Me* was released. It was a fictionalized version of the Mexican Mafia/*La Eme* story and included the character J.D., based on Morgan. The movie raised the stature of *La Eme* and put them on the map just like *The Godfather* did for the Italian Mafia. *La Eme* went from being just a prison gang to being recognized as a bonafide criminal organization. The problem the Mexican Mafia had with the movie was that *La Eme* hero, Rudy "Cheyenne" Cadena, who was represented by the Santana character, got raped on the inside, an event that didn't occur and one that *La Eme* couldn't let pass.

"When they made that movie they actually approached Morgan and supposedly got unofficial permission to make that movie as long as he hired Mexican Mafia advisors and Olmos did in fact do that," Valdemar says. "But when he did that he put himself under the rules of the Mexican Mafia. After the film's release, Morgan filed a lawsuit against Olmos, Universal, and several others seeking $500k in punitive damages." In the court filing Morgan argued that a character depicting him in the film committed crimes he didn't do and that hurt his chances for parole.

Morgan also argued that they didn't have the right to use his likeness or his story without his permission. The case was eventually dismissed, but three people associated with both the film and the Mexican Mafia were murdered after the film was released. The fallout from the movie has caused Hollywood to shy away from any other Mexican Mafia-related projects.

On November 9, 1993, Morgan died of cancer at the age of 64 at Corcoran State Prison hospital. There were two correctional officers in the room with Morgan when the priest came in to read him his last rights. Even as he died, Morgan kept his true character, and dismissed the priest, not wanting to have anything to do with him.

In his book, *From Altar Boy To Hitman*, Mundo described Morgan as "the coldest, most calculating, and brutal son of a bitch you could ever encounter," but he was also "the funniest, most compassionate, and witty person one could ever hope to know." Morgan was a career prison gangster who went hard and helped solidify the Mexican Mafia as one of the most powerful gangs in the United States. Today, *La Eme* controls almost all of the Hispanic gangs in southern California. It is a vast network of *Sureño* gangbangers who do the bidding of their vicious prison shot callers.

After the three technical advisors from *American Me* were murdered, the actor who played JD, William Forsythe, called up Richard Valdemar and asked him, "Hey, am I in trouble?" Valdemar told the actor, "No, they love you. They think you've played him to perfection, so you're not in trouble." Valdemar thought Forsythe did an excellent job. "In fact," he says. "The scene where he's walking onto court with the leather jacket on, if I didn't know that was the actor, I would have thought that was Joe Morgan."

3

NATE "BOONE" CRAFT
EVOLUTION OF A HITMAN

The crew led by brothers Reginald "Rocking Reg," Terrance "Boogaloo," Gregory "Ghost," and Ezra "Wizard" Brown, started out as enforcers and contract killers, but it didn't take long for them to flip the script and start knocking off the drug dealers they were protecting, assuming control of their business operations and morphing into drug traffickers themselves. Nate "Boone" Craft, who confessed to thirty murders, was the Best Friends number one head hitter. He was a man who was as feared as he was lethal. Boone came up hard on the East Side of Detroit, learning to fight and fend for himself at an early age, before embarking on a career as one of the black underworld's elite hitmen.

THE HITMAN'S EARLY BEGINNINGS

"Going from nine turning onto ten, me and my friends, we was more of fighters in the neighborhood," Nate "Boone" Craft recalls. "Everybody knew us and they knew that, well, if you messed with Little Boone, he's gonna come at you with something. He don't come with his fists. He's gonna come at you with a knife or a gun."

Growing up on Continental, between Jefferson and Buell, Boone met Charlie, the man that started him in his life of crime at a young age. A mentor of sorts, Charlie gave Boone packs of heroin to sell. Boone was happy with the two dollars he made off each pack, but he found that his calling was in the enforcement field. Busting heads was just what Boone did naturally and even at a young age he wasn't averse to putting in work. He was willing to do the dirty jobs of the drug trade that others shied away from.

"At nine and ten we were small, but we was very rough," Boone says menacingly. "Everybody knew it. They still even talk about it today. They'd say, yeah, man, I remember you back when you were young, dog. Yeah, okay, we were there, you want a lollipop? You knew me, that don't mean that you truly know of me."

Boone ended up locked down in a boys home as a teen, where it became a daily ritual to prove himself. Survival of the fittest was the M.O. in juvenile hall and Boone found himself in conflict with others from the jump. He was smaller than most of the other boys, due to his age, but that would soon change. In time Boone would become a giant of a man, but he used his time in the boys home to learn everything he could about being a criminal. In that manner he continued to cement his reputation in the criminal underworld as someone who wasn't afraid to do what needed to be done under any circumstances.

DETROIT'S DEADLY DRUG GAME

"He's not scared of stabbing a person or shooting a person. He ain't afraid. He never say anything after he do it. He tried to catch you by yourself so there won't be no witnesses. That's the reputation I earned in the boys' home," Boone says. "I don't need nobody telling on me or watching me do it. Then they got something over my head to blackmail me. That's what I learned inside. I finally got released, got back to the street. Still didn't understand what was going on out there because a lot of things changed for the little five years I was locked up in the boys' home."

The drug game in the city of Detroit was on fire. It was the mid-80's and the crack epidemic was raging in inner-city communities across the country. Trafficking organization's with colorful names like Young Boys Incorporated (Y.B.I.), Pony Down, Chambers Brothers and the Curry Boys ruled the streets and dealers like Maserati Rick, D. Holloway, White Boy Rick and Big Ed moved weight. The talk of the town were the flashy drug dealers who cruised around the inner-city, the epitome of ghetto royalty in high end, luxury vehicles like BMW's, Mercedes and Maserati's. Sporting brand name clothes, dime pieces on their arm, rolls of cash in their pockets, and armed to the teeth, they represented a capitalistic manifestation of the Black Panther legacy.

"When I came home from prison I had all that tension, anger in me, so I went and fought in a tough man contest," Boone says. "Boogaloo, Reg, and all them saw me fight. Maserati Rick came. After the fight, Reg said we want to talk some business. He told me there's money to be made. He gave me five hundred. 'Let's talk privately, just me and you,' Reg said. 'If we gave you ten thousand more will you kill a motherfucker?'"

Boone was looking for a gig and didn't have any qualms about whacking someone out for money. If a person was in the drug business or criminal underworld they had it coming in Boone's mind. It was considered justifiable homicide. There was no honor among thieves in the crack era. It was a vicious landscape of betrayals, double crosses, and duplicity. "Snitches get stitches" was the street code, but other than that, it was anything goes and Best Friends were in the thick of the drama.

"I didn't know Reg had so many enemies," Boone says. "I told them, give me a hit list, let me know, and don't worry about it. When you see that they done disappeared then you know I was on my job, but I don't need you to be there watching me do it. I don't even want anybody to ride with me."

Boone's approach to taking contracts was similar to the assassin in *The Professional*. He was singular and focused. He didn't want any witnesses. He wanted it clean and precise. But Boone discovered that his new partners were like gunslingers in the Old West. Best Friends took the *Scarface* mentality to heart.

THE BUTCHERY OF THE BEST FRIENDS

"Scowling and brutish, Best Friends cut imposing figures, all standing at least six-foot-two and weighing over 230 pounds," explains Scott Burnstein, the author of *The Detroit True Crime Chronicles*. "While its predecessors like Y.B.I. and Pony Down murdered in the name of profit and greed, the Best Friends did it for pure fun. They were burly and intimidating and took pleasure in hurting people."

Best Friends didn't have a problem busting off in shopping centers, at a car wash, or in the middle of the street during the day. Boone tried to teach them a better way to resolve their beefs, but old habits die hard. Boone knew death was always around the corner and being that survival was his main objective, he knew it was only a matter of time before a bullet caught him in the head.

"Most of the time when I rode with them I didn't know if they were going to do anything or not. They'd pull up and everybody is jumping out. Them fools done took me on a shoot out, what they called a drive-by, but these niggas don't drive-by, they jump out and chase the people," Boone explains. "Instead of shooting the fool from the car they'll jump out and run over there—*blam, blam, blam, blam*—they'd hit him or anybody else. That's why I told 'em you all accidentally shooting people that ain't got nothing to do with it or you're shooting people that you all shouldn't be shooting at. The person that you want is that person. I can show you how to get that person without interfering with no one else. You get them from a distance or up close."

With Best Friends taking on all comers—knocking rival dealers off, robbing and killing their connects, and taking contracts on anyone—Detroit's underworld became pure pandemonium. In the chaos two of the Brown brothers, Ghost and Ezra, got murdered. With bullets flying from so many different directions, Best Friends didn't know who was gunning for them, so they just put everybody in Detroit's drug game on the hit list and Boone was happy to oblige. If somebody had money on their head then Boone was coming for them. He was a straight contract killer and money talked.

"At first we all wanted money. Then it turned into power. They wanted to knock off all the other drug dealers so they could take over their territory. They wanted to knock off as many as they can," Boone says. "But the word was out and a bunch of rival dealers had a meeting about knocking off Best Friends. That's when they went after the Brown Brothers. After that we started going after the Curry Boys, White Boy Rick, and the Chambers Brothers. They started putting people on the list, talking about these are all the other people we need to knock off."

Best Friends had little or no regard for human life and their hitman extraordinaire would kill anyone for the right price. "If their goal was to take somebody out, they'd kill everybody and anybody around. Their reign of terror put the entire community, criminals, and innocent people alike, in constant fear," said DEA agent turned federal prosecutor, F. James King. Best Friends would pull up in cars in broad daylight and let loose with an uzi. They had no fear. Under Boone's tutelage they were on some *Grand Theft Auto*-type missions.

"Three days out of the week we'd go riding, spot people, follow them to where they're going and try to find out what they do, how many times they do it, where their house is at, where their safe house is, where they park their car, or where they lay their head," Boone remembers. "Once we find out that info then we'll go there again and do basically the same thing. The third time, that's their ass. They do it a third time, we're at that spot waiting for them."

With all the murders Rocking Reg kept catching cases. He did his work out in the open and had complete confidence that Boone would take care of any witnesses that dared to take the stand against him. When he went to prison, Boogaloo was in charge. One time, Boone and the youngest Brown brother got in a dispute. Boone choked Boogaloo out and told him that he'd cut him into little pieces in the bathtub and flush him down the toilet. But it never came to that. Boone talked to Rocking Reg, and out of respect for him, he let it lie.

There was a lot of money for everyone. Even though Rocking Reg was locked up, Best Friends was knee deep in the drug game, making millions off cocaine. Boogaloo kept his circle small and his associates close, but with the feds circling and his dislike of Boogaloo intensifying, Boone was making plans to get out. He knew other drug barons like D. Holloway were scheming to make Best Friends obsolete.

"D. Holloway didn't want no dealings with Best Friends even though he knew us," Boone says. "But behind our backs he talked about us and told Maserati Rick, 'What the fuck you with those fools for, man? Those fools are gonna fuck around and try to take everybody down; they doing crazy shit.'"

Best Friends eventually had Maserati Rick shot. When he didn't die they paid a visit to his hospital room and finished the job. D. Holloway was eventually also murdered. He was shopping at his favorite store, Broadway, for designer socks with thousands of dollars and a gun in his pockets. That was Detroit in the 1980's—money and violence.

"We had the money count machine sitting there in my house. Boogaloo brought a van and we unloaded it all in my house while he was sitting there running the money through the machine. When he got to $1.6 mil he said, 'Okay, bag it up.' He got to meet up with the Columbian and get more shit. I was like, damn," Boone says. "I want to know if I shoot all these niggas would anybody miss 'em, cause money was power to me and I knew that they would do it to somebody else anyway. He bagged it up in duffle bags and bounced. I think after that he got kind of nervous of me. I think he might have peeked a move on how I was looking at him."

Despite his own scheming, Boone stayed above the fray and kept tabs on what was going on through law enforcement's go-to-guy for drug dealers, corrupt homicide detective, Gil Hill. A major figure in Detroit's criminal underworld and on the political front, Hill not only appeared in Eddie Murphy's *Beverly Hill's Cop* movies, he also effectively called the shots in the city's drug game. With a cadre of corrupt cops, and allegedly reporting straight to the mayor, Hill was a powerful figure in the Detroit underground.

"If you made our list, you was going to be killed. But Gil was like, nah, don't mess with this one, I'm working a deal with him," Boone says. "I can't ask no more questions, because that's not my job. My job is only to do what they ask if they've got the money. I would leave, but the other drug lords would tell everybody, hey, don't mess with this person. Gil don't want us to fuck with 'em. Gil got something up on him or he's gonna do a favor for Gil or Gil gonna do a favor for him. So, he made the don't touch list."

The homicide detective put money on people's heads, approved hit lists, arranged protection for dealers, made cases disappear, and got dealers to help set up rival dealers. Amazingly, even though Hill was a suspect in the FBI's investigation, he didn't go down in the early 90's police corruption probe in Detroit. He manipulated the criminal justice system to suit his own purposes. He was the real untouchable in Detroit's underworld.

"He would tell us to put a gun in somebody's car—one of our enemies," recalls Boone. "Then he'd have the police pull up on 'em and say, wait, is that a gun on your seat? Cause the people don't know we just sneaked a gun in their car. Same way we did with drugs. He used to tell us to set people up with drugs. We'd go put some drugs in the motherfucker's car. We'd go throw a half a brick in there or something, then we'd tell the cops."

BOONE BECOMES AN INFORMANT

Eventually the gig was up. The empire the Brown brothers created was floundering. Ghost and Wizard were dead. Rocking Reg was serving life in prison for allegedly murdering one of White Boy Rick's partners. Boogaloo was on the run, a fugitive from justice. He knew his number was up. It was all coming back on Best Friends and karma was a bitch. The assassin was ready to go down, but then he found out Boogaloo had something to do with his little brother getting killed.

"If somebody killed one of your family members you are going to try to go at them or you're going to tell the law," Boone says. "Unless you just don't give a damn about your family being killed. Some people will do that, but I couldn't. I already knew that Boogaloo was behind the killing of my little brother. I couldn't get to him, so I went to the DEA and told them I can help you get this motherfucker. I figure if we get him we send him to prison and my friends in there are gonna butcher his ass. And they said that they would like to get him in there anyway, cause he had a contract on his ass in prison."

Boone was in damage control mode and instead of facing life in prison for his crimes he was looking to make a deal with the feds and get revenge. In his mind it was justifiable because he wanted Boogaloo dead. But Boogaloo was trying to tie up loose ends and had Boone shot up, but he didn't die from his wounds.

"To give up Boogaloo and Best Friends the Feds gave me immunity across the table for any of my own crimes. I admitted that I was involved with thirty murders," Boone says. "They said okay, but we're just going to find you guilty for these two, but you have to tell us who they was, where you did them, who all helped you. I gave them the detail on all that. The judge asked, 'can't you find somebody else to make the deal with?' But the papers were signed and they knew I was the only one who was willing to give them Best Friends. I gave them up. They killed my little brother and then they tried to kill me.

"I was involved with approximately thirty murders. They gave me immunity. Everybody was like, 'How the hell can they do that?' But they wanted Boogaloo more than me. They wanted these people that I was gonna give them more than me and they figured they'd get them to flip on somebody even bigger. That's what they were planning on doing: try to eat up the chain. I was just giving them these people, that's all. The rest of the people I know about I wouldn't have given them up. They didn't have nothing to do with me going to prison or me getting shot up or killing my little brother, so I kept my mouth shut."

The feds wouldn't get Boogaloo though. He was killed by one of his own guys. A long time crew member murdered Boogaloo and stole the buy money for a one hundred kilo load of cocaine. The remaining Best Friends were tracked down and also charged for that murder. Boone didn't have to testify against anyone. He was shipped off to do his time in the federal Witsec program—a secret program in the federal Bureau of Prisons where high-profile witnesses can do their time safely.

"The state gave me twelve-to-twenty. The feds gave me seventy," Boone says. "The state and the feds came up with an agreement that they'll run the sentences together. I wouldn't do no more than twelve and a half years, then I'd be released." In 2008, Boone was released from prison and moved back to his old Detroit neighborhood where he still resides today. Unafraid of anyone connected to Best Friends or Detroit's police force trying to kill him, Boone moves around the Eastside freely.

"We was young fools then," the imposing six-foot-three, three hundred pounder says. "I wish I could turn back the hands of time and just stay straight and start a small business. When you become a gangster or hitman you get shot up. You get tore up. There is no such thing as retirement. Prison, death or getting crippled is your future. I've been to prison. I'm crippled. I can't even move my hands. Leg, tore up. I have to walk with a cane. Shotgun blast. They hit me with everything, nine in the back, but yet this is me. I'm free."

4

GRISELDA "BLACK WIDOW" BLANCO
COCAINE'S GODMOTHER

Heroin was the drug that initially dominated the headlines in the 1970's as it devastated communities, especially the inner-cities. Cocaine hit the scene under very different circumstances. It was a party drug used primarily by the Wall Street jet-setters and discotheque crowd. In the 70's, cocaine was an exotic, champagne drug that gave people an aura of cool, and all the hip and trendy people were getting into it.

"It didn't hold the negative stigma attached to drugs like heroin and was often done openly within the party circuit, early on," says Kevin Chiles, the author of *The Crack Era*. "However, America's appetite for illicit drugs ultimately dictated the supply and evolution of the Colombian cocoa farmer into full fledged drug cartels." And surprisingly enough, a woman would lead the cocaine invasion for the South Americans.

SPINNING A DANGEROUS WEB

"Griselda Blanco had a tough childhood," explains Niko Vorobyov, the author of *Dopeworld*. "She was into prostitution and petty crime since she was a kid. That made her one tough, ruthless bitch." Blanco came up on the streets of Medellin as a thief and hustler, eventually transitioning to the drug trade. She was not against killing her adversaries, earning big kudos in a world dominated by brash and violent men.

"Blanco's rise to narco infamy began with an abusive childhood that eventually took her to the streets, moving from prostitution to extortion and other crimes," explains Christian Cipollini, the author of *Murder Inc.*. "The drug business endeavor really kick started when she met second-husband Alberto Bravo. He was already involved in the drug trade and the pair fully exploited the business after they illegally moved to New York in the 1970's." The drug dealing duo quickly built up a sizable marijuana and cocaine distribution business, headquartered in Queens, NY.

"Blanco's femininity was a fascinating counterpoint to the macho gun-toting stereotypes associated with drug lords, but it was her innovative thinking that changed the game," explains Pascal Hughes, who hosts the *Real Narcos* podcast. "She revolutionized drug smuggling methods, using a network of female drug mules to flirt and beguile their way through US customs with contraband stashed on their persons in special-made brassieres and girdles." But in 1975, Blanco and Bravo were part of the first major federal indictment for cocaine distribution in the United States.

"They fled back to Colombia before they could be arrested," says Tiffany Chiles, the editor/founder of *Don Diva* magazine. "That same year the marriage and partnership came to a dramatic end when a gun battle between the two left Griselda with a gunshot wound to the stomach and Alberto dead." Blanco, who assumed the *nom de guerre* Black Widow, quickly returned to the states with a new base of operations in Miami and resumed her duties as a trusted member of the Medellin Cartel.

"Griselda was one of the early pioneers of drug traffickers," says Ron Chepesiuk, the author of *Queenpins*. "Being a woman, I think was to her advantage, especially in the early stage of her criminal career." She allegedly had a close relationship with Pablo Escobar, but Blanco's ruthlessness separated her not only from other women, but from most other men. Alongside her use of charm and seduction, Blanco was completely brutal.

"She was incredibly violent and cruel, even by the standards of her industry," Hughes says. "She had a checkered past and a grim upbringing. But even so, her viciousness, her sadism, begs the question, what makes a person like that?" Pablo Escobar was the world-famous super-villain and narco-terrorist, but Griselda Blanco was actually one of the founding members of the Medellin Cartel.

She was a trailblazer and oversaw some of the first distribution routes in North America for the cocaine exporters. "First from New York in the 1970's when the cartel was pushing marijuana and then in Miami in the 1980's when the cartel's product turned to cocaine," says Scott Burnstein, the author of *The Detroit True Crime Chronicles*. "She was notoriously blood thirsty and power hungry."

Alleged to be responsible for up to two hundred murders, including the infamous Dadeland Massacre, which ushered in the "Cocaine Cowboy" era in Miami, Blanco was as vicious as the most deadly mafioso—a mistress of murder and cocaine who didn't take any shorts and won by any means necessary. "The numbers surrounding her reign in the drug game are staggering," Burnstein said. "She was responsible for hundreds of slayings and hundreds of thousands of kilos trafficked."

IMPORTING 'THE MOTORCYCLE HIT'

According to drug trafficking lore, Griselda Blanco was the inventor of the motorcycle drive-by shooting. In reality, as with most urban myths, that's not actually the case, but you could get away with saying she was the first to deploy it as a regular tactic and making it her signature move.

Drug lore holds that she ordered her men to ride motorbikes because they kept getting stuck in traffic when they were looking to kill the Black Widow's enemies. "Blanco never invented the motorcycle hit," Chepesiuk says. "*Sicario's* had been using it for some time in Colombia. I think she can be credited with importing the motorcycle hit to Miami and the US, though."

In the late 70's and 80's, the violence in Miami was off the charts as the cocaine trade exploded in the US. The city was the main point of entry for the Colombians and they were making crazy money. In the early days different crews, both Colombian and Cuban, clashed over the markets and territories, trying to establish who would control the trade. The Black Widow was in the mix, calling shots and giving orders.

"Given the money to be made, gangsters in South Florida jockeyed for position and this led to an explosion of violence," says Chepesiuk. "Griselda was willing to do what she had to do and this contributed to the explosion of violence." The streets of Miami became a war zone. People think *Scarface* is just a movie, but all that was real and the Black Widow was at the center of all the action—

be it kilos of cocaine, houses full of money, strategic and retaliatory assassinations, or luxury items and property.

THE WIDOW DODGES DEATH'S ROW

It wouldn't last though. Blanco was arrested by the DEA in 1985 and indicted in Miami on drug and murder charges, but the case fell apart. Her former hitman was ready to testify against her and the feds were looking at the death penalty, but the case "spun into a scandalous fiasco when her former hitman-turned-witness and an alleged boyfriend both engaged in phone sex calls with staffers in the prosecutor's office," Cipollini says.

"Whether or not the scandal was another methodical effort put into motion by Griselda or simply a bizarre happenstance, the scandal wreaked havoc on the prosecution's case and gave the defense a huge advantage in challenging the witnesses credibility." Blanco went from looking at the death penalty to looking at a decade of prison, a fortunate turn for her.

And it wasn't bribery or cunning that helped Griselda avoid death row in the United States, Hughes related. It was pure luck. "In a situation of extraordinary farce, out of nowhere, news broke that a secretary for the lead prosecutor at the state attorney's office had been fired for having phone sex with a key witness for the prosecution. The state attorney's office had to recuse themselves from the investigation into Griselda Blanco. The murder case against her was totally compromised."

Ultimately, Blanco plead guilty to trafficking charges from the 1995 indictment and got a light ten year sentence, a relative slap on the wrist when you consider the extent of her criminal behavior in a global context. "The Feds never pinned any homicides on her or brought her to justice for any of the alleged killings she ordered, some of which were of her husbands and lovers," says Burnstein.

While she was serving time in the feds, Blanco was still dabbling in the drug game. She recruited a significantly younger African-American lover, Charles Crosby, to run her new network in LA—plugging him in with her contacts back home who supplied him with unlimited kilos to sell on the California black market. Blanco figured if she was doing time for cocaine she might as well keep making money from cocaine.

La Madrina (The Godmother) avoided death row, didn't serve the full term she was sentenced to, and in 2004, was released and deported back to her hometown of Medellin in Colombia. Back on home soil, in true style, she vanished without a trace. For eight years she was in hiding. An alleged cell phone photo of her in 2007 showed she was still alive, although some theorized her days were numbered. It was obvious that Blanco was laying low. "She'd made a lot of enemies in Colombia over the years, and old grudges hadn't been forgotten or forgiven," Hughes said.

"Apparently she'd retired, but you can't cut a path through the cocaine underworld like that and not make enemies: grieving relatives, angry business partners," Vorobyov mused. "A lot of very dangerous people and they all wanted her dead." Back in Colombia and with the Medellin Cartel a thing of the past, Blanco no longer had the power or generated the type of fear she did in her heyday. As Blanco was trying to stay alive, a documentary film that gained worldwide acclaim was released in 2006.

AN ORIGINAL 'COCAINE COWBOY'

The documentary *Cocaine Cowboys* introduced the legend of Griselda Blanco to the general public. The public was previously unaware of any women serving as major drug lords within the cartels, let alone one as ruthless as the Black Widow, who killed her husbands and lovers at will.

"The documentary was the beginning of the legend and *Cocaine Cowboys II* focused solely on her exploits," Chiles said. "She named her youngest son Michael Corleone and her three oldest sons were killed once being deported back to Colombia."

On September 3, 2012, as the legend of Blanco was becoming more mainstream, she was gunned down outside a butcher shop in Medellin. This was a rare trip out in public for the godmother. As she stepped back onto the street, she looked up to see two men on a motorbike speeding towards her.

"A *sicario* rode up on a motorbike and blew her brains out," Vorobyov said. "The same kind of ride-by shooting she used to be known for." Unbeknownst to the store clerk, who was shocked at seeing an old lady being murdered in cold blood, the victim was responsible for hundreds of murders.

Now, *La Madrina* is buried in the same cemetery as Pablo on the side of a mountain overlooking Medellin. "Griselda's past caught up with her," Chepesiuk said. "She had killed a lot of people and created a lot of enemies. I was not surprised when she was killed." Blanco had just signed with a major Hollywood production company, along with her son Michael, to sell her life rights and the motion picture is still presently awaiting production.

"Beside her authorized story, Catherine Zeta-Jones starred in a story about her life and Jennifer Lopez has announced that she is planning to star and produce a story increasing and continuing the legend of *La Madrina*," Chiles said. Her legacy still rings loud in underworld circles today, mainly for the fact that she was a woman whose reputation for ruthlessness rivals any male figure of the infamous Cocaine Cowboys era in South Florida.

The fact that Blanco lasted so many years was extraordinary. "Her twenty-odd years at the top of the cocaine trade was pretty much unparalleled," Hughes concluded. "This longevity, the fact that she evaded the authorities for so long, gave the time and space for her cult of personality to develop."

"Plain and simple, she was the most powerful female criminal figure of our time," Burnstein said. "The mythology surrounding her reign resonates far and wide today and positions her as an iconic player in gangland history. She was just a force of nature in every way possible."

IN NARCO GANGS

In the narco world, women usually play minor roles, if any at all. This makes what Griselda Blanco did even more amazing.

The United Nations Office on Drugs and Crime produced a report in October 2019 that investigated what roles women play in drug trafficking organizations in Colombia. It suggested that women generally work preparing food for labourers, as coca leaf pickers, and as chemists using chemical processes to extract cocaine from the raw materials. They also worked as mules at the trafficking end of things. Of course there have always been exceptions like Griselda Blanco, but women tended to be employed in supportive capacities further down the hierarchy, whereas the organizational and management side was still mostly a patriarchal affair.

"It was extremely unusual that Griselda Blanco, a woman from an impoverished background, became such a key player in the cocaine trade," Pascal Hughes said. "As Robert Nieves, one of the DEA agents in our show *Real Narcos*, put it: 'I think initially there was a bit of surprise from all of us that a woman would be sitting at the top of a criminal organization. I don't want to sound chauvinistic, but it was surprising at that time to hear of a woman who was running a criminal organization, engaged in the violent end of the business, in other words the 'Al Capone' side of the business.'"

On *Real Narcos*, historian Elaine Carey, made the point that there were very few women who were the architects and designers of highly sophisticated organized crime entities, but Blanco was one.

"The fact that she had a low level of literacy and created these highly sophisticated organizations was exceptional," Carey said. "The ability to overcome this and develop this highly sophisticated criminal mind is pretty amazing."

MIAMI'S COCAINE WARS

The coke wars that raged in Florida had everything to do with 'control' of the outrageously lucrative cocaine trade.

The era of the "Cocaine Cowboys" began in the late 1970's when cocaine blossomed into a glamour drug in the United States. The drug was expensive but in high demand, and Miami geographically was the prime location for importation into the United States. The era has been glamorized everywhere from *Scarface* to *Grand Theft Auto* and the reason for the bloodbath was that Blanco and the Medellin Cartel weren't the only game in town.

"Colombians, Cubans, the Mafia, corrupt law enforcement, politicians, investors, bankers, and just about everyone had a hand in the thriving business of cocaine," Christian Cipollini said. "But that of course quickly led to an unprecedented level of violence in the region, where everyone was vying for power and control." In the early 70's, the cocaine business in Miami was run out of Little Havana. The Cubans handled distribution for the Colombians at first because they had connections to the locals who would buy the cocaine.

"You had these Cuban mobsters who'd been chased out of their country by Castro and already set themselves up in the coke and gambling rackets. They weren't too happy about these Colombian upstarts moving in," Vorobyov said. "Some of the Cubans even had CIA training from the Bay of Pigs. But the Colombians were more ruthless. But it wasn't just the Cubans, the Colombians fought each other as well. The Dadeland Mall massacre took place after gangsters in Blanco's crew had a falling-out over money. The murder rate doubled, and apparently at one point there were so many corpses they even ran out of space at the city morgue."

5

EUGENE "NICK THE BLADE" GESUALE
A REAL LIFE GOODFELLA

When people think of the Italian Mafia they usually think of New York, but at one time the Five Families had factions in cities all across the nation—especially East Coast hubs like Pittsburgh. In Western Pennsylvania, the mob has been active since the 1920's, when young Sicilian and Italian immigrants got into bootlegging—securing a power base for future generations. The Pittsburgh branch of the Genovese crime family has been recognized as one of the twenty-four traditional mafia families in the United States—running drugs, gambling, loansharking and infiltrating labor unions in the Steel City for close to five decades.

Eugene "Nick the Blade" Gesuale was one of the areas most influential and high profile mobsters. A towering and infamous figure, he was a "gangster's gangster"—an old school *mafioso* who made his bones in the 1960's, carved out a drug empire in the 1980's, and spent almost thirty years in federal prison for his prohibition-related crimes. Nick the Blade was a player in the Pittsburgh mob for multiple decades, even earning a mention in the classic gangster film, *Goodfellas* as Henry Hill's "Pittsburgh connection." But like everything in the criminal underworld, Nick the Blade and the Pittsburgh Mafia were eventually rendered obsolete by a relentless law enforcement campaign that was destined to wipe them out.

MAKING HIS BONES

Gesuale grew up running numbers in the East Liberty section of Pittsburgh. A Larimer native, his father worked for Bell Telephone. After dropping out of Central Catholic High School in the tenth grade, he attended the Pittsburgh Beauty Academy studying to become a hairdresser, a skill he would fall back on when he went to prison. A strange skill for a tough guy, but regardless, Gesuale was as tough as they come. Police arrested Gesuale thirteen times between 1959 and 1981, but none of the cases ever resulted in a conviction. "That's because witnesses would never testify," a local prosecutor explained.

A young and fearsome mobster, Gesuale earned his nickname "Nick the Blade" after a pair of knife wielding altercations. Legend holds that he cut a man's face for checking out his girlfriend at a movie theatre and that he stabbed another man after a fight broke out in a basketball game he was playing in. Pittsburgh police arrested him for numerous assaults in the 1970's and 80's, including a brawl in Shadyside, a shooting in a Downtown parking lot, and an attempt to kill a man by running him over with his car. But each time, the victims refused to cooperate and the charges were dropped.

"Chaz, as we called him in prison, was a throwback gangster," recalls Zach, a convicted drug dealer who did time with Gesuale in the Bureau of Prisons. "He didn't mess around. If he had a problem with you, he would tell you. If it was serious he would just strap up. You wouldn't even see him coming. Even at seventy-years-old he was talking about getting dudes hit."

By the 1960's, Nick the Blade was running rampant in East Liberty and dealing heroin, according to the FBI, Pittsburgh police, and the former Pennsylvania Crime Commission. He proved a cunning and slippery adversary for law enforcement. When Big John La Rocca, the region's longtime Mafia don, named Michael Genovese as the head of the family in the late 1970's, his drug-friendly atmosphere proved paramount to Gesuale's ascension in the ranks of the Three Rivers mob. Unlike most mafia dons of the day, Genovese actively encouraged narco activity amongst his troops.

According to FBI records, Gesuale "made his bones" in the gangland slaying of Pittsburgh mob flunky Alphonse Marano in December 1967. Marano had unknowingly brought in an undercover IRS agent and introduced him to soon-to-be underboss, Joseph "Jo Jo" Pecora, who was in charge of West Virginia's rackets and casinos. With the undercover agent in place, a string of raids occurred on December 23, 1967 and Pecora was arrested at the mob social club Marano helped run on the evening of December 27th on interstate gambling charges.

Genovese blamed Marano for the pinch, the loss of revenue, and the infiltration. The next morning Marano was found dead in the trunk of his car on an abandoned road in Westmoreland County, shot three times in the back of the head— a classic mob rub-out. Gesuale was picked up for questioning by authorities in the investigation, but never charged. In 1973, the "Lebanese Connection" case accused Nick the Blade and ten others of smuggling heroin into Pittsburgh from Beirut. But a federal judge tossed the case due to lack of evidence.

"Chaz had a long run in the drug game," Zach said. "He made a lot of money. Money that sustained him through his twenty-eight years of incarceration. When it came to paper, he didn't play. He was about his business, in the streets and in prison—a serious *mafioso* and drug kingpin. He was like the Teflon Don for a long time before they got him."

Throughout the rest of 1970's and into the mid-1980s, Nick the Blade was one of Pittsburgh's biggest narcotic traffickers. He was also the go-to enforcer for Steel City mob brass. Like his mentors in the family, future crime family underboss Chuckie Porter and Penn Hills Capo Louie Raucci, as well as syndicate godfathers, Sebastian "Big John" La Rocca and Michael Genovese, Nick the Blade was a mafia lifer who followed the code of *omertà*. He also acted as a liaison between the local LCN and the area's outlaw bikers.

FEARSOME DRUG KINGPIN

Gesuale, formerly of East Liberty and Highland Park, headed a marijuana and cocaine distribution network in the late 1970's and 1980's with ties to both Western Pennsylvania's LaRocca/Genovese *La Cosa Nostra* family and the Pagans motorcycle gang, the Pennsylvania Crime Commission wrote in a 1990 report. Particularly close to Michael Genovese, Nick the Blade seemingly had free reign to do as he pleased. John LaRocca, the mob boss for many years, was once asked why he kept around someone as volatile as Gesuale. "He keeps the heat off of us," he replied.

"Eugene Gesuale was a kilo-weight drug dealer, a thief, and a violent criminal," recalls Allegheny County Common Pleas President, Judge Jeffrey A. Manning, who helped prosecute Gesuale in the 1980's while working as an assistant US attorney. "He was vicious. He was amoral. It wasn't about what was right and wrong. He did whatever he wanted. He was as bad as it gets. He was the ultimate thug. He loved playing the role of the mafia capo, the don."

Between 1978 and 1982, Gesuale made in excess of one million dollars from his illegal operations, an Internal Revenue Service investigation determined. That equals roughly three million today. According to prosecutors, that bankroll allowed Gesuale to live in a twelve hundred dollar a month penthouse apartment on Bunkerhill Street in Highland Park under an assumed name, wear a different pair of Gucci shoes everyday, dine at the best restaurants Pittsburgh had to offer, buy his girlfriends fancy gifts at New York boutiques, fly first-class all over the world, drive Cadillacs and Jaguars (often registered in his mother's name), and pay cash for big losses at Las Vegas casinos.

Along with high-level drug dealing that helped him to control the majority of the cocaine and heroin markets in Pittsburgh, Gesuale was involved in bookmaking, loan sharking and extortion, the commission reported. He also ran a prostitution business in Manhattan's "Little Italy" section, with the apparent approval of New York City mob families, and most afternoons, Gesuale could be found making deals out of a bar in Swissvale, a former Gesuale cocaine dealer and bike gang member testified in court.

"Chaz loved to gamble and be in the middle of the action," Zack says. "Even in prison he always played poker and bet on games. And not just a couple of stamps like most dudes. He would bet $500-$1000 a game, every Sunday during football season. And he'd win too. You'd always see Chaz out at rec playing poker after he worked out. That was just what he did."

FBI surveillance logs from that time period noted Gesuale acting as "top-muscle" for Porter and Raucci. His name surfaced in the press for a "shakedown turned violent," when he and Billy Porter beat up Pennsylvania policy kingpin Harry Martorella with a baseball bat and accidentally shot a passerby on December 20, 1978. The attack took place at a downtown Pittsburgh parking structure Martorella owned.

Martorella co-owned the property with his two brothers, who were partners in a robust citywide numbers lottery that catered to both street figures and a more civilized clientele. Their refusal to pay a monthly tribute to the mob led to the broad daylight assault that cost Gesuale and Billy Porter almost two years apiece in jail. But the beatdown let others know what would happen if they didn't pay.

FBI agent Roger Greenbank, who worked to dismantle the Pittsburgh Mafia since the late 1970's, called Gesuale, "a crude and fearsome narcotics kingpin" who had "absolutely no redeeming qualities." The six-foot-four, two hundred-fifty pound East Liberty mob enforcer and drug dealer once was seen on surveillance snorting cocaine with one hand and urinating off a balcony with the other. He was the John Belushi of the Mafia, albeit with a severe violent streak.

GOODFELLAS CONNECTION

Nick the Blade attained a level of pop culture fame as the infamous "Pittsburgh connection" from the Oscar-nominated film *Goodfellas*. Gesuale supplied wholesale cocaine to real-life New York Lucchese mob associates Henry Hill, James "Jimmy the Gent" Burke, and Thomas "Two-Gun Tommy" DeSimone, portrayed by Ray Liotta, Robert De Niro and Joe Pesci in the Martin Scorsese helmed gangster flick. The person referred to as the Pittsburgh connection is never seen in the film, but Nick the Blade was the Mafia drug dealer hooking up Henry Hill.

"Chaz used to love the notoriety that film brought him," Zack says. "He was locked up when it came out and he reveled in the infamy. He used to tell people all the time, 'I'm the Pittsburgh connection from the *Goodfellas* film.' He was very proud of that little bit of fame. It made him feel like a star, but he would always make it clear that he wasn't a snitch like Henry Hill. He hated rat motherfuckers."

The Lucchese crew met Gesuale via a former prison cellmate of Hill's, Pittsburgh Mafia associate Paul Mazzei. He was affiliated with Chucky Porter and his younger brother Billy, but Mazzei worked under Nick the Blade moving coke, heroin, and marijuana. Mazzei, like Hill, became a federal informant and was implicated in the 1970's Boston College men's basketball point-shaving affair, the national scandal involving B.C. power forward and Pittsburgh-native Rick Kuhn.

"Chaz used to tell us all the time that he ran that Boston College point shaving scheme," Zack says. "He said he made tons of money betting on the games and that Mazzei and Hill reported to him on that venture, getting his okay for every move. He loved sports and gambling so much that I wholeheartedly believed him, even though he wasn't indicted on the case."

BUSTED

The indictment that eventually brought down Gesuale was filed in January 1985 and included Pittsburgh wise guy John "Johnny Three Fingers" Leone, Pagan motorcycle gang boss Daniel "Danny the Deacon" Zwibel, and Roy Ingold, a Pittsburgh Press truck driver, who would later testify against him. Prior to the indictment Gesuale was tipped off by FBI secretary Jacqueline Wymard, who leaked information about the case to her boyfriend, mobster John Carrabba, who in turn tipped off Gesuale's guys allowing Nick the Blade to disappear.

When the US attorney's office brought its case, Gesuale's life of high-living by way of crime finally ground to a halt. He was being charged with numerous offenses including, "engaging in a continuing criminal enterprise." Judge Manning, who tried the case with Assistant US Attorney Bruce Teitelbaum, summed up Nick the Blade, "He's a hustler, a gambler, a spendthrift, a man with a violent temper, and a man with expensive taste."

On Jan. 4, 1985, a fugitive warrant was issued for his arrest, following his failure to show up for trial. He landed on the US Marshals Service's fifteen most-wanted list. The feds said he fled with almost six hundred thousand dollars in cash and was running his drug empire from Jamaica. He was finally arrested in July 1986 in Montego Bay. The United States Marshal Service worked closely with Jamaican Police in his arrest and shipped the fugitive back to the United States to face trial.

Ingold was instrumental in snitching Gesuale out and giving agents his location. Investigators knew Gesuale was a big basketball fan, and at that time, there were only two satellite dishes on the island. One was installed at a Montego Bay hotel. For Nick the Blade, the gig was up. His love of sports doomed him. Authorities flew him back to Pittsburgh on a Learjet in July 1986 and he was taken to trial later that year. Five days into trial, Gesuale decided to plead guilty. US District Judge Donald Ziegler sentenced him to forty-five years.

Using a combination of informants, wiretaps, and surveillance the feds systematically worked their way up the chain of command by using drug dealers Marvin Droznek and Joey Rosa as government witnesses to provide details of the mob's inner workings. Their testimony ultimately led to the prosecutions of more than forty people. The top dogs were Raucci and Porter, Nick the Blade's two main running partners. After the 1990 trial, the two men and their associates went to prison.

"I like [former US Attorney] Tom Corbett's statement on the night of the convictions on the courthouse steps," said FBI agent Greenbank. "'We have successfully severed the head from the body of *La Cosa Nostra* in Western Pennsylvania.' And I think he was right. We took off the largest money makers for the family. It was an awful lot of hard work by a lot of people."

In his underworld career, Gesuale was the subject of numerous drug, gambling, loansharking, extortion, and murder investigations, dating back almost a half-century. He was a main player in the Pittsburgh mob. Chuckie Porter and Louie Raucci, his peers, were convicted of a RICO and drug conspiracy in 1990. Porter defected to the government and entered the Federal Witness Protection Program. Raucci died in prison in 1995. But Nick the Blade did his time. Waiting patiently, like men in prison do, for his return to society.

HOMECOMING

Gesuale's older brother, Anthony who lives in Ohio, lost contact with his younger brother while he was behind bars, but he doesn't like the FBI's rundown of his brother's life. He thinks his brother's life was ruined by drugs and that informants set him up. "It's a terrible thing, drugs," he said. "It all boils down to drugs. He was a victim of the drugs."

Anthony noted that prior to getting involved with cocaine, Eugene was a successful hairdresser in Squirrel Hill. His brother was also a good student when they went to Catholic high school together. But later on drugs consumed Eugene and he became an addict. Even in prison, Eugene was using and never got the help he needed for his addiction.

As for his criminal life, Anthony said Eugene was not the drug kingpin the FBI said he was and that his sentence was harsher than sentences given to other people, as a result of the war on drugs. Eugene served more time than murderers. "He never killed anyone," Anthony said. "Yes, he may have stabbed a few people, but those were neighborhood disputes. It's unjustifiable what they did to him."

After serving twenty-eight years in prison, Gesuale was released from custody on October 31, 2014. Prohibited from returning to Pittsburgh, due to threats he made against law enforcement figures during the time of his conviction, Nick the Blade relocated to Florida, where he'd once been active in the drug underworld. At 72-years-old, his days as an active gangster were over, but he still carried it like the *mafioso* of his youth.

"Chaz had a Rolls Royce at the halfway house when he first got out," Zach said. "He used to park it right in front of the halfway house. It was a bad-ass Rolls that he bought for one hundred grand in 1985. His sister held onto it that whole time for him. He still has money stashed from back in the day too. Chaz was definitely a big deal and liked the attention."

Too old for the mob and too old for crime, Nick the Blade was interested in shopping his story to Hollywood. In prison, noted gangsta rapper T.I. had taken an interest in Gesuale and told the old gangster that he could get millions for his story. With that thought foremost in his mind, Chaz was interested in looking for a blockbuster movie deal. The mafia capo, who'd never snitched on anyone and followed the Mafia's code of *omertà*, wanted a movie made about his life, like *Goodfellas*.

"They made a movie about that fucking rat," he said. "They need to make one about a real gangster like me." During his time in prison, Chaz would regale prisoners, including T.I., with stories for hours and hours. He'd have his fellow prisoners rolling on the cell floors laughing at his tales. He had a serious mob story, but the way he told it was both comedic and tragic. Because to Chaz it wasn't about how bad or how tough he was, it was about all the crazy and ridiculous situations he got himself into during his life. Drugs, women, money, booze, and violence—his life was a never ending cacophony of chaos, unorganized, and off the hook.

DEATH OF A GANGSTER

"Taking Gesuale down was one of the first major victories for the feds fighting the mob in Western Pennsylvania," Manning said.

Though Genovese was never convicted, his condoning narcotics trafficking in the Pittsburgh mob led to convictions of his top people plus much of the younger members and his associates, destroying the organization's line of ascension. Those convictions and the old age of the other mobsters proved to be the downfall of the Pittsburgh family. "Whoever is left, organized crime doesn't exist in Western Pennsylvania anymore," Manning said. "It's a bunch of old men, and that's a good thing."

Eugene "Nick the Blade" Gesuale, was at Past Times Restaurant and Bar, "when he suddenly fell over" at the end of July, bar manager David Ruiz said. At the age of seventy-three, he dropped dead of a heart attack while enjoying his usual glass of pinot grigio. "He was on his cellphone and it looked as if he was having a seizure. I called 911," Ruiz recalls. Gesuale was a regular at the S. Nova Road bar.

Gesuale usually arrived at the bar alone and Ruiz described him as friendly and talkative. When Gesuale entered the bar, Ruiz would set up a glass of his preferred white wine. The old mobster would drink and talk on his cell phone. Gesuale's residence is listed in The Falls community off of Clyde Morris Boulevard in Ormond Beach, the police report noted.

The incident report, as the *Journal Online* noted, described how "while police were on scene and he was being given CPR by another bar patron, his cellphone rang and it was a Facetime call from a cousin who identified himself as Geno." The cousin, once informed of what was happening, asked that Gesuale's car keys and phone be given to the bar's owner.

"I was surprised he was nursing such a girly drink," said Roger Greenbank, the retired FBI agent who helped send him to federal prison twenty-eight years during the Mafia crackdown of the 1980's. "Would have thought something more macho would have been his style." At the end of his life, his former adversaries in law enforcement had nothing but jokes for Chaz.

"I don't think he was a wine guy when he was in Pittsburgh," said Bob Garrity, a retired FBI agent who investigated organized crime in Western Pennsylvania in the 1980's and 1990's. "He seemed more like a shot guy." But now Nick the Blade is a dead guy, though he lives on in Mafia legend. He doesn't have a movie or a tell all book, because he wasn't really that type of guy, despite the enticement he felt in his old age. He was an old school gangster that came up the hard way, when men were men, and *mafioso* had to kill someone to get in.

FEDS VS. MAFIA

For decades, the Mafia ran the rackets, infiltrated labor unions, and paid off politicians and police. With the advent of the Racketeer Influenced and Corrupt Organizations (RICO) Act, federal officials could prosecute an entire network of criminals on a pattern of inter-related crimes. FBI agents like Roger Greenback became students of mafia culture, watching films like *The Godfather*, *Goodfellas* and other gangster flicks to gain an insight on the mob.

"Surveillance gave us an insight into their character," Greenbank said. "There were a lot of conversations about their peppers. Or what they watched on TV last night. You saw a more human side to them. You also saw the treachery. Three guys would be talking and one would leave the room and one would say, 'You know, I never liked [him]. Why do you keep him around here?' The guy would come back in, and everything was okay."

CRIME BY THE NUMBERS

$100 MILLION
Hill and Gesuale made a lot of profit from pushing cocaine

$15 - 40K A WEEK
The mobsters usually blew this on slow horses, women, drugs and rock-n-roll.

95% ACCURATE
Was how Henry Hill described the life of mobsters depicted in *Goodfellas*

5 - 10 KILOS
The amount of cocaine or heroin Henry Hill usually got from Nick the Blade.

$50 - 60,000
What Henry Hill paid for a kilo of cocaine or heroin from Nick the Blade.

1981
The year the the Boston College point shaving scandal hit the mainstream.

$2500
What the mobsters paid the BC ball players to control the outcome of the game.

71 - 64
The score of the BC-Fordham game, that was point shaved.

6 GAMES
Out of the nine games they attempted to fix, Hill and his associates won bets on only six.

2006
The year crime boss Michael Genovese died as a free man.

28 MONTHS
The time served in prison by Rick Kuhn, inside guy for the BC point shaving scandal.

6 TIMES
The number of times the word "fuck" is uttered in *Goodfellas*.

5 MURDERS
The number of mob murders depicted on screen in *Goodfellas*.

28 YEARS
The number of years that Eugene "Nick the Blade" served in federal prison.

TOP 15
In 1985 Nick the Blade was placed on the US Marshals Top 15 Most Wanted Fugitive List

1984
The year crime boss John LaRocca died as a free man.

1967 TO 1990
The years the racketeering case covered that took down the Pittsburgh Mafia.

9/30/2005
The date that Nick the Blade was charged with possession, adding 18 months to his sentence.

6

DAWOOD IBRAHIM
THE BOMBAY DON WHO BECAME A TERRORIST

The Italian Mafia gets all the props in the chronicles of gangster lore, but Dawood Ibrahim and D-Company have ruled India's criminal underworld for decades.

Like an Indian version of Al Capone, Dawood Ibrahim would claim he was just a simple businessman, portraying himself as a local boy done good, despite being the leader of D-Company, the pre-imminent organized crime syndicate in Mumbai (Bombay). With an estimated net worth of almost seven billion, the celebrated "Goonda" made *Forbes'* infamous "Top Ten Deadliest Criminals List." The Indian gangster headed a vast empire and global mafia that controls a number of rackets including drugs, gold smuggling, Bollywood films, gambling, diamond trading, contract killing, extortion, counterfeit currency, and terrorism. Legend holds Ibrahim murdered his way to the top of India's underworld by killing all of his rivals for the throne. Cementing an empire on par with the Italian Mafia and Mexican cartels.

Ibrahim, known as "*Bhai*" or "*Dawood Bhai*," which means brother or don in India's criminal underworld, is the son of a police constable. Some say the police's favorable view of his family helped his rise. But currently he's one of the world's most wanted men. Blamed for orchestrating the deadly 1993 bombing against the Hindu majority, Ibrahim, a devout Muslim, has been hiding out in Pakistan. From there, the powerful gangster ran his criminal network and used his organization to help terrorists like Al-Qaeda. With properties and legitimate businesses in more than ten countries, Ibrahim is an international crime lord. Former Mumbai Commissioner of Police, Amarjit Singh Samra, said of Ibrahim, "In ten years, this ordinary looking son of a police head constable had become virtually omnipresent in any crime. These people are the mafia, they kill people."

INDIA'S MOST WANTED

"He's the most wanted man in India. He's a man that India would like seen brought to justice," said Shobha De, a columnist in India. The 61-year-old gangster is wanted for the aforementioned bombing attack that killed 257 and left almost 1,500 injured in Mumbai, transforming him from mafia don to global terrorist. According to Indian authorities, the bomb and grenade attacks were retaliation for the anti-Muslim riots and atrocities that were taking place in Bombay and all across the country in the early-90's.

"A pregnant woman was pulled out and a sword was put through her tummy," said Pinki Virani, author of *Once Was Bombay*. "Her child was pulled out and hacked to pieces because they didn't want anymore Muslim children to be born in this country. They planted bombs all over the city because it's the financial capital of the country, to bring the government down and get them to apologize to the Muslims in India."

One of Ibrahim's accomplices, Yakub Memon, was punished by hanging for the atrocity and there's a twenty-five million dollar bounty on the crime lord's head. "The most wanted man," said Murph, an American ex-con who's spent a lot of time in India. "A Muslim whose been cooling his heels in Karachi, Pakistan. He ran all the game in Mumbai: gold smuggling, extortion, land-grab, prostitution, drugs, and all else. Dawood is D-Company. Now he's an old, fat fuck." But he was still an extremely dangerous man.

After the bombings, D-Company and the rest of the Bombay underworld splintered into factions among religious lines. Chhota Rajan, a Hindu and Ibrahim's right hand man, broke off with his former boss and vowed to kill him. "So we have the two kings," Virani said. "Who earlier were the best of friends and fell out over the bomb blast. Not just the people, but the underworld was divided over religion."

As the criminal underworld erupted into a deadly feud, Ibrahim became public enemy number one. With every police force in the world looking for him, he's safely tucked away in Pakistan, even though they deny his presence. The Indian government has considered assassinating him, but never pulled the trigger. In the last couple of years the Don of Bombay has reportedly lost a lot of power, as his most trusted associates, which include his brothers, have been killed, imprisoned, or lost influence. Recently, there's been rumors that he's at death's door.

JOURNEY INTO THE UNDERWORLD

"Dawood is so clever," explains Sumit Ranaware, an Indian filmmaker with Five Bird Productions. "His father was in the police, so he had no fear of police." Born in 1955 and brought up in the poverty stricken Dongri area of Bombay, Ibrahim got involved in street crime as a youth. "His first trick was to offer a customer an expensive foreign watch," recalled a member of his youthful gang. "After taking the money, he would vanish, while the customer would be discovering that Dawood had switched the watch for a stone or some such worthless object during the wrapping."

Turning to crime full time, Ibrahim became a smuggler. By his late teens, he started D-Company. Embroiled in a vicious underworld wide gang war and leading excursions against the enemies of Haji Mastan, the infamous Mumbai gangster and Ibrahim's predecessor, the young thug gained stature in Bombay's gangland. As time went on, he got more and more involved and other gangsters, both Muslim and Hindu, flocked to his banner. In the legendary gang war against the Pathan gang, under Samad Khan, Ibrahim cemented his reputation. A killer, a thinker, and an earner, he was the whole package.

"The Pathans, they're originally from Afghanistan," Murph relates. "They wrestled control of crime in Mumbai from the Hindu gangs. Great vendetta shit. This was the epicenter of gangland and the blood flowed. Assassinations. Police extrajudicial killings. Old school shit in the slums and in high-end real-estate. It's a fucking strange world over there."

As the gang war heated up and bodies started dropping, Ibrahim's brother was murdered. After going all in and avenging his brothers death, he was forced to flee India in 1984 as murder charges were filed against him. He holed up in Dubai and ran his rackets from there through intermediaries. In his absence, but through his guidance,

D-Company became the "top boys" in the streets of Bombay—locking down all the rackets and more for Ibrahim.

"Mumbai saw one of the deadliest gang wars in the city," Ranaware says. "Dawood finished all the members of the Pathan gang and after Haji moved into politics, Dawood took over the gang and became bigger than Haji." Between 1983 and 1988, Ibrahim became all powerful. Even the aged don of the Pathan gangs, Karim Lala, was forced to sign a truce with him. After shifting his operations to Dubai, Ibrahim expanded into legitimate businesses, including shipping, which he used to smuggle explosives, arms, drugs, and gold into India. But by 2003, when one of his gang members was murdered publicly in the trendy India Club, Ibrahim was kicked out of Dubai and relocated to Pakistan.

RACKETS AND CRIMINAL ENDEAVORS

"India is a gold obsessed country," De said. "For a lot of middle class Indians, gold is their only hedge against inflation. Gold smuggling was a way that a lot of the gang lords got into the act." Ibrahim also got involved in drug trafficking and providing transportation for illegal activities. He'd smuggle goods from abroad, take part in extortion and murders, and even started betting on cricket when some of his associates took him to the games. Ibrahim was an equal opportunity gangster. If there was money in it, he had his hands in it.

"I think very early on Dawood understood there wasn't too much money in this environment and walking on the straight and narrow," Virani said. Through D-Company, Ibrahim was elevated to don. He ended the gang war with the Pathans by using a female associate to lure rival Samad Khan into a false sense of security that ended up getting him killed. Through murder and control of the rackets, D-Company generated capital which Ibrahim used to diversify their interests, sinking money into more and more ventures, both illicit and legal.

"The smuggling of illegal goods became the center of a thriving criminal industry," Manjeet Kripalani, a journalist, reported. "India was a socialist country and you couldn't get quality goods and services. And so goods were smuggled into India from the shores of Bombay." And D-Company controlled everything that came in and everything that went out. Ibrahim would smuggle in anything that could make them money. It didn't have to necessarily be drugs. If he could make a profit, he'd smuggle it into Bombay.

"Maybe among his supporters in the community he may seem like a Robin Hood kind of figure," De said. "But certainly not to the public." But the crime lord still controls large parts of Mumbai's underworld. Centered in Dongri, the D-Company holds sway from Bombay to Nepal, Bangladesh, Pakistan, and more. With over five thousand hard core members and over one hundred thousand associates, both in and out of prison, the organization can reach out and touch someone at a moment's notice. The gang has interests in South Africa, Malaysia, Singapore, Thailand, Sri Lanka, Germany, France, United Kingdom, and United Arab Emirates.

A GANGSTER IN BOLLYWOOD

"The link between Bollywood and Indian organized crime is as old as India itself," Gary K. Busch wrote on *Gangsters Inc*. "The film industry's intimate relationship with the Indian underworld is considered one of the country's worst kept secrets, with origins that can be traced to a government regulation that rendered the cinema industry ineligible for legitimate forms of financing."

Haji Mastan, Ibrahim's predecessor as don, was very involved in the movie industry. He funded and produced films to promote his mistress' acting career. A lot of filmmakers and industry insiders had deep times with Mumbai's gangsters. It was a mutually beneficial relationship. The producers needed investment money for their projects and the gangsters needed to launder dirty money and make it legitimate.

In Bollywood, Ibrahim was famous for wine, women, and horses. The gangster financed several movies in other people's names, taking his share of the profits when the receipts came in. He was allegedly so powerful that every person in the industry needed his blessing. Bollywood stars were expected to be at his parties and play the role of lifelong friend. He even dated many Bollywood starlets, including Mandakini. Until the 1993 Bombay blasts, no one in their right mind would refuse him.

"Funny thing, India's Hindi film capital is in Mumbai, Bollywood," Murph relates. "They've made many films about this guy and the bloody exploits of the 80's and 90's. Kind of visual *narcocorridos*, Indian style, with requisite goofy Bollywood dance and song numbers, usually five throughout the film."

Ibrahim loved being in the public eye as a modern-day Tony Montana/James Bond that reveled in his notoriety and was certainly on a different echelon in the world of crime. He wasn't going to hide or look for cover, he would wine and dine with the best of them, experiencing everything in first class luxury. With the stars catering to him, Ibrahim dazzled Bollywood with his flamboyant nature. The parties he hosted were legendary and still talked about in Bollywood today. But there was a dark undertone to his presence as stars and industry power brokers were told in no uncertain terms that it'd be in their best interest to attend Ibrahim's festivities.

"Some view Dawood as a hero," Murph says. "He is a mythical figure, but he's killed many Hindus, many Indians. To some government officials he's a money tree. And in Pakistan he's a cash cow. The Pakistanis use him for their own purposes. But in Bollywood at one time, he was calling the shots."

And if things didn't go the gangsters way financially, Ibrahim and D-Company would resort to extorting Bollywood's cinema elite—targeting and even killing the movie business' biggest names when they refused to give into extortion demands and a point needed to be made. And even though Ibrahim doesn't control Bollywood like he once did, there are reports that he still has his hand in on the action through intermediaries. And his exploits have already been lionized on the big screen in the Hindu movie, *D-Company*. It remains an everlasting piece of visual imagery that speaks to the legacy of the Don of Bombay.

MAFIA DON OR GLOBAL TERRORIST?

Accused of ties with Al-Qaeda in 2003, Ibrahim was declared a global terrorist.

Unlike many mafia don's, Dawood Ibrahim, has the unlikely distinction to be named a terrorist. And not a *"narco-terrorista"* like the infamous Pablo Escobar, who is no stranger to setting off bombs and even blowing up planes, but more along the lines of Osama Bin Laden. But a lot of times it seems that governments put these kind of tags on criminals or drug lords that they can't catch, control, or impose any kind of sanctions on. It's like a last gasp effort for authorities to corral the so-called "bad guy." Not to say that Ibrahim is not a bad guy, but like anything in life there are levels of bad.

Everything is not always black and white. If the 1993 bombing attacks in Mumbai where Ibrahim's entrance into the world of terrorists, he had good reason in his own mind. The Hindu/Muslim problems in India were around long before Ibrahim. He was just the one with the will, resources, and way to strike a blow back at the Muslim community oppressors.

7

JOSÉ MIGUEL BATTLE, "EL PADRINO"
CUBAN GODFATHER OF THE CORPORATION

In the 1960's, the Cuban Revolution and Fidel Castro dominated news headlines on a regular basis in America, creating a political dynamic between Cuba and the United States, as exiles schemed to take back Cuba from Castro, making backroom, handshake deals with shady government operatives. That was a running theme that continued for a long time. The Cuban exile community in the United States was used by the CIA to do a lot of dirty political deeds over the many decades, walking in the grey areas of legality, where gangsters called the shots, and politicians made moves that intertwined with those of organized crime.

The story of The Corporation and José Miguel Battle, "*El Padrino*" (The Godfather), encompasses all these elements. El Padrino's reign stretched forty years. Beginning as a cop in Havana, pre-Castro, he fought at the failed Bay of Pigs invasion and served time in a Cuban prison. When the Kennedy Administration secured the exile's release in 1962, Battle settled in New Jersey and became the numbers king. Running New York City's *bolita* racket and controlling the Cuban Mafia from the New Jersey/NYC area all the way down to Miami.

HAVANA VICE COP

"It was in Havana where he learned corruption," says TJ English, the author of *The Corporation: An Epic Story of the Cuban American Underworld*. "He learned how the world operates, how organized crime is a conduit between the upper world—the business and political class—and the underworld—gangsters, vice, money. How whatever money generated in the underworld facilitates to the upper world. Battle developed a very heightened skill at navigating all of that because 1950's Havana was a very corrupt place."

With the criminals and mobsters running many aspects of the entertainment business in Havana, Battle worked in concert with them. The Mafia was making a ton of money in Cuba and a lot of that money was being funneled right back to President Batista and his government. Battle understood how corruption works. He took care of whoever needed to be taken care of within the system. Payment would be made to whoever needed it. He was the type of guy to cross his *t*'s and dot his *i*'s. And he was very good at that.

"He knew Meyer Lansky, of course," English says. "He worshiped the mobsters who ruled in Havana. Lansky and Santo Trafficante, they walked around like royalty in Havana. And he dreamed of being like them in many ways. Battle wanted to be a casino king. Lanksy would give Battle the skim from the casinos to deliver to the presidential palace. Battle was an establishment figure, a cop, but a guy with lots of connections in the underworld.

BAY OF PIGS INVASION

A lot of the Mafia figures and Cubans who were displaced by the revolution were angry. They lost their money, their belongings, and were unceremoniously kicked out of the country. The exiles were angry and they wanted to take it back. And luckily for them they shared a mutual interest with the CIA and the US government who saw the Communist government of Fidel Castro as a threat and wanted to overthrow it.

"All these elements, the Mafia, the CIA, and the Cuban exiles formed a coalition and became determined to kill Castro and take back Cuba," English says. "The biggest initiative in that effort was the Bay of Pigs invasion. That was a covert operation of the CIA that had been endorsed by the Kennedy Administration. A bunch of Cuban exiles, fifteen hundred of them, trained in South America and set out to invade and overthrow Cuba in April of 1961."

But the invasion was both a military and political disaster. Castro knew they were coming, he had inside information leaked to him. The Cuban exiles got slaughtered, many of them got killed, and those who didn't get killed were imprisoned in Cuba. Held in prison almost two years until the Kennedy Administration was able to negotiate their release. One of those men, a member of Brigade 2506, which was the name of the Bay of Pigs brigade, was José Miguel Battle.

"He was imprisoned in Cuba during those years," English says. "When he got back to the United States in 1962, he was determined to get revenge. The survivors of the Bay of Pigs invasion became the generational foundation for what became The Corporation. The politics of that situation led directly to the creation of this criminal enterprise."

Battle started out as a guy who wanted to be involved in taking back Cuba and freeing the nation from what he interpreted to be a Communist dictator, and a despot. His motivations were in some ways political, but as he got into the criminal side of things and built this criminal organization, he became, more and more, just became a gangster, and kind of fell away from the political side of things.

"He was a hero in the Bay of Pigs invasion," relates English. "I've been told this by a number of people. He saved some lives in one particular incident that occurred in Cuba during the invasion. This genuine war hero was revered by a lot of people in the Cuban community. In some ways it's how he was able to start his criminal empire. He had such a solid reputation out on the street that people believed in him and would cover for him."

A lot of Battle's closest associates were still involved in the anti-Castro terrorist activities like assassinating ambassadors from countries that were sympathetic to Cuba and blowing up a Cuban airliner. To try to take down the Cuban government, many of Battle's closest associates from the Bay of Pigs brigade or from his time in prison were willing to do anything it seemed.

"He had all these associates who were involved with the CIA and the efforts to kill Castro," English says. "But he himself got caught up in the gangster side of things. And by that I mean, running a large-scale criminal organization meant having to instill discipline and punishment where it was believed to be necessary. And so he got caught up in a lot of that and revenge."

The Bay of Pigs generation, who had been thwarted in their efforts to get revenge against Castro, seemed to have this oversized sense of revenge. That they weren't going to let anything slip by if they'd been wronged in some way. This was Battle's mindset as he went from cop to war hero to numbers king to mafia don.

THE CUBAN MAFIA

"When he got to the United States he wanted to set up this gambling empire revolving around a numbers racket, what the Latinos call *bolita*," English explains. "A very simple concept but very popular among Latinos of all varieties. Everybody bets the number. You can bet a nickel, you can bet a hundred thousand dollars, a lot of people take part in it. If properly organized, it could be a gold mine."

Part of organizing it properly was making sure everything was cleared with the necessary Mafia figures in the United States. Battle reached out to his old Havana connection, Santo Trafficante, who helped set up meetings with all the key Mafia figures in the New York and New Jersey area. Trafficante was the guy who introduced him to Anthony "Fat Tony" Salerno, who was the boss of the Genovese family in New York, a colorful mob figure from the 1940's into the 1980's.

"Portly guy, always had a cigar in his mouth, wore a fedora," says English. "Every other word was a curse word, really a mobster from the old school. Fat Tony Salerno was the Mafia boss who was designated to be in charge of the numbers racket for all five families in New York. And he was very good at that. He was very good at seeing that things ran smoothly."

Bolita was very popular in the barrio and in Harlem, in particular. Blacks played it and Latinos played it. Having a Cuban organizing it made a lot of sense. The organization at the upper and mid-levels was all Cubans and Puerto Ricans, mostly. But it was done in concert with Fat Tony Salerno and the Genovese family and later with the Lucchese crime family based in Brooklyn.

"This is very much an American story," English says. "I mean, the main character was a cop in Havana in the 1950's, a vice cop. That's where he met a lot of the mob figures like Trafficante who would help him out later getting his criminal business started in the US. This criminal organization was created in the United States and made their money here. They did their business here. A lot of them lived down in Miami, but they still made their money out of the New York City area."

Battle lived in Union City in Hudson County. New Jersey had a long tradition of corruption. Cops being paid off. Public officials being paid off. Battle knew the game and paid off whoever he needed to pay off. He paid off the police inspector in Union City. He paid off the mayor. He learned how to navigate the system like a master chess player. Using bribes and force, he worked to establish legitimacy on both sides of the law.

"Fat Tony Salerno quickly understood the value of having José Miguel Battle and The Corporation organize the numbers racket," English says. "*Bolita*'s known as the poor man's lottery. It's a street gambling game that can be played at a very low level. People with coins in their pockets can partake in *bolita*. People don't realize that numbers was an immensely profitable criminal racket."

Ever since Prohibition, when it was first instituted on a large scale in New York, numbers have been the most profitable single racket after narcotics and illegal booze. If it's properly organized without different organizations vying for territory and fighting with each other, it can be a really profitable racket. *El Padrino* was much more of an old-school mob boss, because of all the connections he had, and his understanding of how the system worked, but his thirst for revenge was frightening.

"Very early on, one of his brothers got murdered by a rival in New York City," English says. "Battle made it his life's obligation to get revenge for his brother's murder. There were other instances in the organization where he felt he'd been slighted in one way or another and needed to make it right and to get revenge. And I'm telling you, the Cubans ... I mean, a lot of different groups have a heightened attitude of revenge, but for Cubans, revenge is like a religion."

BETRAYAL, MURDER, AND REVENGE

The Corporation rivaled the Mafia in scope and body count. They used violence not as a last resort but in many cases as a first resort. Battle was a cop in Havana during the time of the revolution. When there were bombs going off in Havana daily. The police didn't mess around with revolutionary activity. They repressed such activity quickly when they could.

Battle was used to a very high level of confrontation and violence. He wasn't afraid to resort to that. He wasn't even afraid to use his own hands. Even as he got older, into his fifties and sixties, he was still taking part in some of the killings himself. He was a vicious Cuban mobster.

"Battle met Ernestio Torres, who he called *El Hijo Prodigo* (The Prodigal Son) when he was hiding out in Madrid, Spain," English says. "He thought this 19-year-old kid showed talent as a gangster and killer. Battle kind of saw Ernesto as someone he could mentor and shape to take over the organization. Others in the organization couldn't quite understand it because this guy Torres wasn't very bright and didn't seem like the kind of guy who would make a good leader."

Battle saw something in this guy that nobody else did and hired him as a hitman. One of his first jobs was to try to avenge the murder of Battle's brother. It was a job that proved too hard to complete. Jose "Palulu" Enriquez had murdered Pedro Battle, the youngest of the Battle brothers, and Jose Miguel Battle was determined to get revenge for that murder. He initially hired Torres to do it, but when he couldn't get the job done, he hired a lot of other people and finally got Palulu after a dozen attempts over nine years.

"At a certain point, Battle insisted on making Ernesto a banker in the *bolita* organization, which is a higher level of importance in the organization than a hitman," English explains. "All the others didn't think Torres had the talent for that. It takes some brains to be a banker. It's more of an organizational job than being a hitman. But they were asked to put up some money so that Torres could start a bank and bankroll his own little *bolita* business.

"But Ernesto was a disaster as a banker. He was always broke. He was borrowing money from people, and at a certain point, he started to do the unthinkable. He started kidnapping other bankers in the organization and holding them for ransom money. This was a crazy, self-destructive act on his part, and a lot of the other bankers were irate about it. They told Battle that he had to do something about it because this guy was a loose cannon. They wanted Torres taken care of."

Battle first tried to hire out the murder of Torres. Then he took matters into his own hands. Battle flew to Miami, figured out where Torres was, and one afternoon went over to his place, burst in, and shot him full of bullets. Battle administered the *coup de grace* himself, a bullet right between the eyes. Battle went back to New York and told everybody he'd taken care of Ernesto Torres, and that was the end of that.

But Battle was put on trial for conspiracy in the murder case. He got found guilty and it looked like he was going to be put away for a long time. He ended up beating the charge on a technicality and got a lighter sentence. When Torres's former girlfriend made noise about testifying against him in a retrial, the organization took care of that situation by murdering her before that trial could ever take place.

"The Corporation ruled with an iron hand and instilled fear in a lot of people," English says. "And for good reason, because they murdered witnesses who testified against them in court, they were very good at revenge killings, and they had created a kind of reign of terror in the criminal, Cuban, and Latino communities in general. Very few people did talk and live. There wasn't a lot of substance written about this phenomenon of The Corporation while it was happening."

THE FALL

Battle's day-to-day operations were overtaken by his need to right wrongs, get revenge, and exact punishment for certain things on the criminal side. Ultimately, in a way, it's the thing that brought him down. He kinda lost his goal along the way and became hyper-violent. Eventually, Battle was doing killings that didn't really have anything to do with business. He's believed to have killed an ex-girlfriend that he thought might have talked to the police. Battle became super-paranoid and got real out of control in the end.

"Battle kept beating the smaller charges against him, and in Miami there was either corruption on the part of law enforcement, or law enforcement people didn't take it seriously," English says. "They were kind of overwhelmed with the whole cocaine cowboy-era that was happening there. And Battle was believed to be a *bolita* guy, not a narco guy, and so they more or less left him alone while he was there. And, in the meantime, the corporation built up a financial empire."

Battle's son created a network of shell and overseas companies in Switzerland, Panama, the Caribbean, where he was burying the money. Literally billions of dollars over the course of decades, creating a financial infrastructure that really kind of turned The Corporation into a corporation. Up until then, it had really been a grandiose name for a street operation, but the criminal venture evolved into a real corporation with financial holdings around the world. The operation flew under the radar until one law enforcement type took notice.

"David Shanks was a Miami cop who'd come into the story of The Corporation kind of late, really," English says. "By the time he became involved, Battle had moved from New Jersey down to Miami, and The Corporation had been up and running for at least fifteen years or twenty years in the New York area, and was now moving its operations down to Miami. David Shanks had worked organized crime, particularly street gambling and money laundering. He's one of the guys who first comprehended, I think, the full scope of what the corporation was all about."

The key for law enforcement was when Battle went off to Peru and opened a casino in Lima. He was basically using the casino as a money laundering operation. Money from the United States was literally being loaded up on couriers, people sticking it in their underwear and strapping it to their bodies and taking it down to South America to finance this casino. Opening the casino was Battle's dream. He had finally achieved the status of a Meyer Lanksy or Santo Trafficante.

"In Peru, visitors would go to his room in the hotel to try to ask him something in the middle of the afternoon," English says. "They'd knock on the door, come in, and Battle would be sitting on the sofa in his underwear with a shotgun in his lap, and a mound of cocaine on the coffee table. He'd be watching *The Godfather* movies and mouthing along with the dialogue, which he knew by heart. He had it memorized. He was kind of crazy and his desire to play the role of the Godfather was really strong."

But financially the casino was a disaster. It was also the event that led the authorities in the United States to make a racketeering case, a RICO case, against The Corporation. The Miami cop, Shanks, followed the money trail in a way that nobody had before and when he started to pull away a piece by a thread, the more he pulled, the more it started to fall apart.

Shanks discovered a check cashing scheme that connected the money laundering scheme to the organization itself. Shanks was the only one that saw The Corporation had now moved its operations to Miami. He was building a RICO case against the organization. But it would take years to come to fruition.

"It really took decades to pull that off," English says. "When the case finally took place in 2006, it was a massive RICO case that involved prosecutors from both New York and Miami, who tried the case together—tried it down in Miami. They started out with something like fifteen defendants. A lot of people pleaded out.

"Battle himself, who was in bad health at that time, pleaded out before there was a conviction. And so The Corporation was eventually brought down in court in a way that a lot of people never believed it would ever happen. Battle ended up dying in prison two years later." *El Padrino* was dead. Heavy is the head that wears the crown.

THE BOLITA ARSON WARS

In the 1980's, a war that broke out over "bolita" between The Corporation and the Lucchese crime family in New York. The newspapers called it "The Arson Wars."

"There was a dispute over the opening of *bolita* spots or *bolita* holes as they called them. There was a rule, an understanding that the Cubans and the Mafia had," English says. "It was called the two-block rule. You could not open a *bolita* spot that was less than two blocks away from a pre-existing *bolita* spot. It had to be more than two blocks away. Someone violated that rule. There's still some dispute over whether it was the Cubans or the Italians who violated first, but it created a war."

It turned out to be a really violent and gruesome arson war where the two sides were starting fires and burning down each other's locations around the city. Over the course of about a year and a half, there was something like sixty fire bombings around New York and a lot of people got killed. Some of them were just people who happened to be there placing a bet and got trapped in there during the fires and died horrible deaths.

"*Bolita* was not supposed to be a violent racket, but the money was so great that everyone got greedy and it did become violent," English says. "There was a major prosecution and eight or nine Cubans got arrested and tried for the arsons. It brought down a level of media attention that was not good for anybody. The war basically ran out of steam and ended of its own accord."

THE MAN WHO BROUGHT DOWN "THE CORPORATION"

David Shanks was instrumental in bringing down The Corporation. He made a career of it, investigating them for twenty years.

Shanks' mom worked for E. Wilson Purdy, who was the Director of the Dade County Public Safety Department, which is what the Dade Sheriff's Department in Miami was called then. A self-admitted "Dennis the Menace, smart assed to say the least" Shanks' mom arranged a sit down with Purdy and that set Shanks on a better path in life. Early on he wanted to go to Annapolis and become a Naval or Marine Corp aviator.

He was an athlete, a senior patrol leader in Boy Scouts, a senior leader in the Sea Cadets and also joined the Miami Police Explorers. When the Naval Academy didn't work out because of an injury, Shanks came back to Miami and got a job with the police department. The Purdy influence on his life was still there. Once Shanks got into police work, he discovered that he was good at it and that he liked it. Shanks decided to become the best of the best, which meant becoming a detective in either homicide of organized crime, where he ended up in OCB.

David, when did you first hear about Jose Migeul Battle and The Corporation?

I grew up in Little Havana in Miami, Florida, where everyone knew of the hero at the Bay of Pigs invasion who turned into a crime boss. But the first time I learned more about him was when my old uniform partner, Jimmy Leggett, testified in front of the President's commission on Organized Crime about Battle. When we became detectives we went in different directions, but stayed in touch. I had gotten the bare bones of the case and thought that Battle always seemed to be running threw the raindrops.

A lot of agencies had taken a swipe at him, but he always seemed to come out the other side smelling like a rose. Three years later, I joined Leggett in OCB as his partner and began reading all of the specifics. I concluded not only that he had an ability to get out of trouble, but he was a ruthless killer who deserved to be brought down and stripped of all wealth and power.

What did your investigations reveal about El Padrino's personality?

Battle had a huge ego and wanted to be known as the biggest criminal in the world. He had no conscience and to me he was the true face of evil. For instance he had friends from the Bay of Pigs days, who counted on his friendship, when there was a minor business disagreement. Both men came to Battle and asked if every was okay between them. Battle kissed them on the cheek and said they were good. Both were killed within a week by one of Battle's hitmen, on Battle's orders.

What was it like when you finally brought him to justice and how did they avoid prosecution for so long?

After sixteen years of mass arrests and tying up all their cash, we arrested them in 2004. That was the big day for me. When we had the convictions three years later, all of the prosecution team was ecstatic and I was very calm. In those days, to the FBI and everybody else, the Italian Mafia was the big thing. We used to have a saying at the US Attorney's Office: "The Bureau had more mafia soldiers than all of the give families put together." The Bureau was famous for getting what they wanted, case wise, by making ordinary criminals into mafia soldiers. Even though The Corporation had beat the five families the Bureau never got it, until I retired.

8

THE ARYAN BROTHERHOOD
SHAMROCKS & SHOTCALLERS

The Aryan Brotherhood formed at San Quentin prison in the California Department of Corrections in 1967 to protect white convicts from the predatory gangs that were taking root in the system like the Black Guerrilla Family, *La Nuestra Familia,* and the Mexican Mafia. It was a volatile time in the United States and this volatility was amplified a hundred times over in the netherworld of chaos and violence, where it was go hard or check into the hole like a punk—and AB members made sure no one confused them with a punk.

ORIGINS OF 'THE BRAND'

"What really got them originated was the white boys had to come together for protection purposes. The blacks were acting like they ran shit, so the white boys got together to say you can run it, but you ain't running us," Dog, a penitentiary veteran and long time AB associate says. "They formed to take care of the whites in the California system because of the black prison gangs. It was a way for them to make money, a protection racket."

The white supremacist group, which later adopted the moniker "The Brand" due to the shamrock or clover leaf tattoo they used to signify membership, was made up mostly of prisoners with Irish, Nordic, and German backgrounds. Convicts from 1950's biker gangs like the Diamond Tooth and Bluebirds formed the crux of the newly formed organization. The caucasian inmates consolidated under a Neo-Nazi banner to watch each other's backs, show unity, and handle their business on the yard. Representing the white race, they made sure that no whites were exploited on their watch. By 1975, the gang was prospering inside the fences of the CDC, making power moves, calling shots, and protecting their own.

"In the beginning, the AB had one true purpose, to stop blacks and Mexicans from abusing whites. If you weren't picked up by the AB, you were dead," recalls an old-timer, who has done stints in both California and federal prison. "The mentality back then was 'kill whitey.'"

The 1960's were a radical time in America, with the black power movement in full swing and minorities marching and demanding civil rights. Behind the walls of the CDC, where blacks, whites and Mexicans were crammed together like sardines in a fish bowl, racial tensions were definitely over the top.

George Jackson, who legend holds formed the Black Guerrilla Family, wrote the celebrated prison memoir *Soledad Brother* and in his book he describes instances where blacks would attack whites on the tier just because of the color of their skin. The former Black Panther, revolutionary, and celebrated author had an unhealthy hatred of the system and all things white. In the depths of America's gulags, blacks were making a power move.

With the Black Panthers holding iconic status in the urban centers during the radical sixties, that mentality spilled over into the prisons, where race wars raged on unabated. The cauldron of hate created an atmosphere of tension at San Quentin which ignited the disputes that evolved into an all out melee that erupted throughout the whole California system. The end result was the rise of the big four prison gangs, divided along strict racial lines, which provided a measure of safety for their members. Another famous author, Edward Bunker, a white con who went Hollywood when he got out, wrote about life in the CDC in his book, *The Miseducation of a Felon*, which documented how the whites came together to hold their own.

Along with the other race based gangs, The Brand took their place in prison legend and lore as one of the most fierce and violent gangs to ever grace a California mainline. But the Aryan Brotherhood wasn't for everyone. Exclusiveness was the rule. They were very selective in who they let join. Choosing prospective members took a great deal of scrutiny. "You can't sign up for or join The Brand," Dog says. "They have to pick you to join."

BLOOD IN, BLOOD OUT

The Brand's motto was "blood in, blood out," meaning once you spilled blood in order to join, the only way you were leaving was in a body bag. And if you wanted to join, all you had to do was to kill, or attempt to kill, a black or Mexican inmate. The AB offered an exclusive membership to only the most violent, cunning, and loyal convicts—the elite of the white convicts. The guidelines for membership were strictly enforced. Only the most thorough and solid white convicts need apply.

"You have to kill a black to get in—blood in, blood out—there's nothing wrong with that in my mind. We believe in being separatists," Dog says. "We got freedom of speech, freedom of religion. Being a separatist is a form of religion. It's like them old bylaws: blacks can't eat here. AB's do time the way we want. We get high when we want to get high. We drink when we want to drink. And we fight and kill when we want to fight and kill."

The Aryan Brotherhood existed as a brotherhood of soldiers on the front lines of the prison race wars. They conditioned their bodies, minds, and souls to go full blast at a moment's notice. A law enforcement official likened them to special forces members. "The AB are the most lethal killers this country has produced outside of Delta Force," he said. "With their thick bull necks, massive forearms, knit caps pulled low over their eyes, and walrus-like mustaches, they resemble Viking warriors or Old West outlaws. A fearsome sight indeed. An image cultivated to install fear. Necessary in the environment they found themselves in."

"A riot could happen over the smallest thing between races in the California prison system. A misunderstanding that became disrespect could get inmates seriously injured and even killed," says Bumperjack, a long time AB member. "I got involved with The Brand in 1985, thirty years ago at Deuel Vocational Institution in Tracy, California. I had to get a green light on a guy who had jumped me in the county jail with two northern Mexicans and he was the shot caller. They put me in the hospital after I beat him in a hand-to-hand altercation over me not paying rent over a pack of Camel smokes. This hit I made was my indoctrination into The Brand and

I was credited with the initial part of making my bones." Violence was the norm in the system. You either adapted or got eaten up by the piranhas.

"The system in California, back thirty years ago when I entered, was no joke. If you came into the system and had a problem with another inmate you had to get permission from The Brand if you were a white inmate. The prison gangs had control of all the prisons. There were a lot of stabbings and some fist fights," remembers Bumperjack. "In the California prison system as a white guy you didn't have too many options of who to run with. If you become a race traitor you were a target when the first riot jumped off. I was told when I went to prison to stick with your own race because a race traitor was not something you wanted to be labeled as in those days."

The Aryan Brotherhood, although a bonafide criminal organization, has been responsible for organized violence against black inmates in federal penitentiaries at USP Marion in Illinois and USP Lewisburg in Pennsylvania. But despite their racial politics, the AB has become more of a racketeering enterprise over the years. They want to make money first and kill blacks second. Power is the most important thing to them. "It's a criminal organization first and foremost," the law enforcement official said. "The AB has used murder as discipline. They used murder to keep their members in line and to spread fear and terror amongst the prison population." And in the process they became prison celebrities.

A chance to see a AB put in real work was bigger than watching the Super Bowl for those inside the belly of the beast. And The Brand didn't disappoint; they killed by garrote and bludgeon and prison-made knives. They killed blacks, whites who didn't do what they said, and even their own members who got out of line. They were violent, disciplined, and fearless—a prison official's worst nightmare.

"They wouldn't sneak up and stab you," Dog says. "They'd do it right in the open. If a brother told you he was coming to kill you, he was coming to kill you. They were not scared of nothing that I ever saw. Lots of killings. Putting hits on baby rapers and snitches. They don't hide from the police. They're doing life sentences. Even if their guy was wrong, they ride with him. They don't fight fair. They'll all jump on you. Shit they're like the Musketeers, all for one and one for all. They got shanks all over the yard—easy access." And as the gang expanded into the federal system and other prisons across the nation in the 80's and 90's their reputation preceded them.

BIRTH OF A CRIMINAL NATION

The AB's leaders read Machiavelli, Nietzsche, Sun Tzu, Tolkien, and the old standby, *Mein Kampf*. But the AB long ago subordinated its racist ideology to the acquisition of money. "The leadership became much more interested in power than race and started muscling in on the gambling, extortion, and dope rackets," the old-timer says. As part of its bid to exert control over these prison industries, the AB adopted a structure in the 80's similar to the Italian Mafia, with a three man council and a formal hierarchy that sent orders down the chain of command.

The Brand's leaders wielded so much control that they effectively served as power brokers in the CDC and BOP. Maintaining order and dictating who could walk the mainline and the yard. "Prison is where these guys live. We only punch the clock," a correctional officer says. "If you are going to spend the rest of your life in prison, why not be an AB member? They live like kings." They were brutal warlords that maintain their position with an influx of drugs and unrequited violence.

The Brand eventually ran much of the drug trafficking, gambling, and prostitution behind the walls, and plenty more on the outside. They gang operated as a full-fledged criminal enterprise, using murder or the threat of it to enforce their authority and power that was maintained largely by controlling the drug trade. "Selling heroin to fellow convicts generates a lot of money for The Brand," explains the correctional officer. "Several hundred thousand a year from a single prison. And how many yards do they control? You do the math."

In the federal system, they established ties with jailed mafia crime bosses like Oreste "Ernie Boy" Abbamonte, "Little Nicky" Scarfo and the late John Gotti, the Teflon Don. Associates from other gangs like the Dirty White Boys, Nazi Low Riders and Mexican Mafia do their bidding. They flood every compound they're on with heroin, shipping the proceeds back to California to be disbursed between other jailed members and leaders of the gang. The two commissions, one in California and the other in the feds call the shots. Though never vast in numbers, the AB make up for it with their violent acts which have led to a fearsome reputation. Their far flung associates that number in the hundreds exert power on whatever prison compound they are on, trying to further the influence of the gang.

"The state of The Brand in the California system has been letting others do their bidding," Bumperjack says. "They are locked away in Security Housing Units and have indeterminate security housing unit programs, so you can only have control to a certain degree as I see it. In 1989, they built Pelican Bay. In 1988, they built Corcoran to take back control of the California Prison system from all the prison gangs. And they didn't really succeed because The Brand uses others to do their bidding on the mainlines. In the feds, they have all the power of The Brand locked up in ADX Florence, Colorado. Prison officials think that if they take the head then the body will die, meaning the rest of these gangs will fall apart when they lock up the leaders. But The Brand has been around a long time so they have a lot of influence. Overall they have slowly been losing control in both the state and federal prison system due to new cases, infighting and age. A lot of the leaders are dinosaurs."

On August 28, 2002, AUSA Greg Jessner indicted virtually the entire leadership of the gang. The indictment reached back twenty years spanning three decades and thirty-two murders. Forty members were indicted of federal racketeering charges in a 140, 10 count indictment. The majority of the gang members were already doing life sentences, so twenty-three of them were eligible for the death penalty. "This is a homicidal organization," Jessner announced. "That's what they do. They kill people. I suspect they kill more than the Mafia. They may be the most murderous criminal organization in the United States." The indictment was the largest capital case in the history of California and the AUSA indicted The Brand with laws originally passed to target mafia leaders. "Inmates and others who do not follow orders of the AB are subject to being murdered as is anyone who uses violence against an AB member or anyone who cooperates with law enforcement," the indictment read.

RACE WAR

A main component of the case was the ongoing race war with the DC Blacks in the federal Bureau of Prisons. The race wars in the federal system started on Nov 22, 1981 when the body of Robert M. Chappelle, a member of the DC Blacks was found dead in his cell at USP Marion. Thomas "Terrible Tom" Silverstein was the killer and Chappelle's death worried bureau officials who thought it might spark a war, which it certainly did. Raymond "Cadillac" Smith, the alleged national leader of the DC Blacks was the next person killed. Terrible Tom killed Cadillac on Sept 27, 1982 by stabbing him sixty-seven times in the Marion control unit and dragging his body up and down the tier so that those locked in their cells could see.

The race wars against the DC Blacks raged across the feds in the early 1980's and again in the 1990's when two DC Blacks were killed at USP Lewisburg by AB members who stabbed them thirty-five and thirty-four times to death. The feds accused Barry Mills and TD Bingham of ordering the killings at USP Lewisburg from their cells at ADX. The case reached back forty years to include stabbings, strangulations, poisonings, contract hits, conspiracy to commit murder, robbery, and narcotics trafficking. Mills, Bingham, Silverstein, and thirty-nine other members of the AB received life sentences on top of the life sentences they were already serving. The prosecutors won the case, but the jury refused to sentence the leaders to death for their convictions.

"The legacy of The Brand is the most dangerous white prison gang in the world," Bumperjack says. That is undisputed, but Bumperjack concedes that the gang's actions have been questionable. "Over the years, a lot of Brand started killing Brand for stupid, uncalled for reasons in the 1980's. Specifically, I didn't approve of it, but business is business and you have to overlook things like that which is also not right. But there were a lot of things I didn't approve of in my twenty-six years as a member, but we believe in *omertá*, the art of silence when it does not directly involve you."

The truth of the matter is that the Aryan Brotherhood is not as powerful as they once were, but they have spawned imitators and in prison systems all over across the nation the AB has members and associates. And longtime members like Bumperjack have come to see what it's all really about. "If you join a prison gang in California it's, 'blood in, blood out' so in reality you just sold your soul to the devil and should plan on living the rest of your existence incarcerated or getting killed by the gang." He says and that just about sums up the story of The Brand, the most infamous prison gang in America.

THE BRAND'S MOST NOTORIOUS

BARRY "THE BARON" MILLS

The Baron is known as the brain of the Aryan Brotherhood and has been a long time leader. He is responsible for much of their organizational structure and the formation of the three man commissions in the California and federal prison systems. Mills is a tactical and innovative gang leader whose word is law. He isn't afraid to get busy himself when necessary, but is equally adept at delegating and passing orders down the line. He is credited with the longevity of the gangs criminal enterprises and vicious reputation inside the belly of the beast.

Mills is responsible for 14 murders and was convicted of nearly decapitating a man at USP Atlanta in 1979. He has been sentenced to life many times over and seemingly doesn't care, content to live out his life as a career prison gangster. He became involved with the AB in San Quentin prison in the late 1960's after growing up in Northern California and quickly rose through their ranks as he returned to prison frequently as a young man finally getting his first life sentence for the near decapitation of a fellow prisoner.

As a result of a major racketeering indictment in 2006, he was convicted and given life again after a jury deadlocked on the death penalty. He now resides in the Bureau of Prison's Super max facility in Florence, Colorado serving his time in 24 hour lockdown with no human contact. Testifying for himself in one of the many trials he has been convicted at, Mills stated to the court, "We live in a different society then you do. There is justified violence in our society. I'm here to tell you that." Barry Mills is a real icon in The Brand who was there when it all started and has been credited with the gangs proliferation in the federal prison system.

TD "SUPER HONKEY" BINGHAM AKA "THE HULK"

The Hulk is a massive specimen of a man who benches 500 pounds and is known as The Baron's right hand man and chief enforcer. He is part of the three-man commission that controls activity in the federal prison system and was the shot caller who sent out the order to reignite the race war at USP Lewisburg in 1997, leading to the deaths of two DC Blacks, The Brand's arch enemies in the Bureau of Prisons.

Up until the massive 2006 racketeering indictment against the Aryan Brotherhood, The Hulk actually was scheduled to get out of prison after multiple decades inside. But with his conviction in that case he now sits alongside his general, The Baron, at ADX Florence doing natural life in total isolation, with hardly any recreation time, and restricted and limited correspondence. The Hulk is another long time AB member, from Northern California, who made his bones in the California Department of Corrections in the late 60's and early 70's before being released, committing more crimes and graduating to the federal prison system.

The Hulk and The Baron are primarily responsible for consolidating the AB power structure in 1980 and expanding the operations of the organization into federal and other state prisons. The two stalwarts of the gang transformed The Brand from a separatist-protection prison gang to a major criminal enterprise that controlled the drug trade and engaged in racketeering type activities to make significant cash profits. He once justified the life he led to a judge and jury by saying, "There's a code in every segment of society. Well, we have a different kind of moral and ethical code."

THOMAS "TERRIBLE TOM" SILVERSTEIN

Terrible Tom was from Long Beach, California and entered the California Youth Authority at the age of fourteen for juvenile delinquency. He was indoctrinated to the life of crime and never really left it, always trying to prove himself. He was sent to San Quentin at the tender age of nineteen and when he was paroled from that short bid he quickly jumped back into a life of crime and was sentenced to fifteen years for an armed robbery charge and sent to USP Leavenworth, an AB stronghold, in 1977. He got involved with The Brand and murdered an inmate to make his bones. He also got a life sentence for the crime. But Terrible Tom's murdering rampage had just started.

Terrible Tom started the AB-DC Black race war by killing Raymond "Cadillac" Smith, the leader of the DC Blacks in 1982 by stabbing him 67 times in the USP Marion Control Unit, where the worst of the worst inmates were housed at the time. Still, Terrible Tom wasn't finished. In 1983, he killed Correctional Officer Merle Clutts at USP Marion with a prison fashioned shank for disrespecting him. The state raised kid had murder on his mind, but the Bureau of Prisons had something in store for him. They developed a special isolation cell just for him. He was a man considered so dangerous by the BOP that he was totally cut off from the outside world and human contact.

"Within the gangs' lore, Silverstein has become the Christ figure," Assistant US Attorney Jessner, who was the lead prosecutor on the 2006 racketeering indictment, said about Terrible Tom. He currently holds the distinction of being the longest held prisoner in total solitary confinement in the BOP, 28 long years of being deprived of any and all contact with fellow prisoners. At one of his numerous murder trials Terrible Tom said, "I have walked over dead bodies. I've had guts splattered all over my chest from race wars." And for real, no one can accuse him of being a liar.

ARYAN BROTHERHOOD TATOOS

The main tattoo of the Aryan Brotherhood is the distinctive shamrock clover that made members get to signify that they are official and legitimate members. The shamrock is the brand that gives them the name they go by in the pen—The Brand. It's said that when Michael "Big Mac" McElhiney, who had a big shamrock in the middle of his chest, hit USP Leavenworth in the fall of 1994, all he had to do was flash his shamrock and he was handed the keys to the white boy car on the compound. That is the strength of The Brand inside the belly of the beast

And if an AB member finds someone fronting with the shamrock tattoo or showing The Brand's colors or flag they will make them cover up the tattoo, burn it off, or even cut it off if that is what it takes. They are very touchy about who wears that tattoo or any other AB insignia like lightning bolts on the underside of the forearms which is another old school indicator of AB membership.

But AB members sport a variety of different kinds of tattoos besides their colors: tattoos of fierce Vikings, Nazi imagery like swastikas, 666 tattoos, Celtic tattoos, 1488 tattoos, spiderwebs on their elbows, nicknames emblazoned across their backs, dates signifying how long they've spent in prison with hourglasses and prison bars represented the life they have chosen to live as prison gangsters. Most AB members are covered in tattoos and take a certain pride in where they got them and who inked them up and what the circumstances were.

9

KENNETH "SUPREME" MCGRIFF
THE SUPREME TEAM DEFINES THE CRACK ERA

Romanticized, mythologized, and even glorified by hip-hop's superstar elite, the Supreme Team has gone down in legend as the most celebrated crew from the crack era. Their iconic reputation in the drug world inspired hip-hop culture and rap heavyweights like 50 Cent, Jay-Z, Biggie, Nas, and Ja Rule. Born at the same time as crack, hip-hop was heavily influenced by the drug lords that controlled New York city's streets.

In the five boroughs, the Supreme Team reigned as overlords of a crack empire that stretched multiple city blocks. But they weren't content to be just kings of the streets, their efforts played a big part in the birth and success of hip-hop music. Not only did the aspiring rappers emulate members of the Team in attitude, mentality, and swagger, but they were funded in part by the Team who threw massive block parties where the rappers performed, honing their skills in a forum that was receptive to their art form. In the annals of hip-hop history, the Supreme Team holds a special place in the hierarchy of the drug crews that have been lionized in rap, making them a permanent part of popular culture.

THE PEACE GODS

What has become known as the Supreme Team was a crew organized in the early 1980's in the vicinity of the Baisley Park Houses, a public housing project in Jamaica Queens, New York, by a group of teenagers, who were members of a quasi-religious sect known as the Five Percenters. The Peace Gods as they were known, for greeting each other with the words "peace, god" evolved into the Supreme Team, becoming a monster crew that dwarfed other drug networks of the era—but they took their cue from the streets.

The flashy hustlers of the day set the standard and became role models for the neighborhood, flaunting their alluring lifestyle, which was well beyond the reach of working class Queens. "Ronnie Bumps, the Corleys, Pretty Tony on Liberty Avenue, Tommy Mickens on Rockaway, Fat Cat, these were the niggas we looked up to. These were the niggas that set shit up for us," says Bing, a Supreme Team member. "You see it all in hip-hop, but back then, that was the streets."

The working class neighborhoods of South Jamaica, St. Albans and Hollis where the Supreme Team operated their drug enterprise lie in the 103rd and 113th Precincts, which are a 4.8 square mile perfect box encompassing Van Wyck Expressway to the West, Hillside Ave to the North, Francis Lewis Boulevard to the East and a jagged line that runs along the 110th Ave to the South. Around 125,000 people lived within its borders back then with 62 percent of them black.

Under the leadership of Kenneth "Supreme" McGriff, with Gerald "Prince" Miller, his nephew as second in command, the gang concentrated its criminal efforts on widespread distribution of crack cocaine. But they differed from other crews, due to their Five Percenter ideology and the fact that they recruited both Latinos and blacks, which enabled them to bypass larger local dealers like Lorenzo "Fat Cat" Nichols and plug directly into Colombian cocaine distributors due to their Latino members.

Under the red brick towers of Baisley Projects, an around the clock crack cocaine trade operating more like a corporation than a drug outfit prospered, selling 25,000 crack vials a week. The Supreme Team's narcotics operation used dozens of employees, including layers of drug sellers to insulate the gang leaders from the street-level activity, court documents relate. Team members communicated in coded language and numerical systems. To thwart law enforcement efforts further, the Team used armed bodyguards and deployed sentinels with two-way radios on rooftops.

Supreme was the recognized founder and leader of the Supreme Team. Everything was done under his banner. He is credited with bringing the drug crew into existence and overseeing all of their operations. At his pre-1987 peak, it's said he generated $200,000 daily selling crack and cocaine out of his drug spots at Baisley Projects.

There was no free styling. Either you were down with the Team or else. That was how it played out in the streets. And the Team placed a premium on loyalty.

"Supreme is a dude who will rationalize, talk it out. He's very diplomatic and charismatic. I remember the name Supreme as someone who always was spoken of highly. I don't know if it was out of fear or respect. But usually when people spoke that name they were speaking of something greater than themselves," Tuck, a Supreme Team member, says of the man known as the General. Supreme led a team that was said to be over 200 deep and rivaled the Mafia in structure. The Team used a color coded system for the vials of crack. Each color signified whose cocaine it was. A color for every lieutenant of the organization—yellow, orange, red and blue.

With his team supporting his moves, Supreme's power on the streets of South Jamaica grew. The Southside was gradually coming under the sway of the Team. "From '81 to '85 everybody was home," Bing says. "The Team was in full effect and dominated the streets." As they became more entrenched in the drug game, dudes got busted, cases would come and go, and they would lose members to the criminal justice system. But their first run was uninterrupted, and during this time they forged their legend in the hood.

Supreme came up with the slogan, "no singles, no shorts" which his dealers chanted like a mantra, repeating it to crack customers, meaning no dollar bills and don't come short with the money. It's said Supreme had such an aversion to dollar bills that he used to pass out $3000 worth of singles a day, everyday in Baisley Projects. He also had turkey giveaways and funded trips to amusement parks for the kids that lived in the projects. He was like a Robin Hood. But there was another side to the drug dealing life.

THE GAME

Drugs, murder, kidnappings, shootings, more drugs, and more murder were the rule of the day. They called it "the game," but it was a vicious attempt to come up by any means necessary. In the late-80's, the mindset was "get mine or be mine," and nobody embodied this attitude better than the Supreme Team. "Back then the game was the game. Everybody stood by the rules. Soldiers were soldiers," Bing says. "This was the era from which Supreme and the Team emerged. It was a time when men were men, and the consequences of snitching were clear."

In Queens, snitching was forbidden. It was embedded in the young gangster's DNA. *Omertá* played a powerful role in shaping the crack-era hustler's mindset in terms of how they saw the world. Nobody took liberties and keeping your mouth shut became a sign of a go-hard gangster. They took their cue from *Scarface* and ran with it times ten. The hip-hop mafia was in effect.

"In the early-80's when *Scarface* came out, all the young cats wanted to be like that," Lance Fuertado, a drug dealer from the era says. *Scarface* was a movie about them and for them. The Supreme Team embraced the gun culture promoted by the movie. Firearms became a must have fashion accessory. A "shoot or be shot" mentality emerged. The guns gave them a feeling of having juice or power over their rivals.

"It made all of the youngsters dream. All the youngsters wanted to be drug dealers. It gave us a dream," Antoine Clark from *F.E.D.S.* magazine, says. "This was the Bible. It was inspirational. Had people taking risks. Doing crazy shit. Glamorizing sex, guns and drugs." And as big of an impact as it had on the drug world, its effect was equally important on hip-hop culture.

"They saw this come up. To the people in the hood it was a way to get on. Nino was working *Scarface* in *New Jack City*. It made niggas want to get money. It's the classic hustler movie. They went crazy with *Scarface*," Antoine says. "None of us thought we could be Scarface, but we could have that mentality of taking over wherever we went. He gave us that mentality."

Scarface made selling drugs seem cool and lucrative. It romanticized the dope game while glamorizing it and led a whole generation of youth astray. In reality that movie corrupted the black community. It made dudes want to be hustlers and get money by any means necessary. Supreme was one of those who took the mentality to heart.

He dressed in expensive white suits with the crisp white shirt open just like Tony Montana. He embraced the swagger and adopted the fictional gangster's style. He carried himself with the class of an older, more established hustler even when he wasn't. His debonair appearance and demeanor was what made the Supreme Team willing to go to war for him.

"He's very charismatic, he can be the perfect gentleman, but he wants to win at all costs," recalls T, a gangster from the era. "He is not an abrasive dude. He's a good hearted individual." But behind the ghetto glitz and kind heart was a seriousness about hustling that elevated Supreme above his many peers on the streets.

"Not all gangsters are outlaws and not all outlaws are gangsters," Prince says. "Stand up people do not fold or run when faced with difficulty. We analyze and determine the best course of action, holding firm to the principle of never harm another to save yourself. We understand that every action we choose has consequences. Therefore, before we act, we first settle within our hearts and minds that we can handle the consequences, whether it be beneficial or detrimental to ourselves and the lives of those we risk our life and freedom for." For gangsters that is what it's about.

"When we was coming up there was a code of conduct," Supreme says. "The game has been over for a long time. It's a sad state of affairs. It is designed so that the only one who can flourish is the rat. Treason is the betrayal of one's trust or assisting the other side." Supreme and the Team lived by the death before dishonor credo, a maxim that has long held sway in hip-hop and the Mafia.

There were rules in the dope game and prospective dealers or wanna-be gangsters had to prove their mettle to the hierarchy of already established hustlers in their hood. They were tested before they were allowed to put a foot in the door. Not just anybody was allowed to be a player in the game. Dudes like Supreme and Prince had to pay their dues, as did all the members of the Supreme Team.

"Death before dishonor. You get arrested, you closed your mouth and kept it shut and went to jail. That was installed in me as a kid by older guys who I came up under in the streets. The way I grew up and the people I looked up to showed me morals and principles. They told me that when you go out to hustle, you hold your own." Bing says and the Peace Gods were always hustlers despite the religious overtones.

"Niggas was always hustling before they was selling drugs," Bing says. "They were robbing banks, burglarizing, shooting dice, robbing, sticking dudes up, gambling. The Team did banks and shit. That's how they started in 1982. We always had our hustles before we started dealing drugs and we were gangbanging."

GROUND ZERO FOR CRACK AND HIP-HOP

The Southside of Jamaica, Queens became both ground zero for crack and hip-hop, a fertile breeding ground for both rappers and drug dealers. Supreme played a pivotal role in the growth of hip-hop as he used to book early acts like Curtis Blow, LL Cool J, and the Beastie Boys, paying them $1000 a night to play at his lavish gangster parties. In turn the rappers copied his style, swagger, and trends.

American culture loves its bad guys and the legendary figures of the drug game were the province of myth and hearsay until hip-hop artists romanticized their exploits in verse. The Queens underworld has long captured the imagination of the public with the fusion of ghetto and prison culture unique to gangsta rap. The Supreme Team is just the latest in a long line of outlaw heroes immortalized in popular culture.

"The Team was the flyest crew in Queens," Bing says. They talked the talk and walked the walk, becoming lords of the ghetto in the process. The young drug dealers and hip-hop scene that would sweep the nation in the 1990's and popularize Queens' culture owed a debt to these icons. Dripping in gold and carrying guns, with sharp clothes and flashy cars the Team popularized thug culture. "Dudes from Queens always stayed fly," Bing says, "Queens was always fly niggas, getting-money niggas. We had to prove ourselves though."

The Supreme Team had a reputation to earn, a reputation to uphold. A legacy was born, and they embraced and adopted it. That reputation earned Queens a place in the power struggles of the streets and in the rap world. Queens became hip-hop, and the Supreme Team epitomized Queens. Not surprisingly, when Run DMC started making noise in hip-hop in the early-80's they brought b-boy style, Queens culture and the drug dealer mindset to the mainstream. These were all attributes they learned from the Supreme Team.

Queens became where it was at, and dudes from the borough started to stick their chests out. It was a drug game thing; it was a hip-hop thing; it was a Queens thing. It was a growing mentality and attitude that they developed, nurtured, and created. All the neighborhoods in Queens were now being heard together with one defiant voice. Respect was what that voice demanded, and dudes from all parts of the city knew that Queens' hustlers were getting theirs. Queens went from faking it to running it. They were getting their respect in the streets, in the prisons and in hip-hop. "It was the niggas from Queens making all the noise," Bing says. "We started all this gangster shit." But Team members also paid gangster prices.

GANGSTER PRICES

Supreme oversaw the Team during its "wonder years" from the early 80's until his incarceration by the state in 1985 and subsequently the feds in 1987. He served two years in the state and then went home on appeal bond when he overturned his 1985 conviction. But it didn't last, the feds came calling and Supreme pled guilty in 1987 to a "continuing criminal enterprise" charge for running the Supreme Team and was imprisoned again.

After Supreme went to jail in 1987, leadership of the Supreme Team was assumed by Prince. Supreme's nephew was the enforcer and second in command for the Supreme Team. Prince solidified his control by increasing the security force and employing it against rivals and against team members suspected of disloyalty. Prince had a vicious crew and security force that had several drug spots inside and out of Baisley Projects. They sold the yellow top vials of crack, making almost $500,000 monthly. Known as the enforcement wing of the Team, Prince's crew handled all beefs, confrontations, security matters, and inner team disciplinary actions.

Prince became known as Mr. Untouchable in New York City's tabloid newspapers during the late-80's due to his proclivity to beat any and every case the state brought him up on. He beat multiple murder charges including the gruesome quadruple murders of four Colombian coke dealers Prince and his crew tricked into bringing eight kilos of coke to them at Baisley Projects, proceeding to double-cross and murder them instead of paying them for the drugs in the summer of 1987.

Prince was also brought to trial for shooting a rival dealer point blank in the head in broad daylight and acquitted when the witnesses recanted their testimony. Prince was known as one of the most violent and feared gunmen and kingpins in New York during the crack era and had no problems blowing a person's brains out whenever the opportunity presented itself. The wonder years of the hip-hop era had ended as the Supreme Team turned into a full fledged criminal organization that handled all beefs with gun play.

Supreme eventually got out in the mid-1990's and started rolling with Irv Gotti's Murder Inc. crew. He managed to produce *Crime Partners*, a straight-to-video DVD based on a Donald Goines novel of the same name. He rose high in the hip-hop hierarchy, riding shotgun with Murder Inc., during their dominant chart topping years in the music industry, when they were media darlings and MTV/BET staples.

In his 1990's heyday, as hip-hop royalty, he was linked by police to every rap related crime and pursued heavily by the hip-hop cops. The organized crime task force was always conducting continuous investigations regarding him and his dealings also. He has been accused of shooting 50 Cent and allegedly had a hand in the Jam Master Jay murder. He went back to prison in 2001 and has remained there, getting a life sentence on a murder for hire charge for the shooting death of Mobb Deep affiliate E-Money Bags.

Supreme and Prince are now doing life in the federal prison system for their exploits in the drug game. Many other members of the Supreme Team are either in prison with their leaders or did their time and got out. Most of the notable and reputable faces from the crack era are either dead or in jail. The impact the hip-hop hustlers, like those from the Supreme Team, had on rap and popular culture is undeniable. You see it everywhere in music and film today. But the inevitability of their fates is real, they are not walking off the set of a movie or a video. At the end of the day they are getting locked in a cell every night and getting served oatmeal for breakfast in the chow hall every morning. It was fun while it lasted, but the reality of living life in prison is final.

PLAYERS IN THE GAME

KENNETH "SUPREME" MCGRIFF

Supreme was the leader and namesake of the legendary team. They called him "The General" and in the streets his word was law. He was known to be a deep thinker and very diplomatic. He was not prone to violence but understood its uses. But he would only resort to violence as a last option when all else failed. He was in prison as much as he was on the streets during his reign, but his crew had such respect and admiration for him that he was afforded the opportunity to run the drug organization from the various penitentiaries where he was housed during his numerous incarcerations. He has gone down in legend as a gentleman gangster and is one of the most respected men of honor from New York City. Some liken him a black John Gotti.

GERALD "PRINCE" MILLER

Prince was the yin to Supreme's yang. Although Supreme's nephew, he was only two years younger and Supreme and Prince grew up together like brothers. Where Supreme was cautious and careful, Prince was bold and reckless. The two leaders of the Supreme Team were really night and day. Officially Prince was the second in command and leader of his own sub-crew which featured the feared security team and his own drug dealing network which sold yellow vials. When anything jumped off with the Supreme Team you can bet that Prince was usually at the center of it.

TROY "BABYWISE" JONES

Babywise was an original Supreme Team member, a part of what they called "the original seed." He was down since day one and his crew controlled the red top vials. He worked as a lieutenant under Supreme and sold out of numerous drug spots in and around Baisley Projects. He allegedly made 20 to 30 thousand dollars every other day and was a Supreme loyalist and supporter who answered to no one but himself. Babywise was known as a smooth ladies man who kept to himself and avoided the limelight, but would bust his guns when necessary, handling the Team's business. He was one of the only members in the crew who refused to talk business on the phone and this was long before *Goodfellas* and *The Wire*. He didn't take photos or go out to parties, preferring to stay low profile, get money, and handle his business. He was one of the most intelligent members on the team and espoused his values on life, drug dealing, and the Supreme Team freely. His word and advice was highly respected and people listened when he talked. His spots were steady and generated mucho illicit dinero for himself and the team. He was known as a fly dresser that rocked all the latest fashions and luxury automobiles of the era. It's said that it was his crew that sported the infamous matching red Supreme Team jackets.

ERNESTO "PUERTO RICAN RIGHTEOUS" PINIELLA

Puerto Rican Righteous was one of the Supreme Team's top enforcers. He got down with Supreme and the team early in its existence. He was known as a go hard *boriqua* and acted as security for the crew. He was one of the most feared and respected team members and eventually was placed in charge of the security force under Prince. When Prince and Supreme were in jail fighting cases, Righteous handled their business, collected money owed, and enforced their will on the streets: making sure the spots ran smoothly, the connects kicked down kilos, and malcontents got in line by any means necessary. Righteous worked under both Supreme and Prince as an enforcer. His inclusion into the team ensured the future entrance of Hispanic members into the crew. With Righteous and their Spanish members, the Supreme Team was able to bypass the bigger black dealers like Fat Cat, Pretty Tony, and Tommy Mickens and buy cocaine in wholesale quantities directly from Colombians, thus cutting the price down and increasing the quality of the product at the same time. Righteous was said to be genuinely fearless and was very respected for the work that he put in. He played a major part in the double-cross murder robbery of four unsuspecting Colombian cocaine dealers, who were lured into Baisley Projects under false pretenses, and then viciously killed for the eight kilos of cocaine they brought to sell to the team. Righteous allegedly acted under Prince's orders.

JAMES "BIMMY" ANTNEY

Bimmy was a long time lieutenant for the team and got down with the crew right after their inception. He was in charge of the blue top vials and was known as a major money getter and player who all the ladies and rappers flocked around. He was said to punctuate all his sentences with "Word to Preme" and considered Supreme a god. His crew controlled several drug spots in or around Baisley Projects and made almost up to thirty thousand dollars every other day, selling crack and cocaine. Bimmy has always been known as the most well connected Supreme Team member in the music and entertainment business. He was down with the hip-hop scene from day one and ran with Run DMC, Russell Simmons, and LL Cool J when they were still rapping on the block. The rappers were like family to him back in the day and Bimmy also supported a young 50 Cent, who used to hang with Bimmy and Black Just before he became famous.

COLBERT "BLACK JUSTICE" JOHNSON

Black Just was a Supreme Team lieutenant who allegedly started as a worker in Babywise's crew before rising up to run a crew of his own. He was known to be a Supreme favorite and controlled the orange top vials, selling at several drug spots in and around Baisley Projects. It's said he took care of all the other Supreme Team members financially, Supreme especially, as they went in and out of jail, fighting their cases or did their time in prison. Black Just was known as a Supreme stalwart and it's said that he "bled Supreme Team," holding the crew down through thick and thin. He would go visit Supreme in federal prison and relay his orders back to Prince and the crew. When Prince went in, Black Just and Bimmy effectively became the bosses of the team. Black Just was very involved in the mid-80's and 90's hip-hop scenes, going to all the parties, events, and hobnobbing with all the rap superstars to be.

WILFREDO "C-JUST" ARROYO

C-Just was known as a real quiet, soft-spoken dude who never raised his voice. But he was as thorough as they come and ready to put in work at a moment's notice. The Puerto Rican Five Percenter was a vital part of the security team and was very close to both Prince and Supreme. Doing their bidding and making sure the security aspect of the team was always top shelf. He assisted in arranging cocaine purchases, provided security during drug transactions, supervised the processing of cocaine into crack, and delivered crack to sales locations. He also allegedly helped to terrorize Southeastern Queens at Prince's behest, unleashing a string of violence that the feds say included at least nine murders. C-Just was a main player in the crew when they where described by prosecutors as one of the busiest and bloodiest of the trafficking rings that plagued Queens at the height of the crack epidemic.

HARRY "BIG C" HUNT

Big C was known as Prince's right hand man. A real serious and intimidating cat that had dreads, wore dark glasses and tank tops that showed off his huge arms which were like pythons. He was a loose cannon and Prince was the only one who could talk and control him. He was the fear factor that Prince moved and progressed off of. Dudes in the streets were very leery of Big C. But he had a comical side and was fun to hang with despite his menacing demeanor. With C-Just and Puerto Rican Righteous, he formed the core of Prince's security team. The security team had a fearsome and well deserved reputation in the hood and they dressed accordingly. Tales from late 80's Queens claim the army fatigue look was a Supreme Team signature. Their war gear was black fatigues and jackets, bulletproof vests, black Timberlands and hats, the drawstring joints or baseball caps. And their weaponry consisted of AR-15's, Mac-10's, Nines, 45's, 357's, Tech—you name it, they had it. And when they were on a mission, shit got crazy. They would be jumping out of mini-vans like a task force. And when dudes on the block saw them they'd start running and scrambling praying that the team wasn't coming for them.

LYRICAL LEGACY

The Supreme Team has gone down in hip-hop history as one of the baddest to ever do it in the 1980's crack-era in New York City. Their stomping ground, Baisley Projects in the Southside of Queens, became ground zero for both crack and hip-hop. They were ghetto superstars in the extreme in their day and their accolades are profiled in verse.

The Supreme Team became Robin Hood-type figures, very central to the core of rap's lyrical lore. Their legend has impacted the beat, vibe, style, and rhythm of the music and culture. They transformed Queens into a "nightlife Mecca", where drug lords reigned king and the burgeoning hip-hop generation took note turning their 80's exploits into the bling-bling proliferation that came to define rap in the 90's.

In *Ghetto Qur'an,* 50 Cent called Preme the businessman and said he was very well respected in the streets. Supreme has been mentioned in numerous other raps by Ja Rule, Noreaga, and others. The characters Nino Brown in *New Jack City* and Majestic in *Get Rich or Die Tryin'* are said to be based on Supreme.

Prince is mentioned in several rap songs including *Get Down* by Nas on *2002 God's Son* and 50 Cent's *Ghetto Qur'an* where he is described as the killer to Supreme's businessman. 50 raps that "nigga's feared Prince and respected Preme." Prince was infamous for always wearing a bulletproof vest and baseball cap everywhere he went, driving a tricked out James Bond enhanced bulletproof BMW and for having the whole projects working for "50 on 500." That means for every $500 worth of crack they sold, the dealers got $50. The rest of the money went to Prince. Prince was notorious for making potential witnesses to his and the Team's crimes disappear or recant their stories.

Black Just, or Blackie as he was called on the team, used to hang out in Harlem a lot. He was down with Rich Porter and Alpo back in the day and used to go to all the trendy clubs of the era like The Rooftop, Latin Quarter, and The Tunnel. Blackie was a very smooth character and dresser who was known to change cars like other people changed shoes. Driving Porsches, Beamers, Benzs, Land Rovers, and other luxury automobiles from the 80's and 90's. He was killed by Mobb Deep affiliate E-Money Bags in a 1999 shootout on the streets of Queens. Supreme drove him to the hospital, but it was too late—Black Just had bled to death.

Black Just was very instrumental in the young 50 Cent's early drug dealing career and ran a boxing club in the hood that 50 frequented. 50 Cent has mentioned Black Just numerous times in magazine interviews and rapped about him on *50 Bars of Pleasure, 50 Bars of Pain*. The Supreme loyalist stayed true to his boss till the end, dying right next to him in the shootout with E-Money Bags, possibly even taking the bullet meant for Supreme. It took Supreme a couple of years, but he got revenge for Black Just by having a hit squad kill E-Money Bags *Dead Presidents*-style in 2002. After the hit Supreme allegedly told friends that, "Blackie could finally rest in peace."

Babywise was mentioned in 50 Cent's *Ghetto Qur'an* and other songs. He was known as one of Supreme's main men and allegedly shot another crew member, Green Eyed Born, in the leg for having a disagreement with Supreme. Babywise was one of the originals and has remained loyal to Supreme and flown the Supreme Team banner since the jump. His name has gone down in legend, even as he has attempted to stay in the background and let other members of the team get all the hype and accolades.

Bimmy has been known as a longtime Supreme Team lieutenant and Supreme enthusiast who had one foot firmly entrenched in the entertainment world and one foot squarely planted in the criminal realm. He has been around since the beginning of hip-hop and has managed to move between the two worlds successfully, at the same time inspiring rappers like Run DMC and LL Cool J, who adopted his street styles, attitudes and mentality. He has always been a familiar figure around the Southside of Jamaica cruising in his BMW or Mercedes Benz. Although not known to bust his gun, he has always been a serious money getter and hustler extraordinaire. At one point, Bimmy worked as an A & R man in the music industry and had his own venture,

3 to Life Entertainment, which helped him to make inroads into the industry. He has always stayed fly and in fashion and rocked luxury whips and sported dime pieces on his arm. His nephew is rapper Waka Flocka Flame.

Puerto Rican Righteous is mentioned in 50 Cent's *Ghetto Qur'an* and became infamous as a turncoat when he switched sides and decided to testify against Prince and his former comrades. He has gone down in the chronicles of gangster lore as a rat of the highest order—one who betrayed the trust of his homeboys by breaking weak and snitching to save his own ass. He has told people that he testified against Prince because Prince slept with his wife when he got locked up, implying that Prince betrayed him first. Righteous was also known as a loose cannon who perpetrated the worst of the Supreme Team's heinous and violent crimes and then flipped the script on his comrades and blamed them for his actions.

The Supreme Team has been romanticized and glorified in hip-hop, but the truth of the matter is that most of their members are currently in prison for life or have spent decades of their prime years behind bars. The team and its infamous leaders, Supreme and Prince, have been profiled on BET's *American Gangster* series, in Ethan Brown's *Queens Reigns Supreme* and Seth Ferranti's *Street Legends Vol.1,* and in street magazines like *Don Diva*, *As Is* and *F.E.D.S.* Currently Prince is serving seven life sentences at USP Allenwood inPennsylvania and Supreme is serving life at USP Lee inVirginia. Their tale is one of turns, twists and fate, but their influence and relevance has left a lasting impression. The drug game influenced the style and swagger of street culture, hip-hop and gangsta rap and made the Supreme Team icons in the annals of gangster lore.

10

"LITTLE VIC" AMUSO & "GASPIPE" CASSO
THE CREW THAT TRIED TO "WHACK JERSEY"

The order came down, "whack Jersey." It was as unprecedented as it was insane. But from the New York side at the time it was expected. From all accounts, Vittorio "Little Vic" Amuso and "Gaspipe" Casso were madmen—power hungry and ready to murder anyone who they thought was standing in their way. Both were paranoid and violent, killing friends and enemies in equal turns. They put the murder in the Mafia.

THE NEW KIDS ON THE BLOCK

"Anthony 'Gaspipe' Casso was extremely cunning," says Philip Carlo, author of *Gaspipe: Confessions of a Mob Boss*. "He was in a very real sense, born into mafia culture, absorbing the mindset and belief system in a neighborhood in South Brooklyn where a lot of *mafioso* come from."

Little Vic and Gaspipe, the new kids on the block were steeped in Mafia culture, old enough to know the glory years but young enough to be enamored with the romanticism of the mob that Hollywood infused. They took over when Tony Ducks Corallo, the don of the Lucchese family, went to prison. Weirdly enough they were handpicked to lead the Lucchese family by the highly respected and smart Tony Ducks, who was sentenced to one hundred years in the famous Commission case.

The mob's history is one filled with violence and murder, but Casso and Amuso stand out as being among the most bloodthirsty and ruthless gangsters ever to have their finger pricked and become a made guy. After Corallo went away, the family descended into bloody chaos. Lucchese mobsters ended up dead all over the place. Based on rumors and innuendo, Casso and Amuso ordered dozens of mobsters whacked and then they turned their attention to the Jersey crew.

New York wise guys have always thought of the Jersey guys as farmers and when Anthony "Tumac" Accetturo, a Lucchese old-timer running the show in the Garden State, refused to up his tribute to the New York faction's new bosses, it was on and popping. These guys were going to the mattresses. It was death before dishonor.

Tumac was an old-fashioned *mafioso*. He believed in *omertà*, the Mafia's oath of loyalty and the code of honor. He'd come up in the Mafia's heyday and was a man's man, equally apt to shoot you and kill you as well as fight you. He was raised a street fighter that took care of business and gained his nickname "Tumac" from the caveman in the 1940's film, *One Million BC*.

He was an earner too. Tumac had houses in both New Jersey and in Florida, he had multiple rackets going on in both states. Tony Ducks loved Tumac. They'd been in business for a long time, a relationship stretching over thirty years because basically Tony Ducks let Tumac run Jersey for the Lucchese's.

"The New Jersey faction, at that time, was led by Tumac. He ran rackets in the Garden State and down in Florida, everything from unions and gambling to drugs. Accetturo had, as he called it, a great relationship with Tony Ducks enabling him to kick up just a small percentage of the crew's earnings to the family leadership," explains David Amoruso, a mob expert.

But when Little Vic and Gaspipe took over it was a different story. They wanted their money and they weren't going for the same arrangement that their boss Tony Ducks had with Tumac. The Jersey gangster was making several million a year from his rackets, having a stake in numerous legitimate businesses along with narcotics, extortion, loan-sharking, and gambling, all mafia mainstays. The new New York bosses saw all of this money and wondered why they weren't getting their cut. They wanted in on the action ASAP.

But Tumac was an old school gangster raised in the neighborhood. Jersey was his turf, as was Florida. He had worked from the ground up and established himself in the criminal underworld. He wasn't giving up what he'd earned, especially not to what he considered violent upstarts. Tumac was old-school. He wasn't going for all the woofing. He'd been in the game too long. He wasn't a rah-rah type of *mafioso* and he considered Little Vic and Gaspipe cowboys.

"TOP COP" BOBBY BUCCINO

Tumac grew up with another local tough guy, Bobby Buccino, who became first a state trooper and would later end up connected to the State of New Jersey's Attorney General's office. His speciality was supervising cases against New Jersey *mafioso*. Buccino had grown up in the neighborhood and knew what the score was.

"I grew up with Tumac. He was a year younger than me. His older brother Rocco was a good friend of mine and I grew up with him. He was in the neighborhood and I used to kick his ass," said Buccino, author of the book *New Jersey Mob: Memoirs of a Top Cop*. "Back in time when Tumac first came to view, when I heard he was involved in organized crime, I figured he had to be a laborer or something."

The future top cop in New Jersey wasn't very impressed with Tumac as a kid. He never thought he would rise in the ranks of *La Cosa Nostra* but Tumac proved that he was super capable when it came to crime and running a LCN crew.

"I don't think he passed the third grade in school, but the fact of the matter was he was a very wise guy, a very smart guy, and he was meeting with bandits from all over the country. He started with the Indian bingo and he started doing things and he was smart enough to share his profits with other families, so he was really testing to be the new boss," Buccino shares. "Matter of fact he took care of Ducks Corallo on his deathbed. Tumac was a pretty smart and tough guy. He was also very demanding of money. He liked green. He made sure that he got a ten, no matter what happened with the New Jersey faction."

Buccino was a lawmen's lawman. He'd worked his way up the ranks just like Tumac. Though polar opposites they had that connection from their youth. It was a tie that Tumac would ultimately utilize when the homicidal antics of Gaspipe and Amuso multiplied exponentially.

When Casso and Amuso assumed control they were utterly disgusted with what Accetturo kicked upstairs. They demanded a fifty-percent cut. Accetturo refused. Tensions were already high. Lucchese gangsters were dropping like flies at the hands of their fellow brothers, and when Accetturo refused to attend a meeting with Casso and Amuso the fuse was lit.

WHACK JERSEY

"The story behind the so-called 'Whack Jersey' directive was revealed to the public during the trial of Lucchese crime family boss Vittorio Amuso," says Christian Cipollini, author of *Lucky Luciano*. "Alphonse D'Arco, who became acting boss in early 1991, struck a deal with the government that same year. Amuso and his underboss Gaspipe had gone into hiding mode, which put D'Arco in the top position, but really only as an 'acting' boss or figurehead. Amuso was calling the shots. By 1992, Gaspipe was still on the run, but Amuso had been caught and brought to trial, whereby D'Arco spilled the details on, among many other sinister activities, who and why the New Jersey faction was being targeted during the 1980's."

The New Jersey faction of the Lucchese family had a chronic problem of paying the New York based boss, Amuso, on time or in full. Little Vic and especially his underboss Gaspipe were not known for having good temperaments. Their M.O. was shoot first, ask questions later. They'd killed people frequently and for less. Casso was a hands-on kind of guy, seemingly obsessed with murder.

The Jersey crew was made up of approximately fifteen mobsters led by Tumac. Sometime in the late 1980's, when the payment lag situation began, Amuso's hatred for Tumac and his son in particular grew. He viewed both as disrespectful. He was the boss and they weren't paying their proper respects. Eventually that disdain turned into an edict – kill all the Jersey crew guys. "Whack Jersey" was in effect. It was the first time a whole mafia family had been green-lighted.

Some of the Jersey crew members, including Tumac and his son, were invited to discuss the problem with the New York guys, but if the meeting location was suspicious, like a basement, the Jersey guys would refuse or back out of the meeting for fear of being set up to be killed. They knew what was up when it came to Little Vic and Gaspipe.

"The vicious bosses put out contracts on Tumac and his son, who was also a made member," Amoruso explains. "Other members of the Jersey crew became anxious as well. When they were summoned to a meeting, they talked outside and voiced their fears of a set up.

Within minutes all men were driving their cars back towards New Jersey. When that happened it was the straw that broke the camel's back. Casso exploded and yelled, 'That's it! Kill them all!'"

KILL THEM ALL!

With his crew loyal to him, Tumac and his son went down to their Florida haunts. He had a couple of street bosses run New Jersey for him. The Taccetta brothers were adept at both avoiding Gaspipe's hitmen as well as running the New Jersey crew's rackets while keeping Tumac's fingers in every pie.

"Michael and Marty Taccetta fell under Tumac's wing," Buccino says. "From when they were young punks robbing vending machines. Tumac had gone to Florida and his headquarters was at the Marco Polo Lounge in Fort Lauderdale. The Taccettas worked for him and they start becoming his muscle and one thing lead to another. They got made and they started to bring back the New Jersey faction Lucchese crime family."

Through the Taccettas, Tumac remained in control of the numbers rackets, sports betting, and the loan sharking business. The Taccettas were very well respected and serious mobsters. Their loyalty to Tumac was unconditional. Overtures from Little Vic and Gaspipe, who tried to get them back in the Lucchese fold, were rebuffed.

"I was deeply involved with them taking over businesses," Buccino recalls. "I would hear that there was a business in trouble, you know, I would go out and meet with the business people and tell them I could take care of that problem by locking the mobsters up. Michael Taccetta was always very respectful to me, always respectful. He hated my guts, but he also respected me. I once served a subpoena on him. I said to him, 'You're a mob guy and I'm a cop, but you can't bribe me or anything.' Taccetta goes, 'Oh, no, we would never try to bribe you because you're no phony.'"

As Buccino and New Jersey state officials investigated Tumac's operations, Gaspipe gave New York based hitmen photos, names, and addresses of all the Jersey *mafioso* that were loyal to Tumac. The war was on. But it was a hurry up and wait situation as the New

Jersey guys stayed under the radar and out of sight from the Luccsese hit squads sent into Jersey and Florida to kill them.

"The New York guys referred to them as country boys. They never accepted them as a viable crew," Buccino says. "There was always friction between them. Tumac did nothing but provide services for the family, so he always had that problem, big boys with the little boys, you know. And in the meantime the New Jersey boys were doing pretty well financially. They were doing some good operations.

"There were always problems coming up between the New Jersey faction and the New York faction. Prior to the Whack Jersey statement, the New York guys came over and opened up a company, it was a trailer in the Jersey area. They were organizing the transportation of garages from New York and New Jersey to Ohio and Pennsylvania. They didn't let the New Jersey faction in on it—just moved over. That created friction, but it was a continuous thing between them. And then, New York as everybody knows started killing everybody, even their own soldiers."

It was a tense situation in mob land between the Luccheses. As the feud escalated the mobsters focused more on killing their comrades than their business operations. Law enforcement was getting a lot of info on the crews at this time as their interests were focused more on each other instead of staying out of law enforcement's way. The hit teams were running rampant, dropping bodies and causing problems, even if they weren't "whacking Jersey" as ordered.

"Tumac actually made a statement about that, he said, 'What kind of army kills its own soldiers?'" Buccino says. "So it became very violent in the New York end and they were demanding that the New Jersey faction declare all the businesses that they had some influence on. New Jersey didn't want to do that, didn't want to give that up. And so it came upon a time, I don't remember exactly the date, but Tumac's crew were called into New York. They were supposed to meet at a meeting with the New York faction to solve the problem. When they went to a location they were supposed to meet at, they said as soon as they saw an old car pull up they realized then that they were going to get whacked. So they just left. They turned around and went back into New Jersey. They didn't go to New York any more. That was it and that was really the break between the factions. When they came back to New Jersey they used money from the vending machines that they had control over to buy all kinds of weapons in preparation to fight the New York faction. It didn't cop out—nobody got arrested, nobody cooperated, that's the best of my recollection of it."

ALL OUT WAR

The war was on and the Jersey crew was arming. Anybody in their right mind would not be dealing with Gaspipe and Amuso. They were capable of anything. Not only were they power mad and brutally violent, they were legitimately crazy, ready to kill off their whole family if necessary.

"Yeah, we felt there was going to be some action. We also had informants in place. It got to a point where everybody was cooperating, so we were getting in a lot of intelligence on it, a lot of information," Buccino recalls. "We also realized, like Tumac had said, that they're killing their own soldiers. We all could have just sat back and watched. They were doing it. The Colombo Family was doing it. The Bruno Family in Philadelphia, they were all killing their own people, so they really weakened their whole operation and when they all started cooperating I realized at that time it was coming to an end."

While Lucchese mobsters were hunting their colleagues, many mobsters began questioning their loyalty. Why would they remain loyal to bosses who were trying to kill them over petty bullshit? Why would they remain loyal and risk ending up in one of Casso's paranoid thoughts? With two serial killers at the helm of the family, everyone was at risk of getting whacked at any moment. It all resulted in countless mobsters flipping to the government's side and becoming a witness against the Mafia.

The beef and the crazy antics of Gaspipe and Little Vic had Tumac and other made men questioning the hierarchy as they kept their heads low and tried to avoid their bosses and law enforcement. A lot of Tumac's crew were in Florida where a New York hitman couldn't creep up on them like he could in Jersey. The Jersey side weren't scared, they were just cautious. War is war. When someone yells, "whack Jersey" and it's the infamous Gaspipe, you get ready.

"Yeah, they were very concerned about that," Buccino says.

"Because that would have been an all out war between the two crews. I bet they didn't go to mattresses or anything like that, like you see on television. They were around, but they traveled together and had some heavy arms."

At the same time, the Jersey crew was fighting indictments. The whole Lucchese faction had already been to trial once against the feds and famously won. Vin Diesel made a film about the case, portraying Lucchese mobster Jackie DiNorscio in the 2006 movie, *Find Me Guilty*.

"It was the one where they took out the whole family. They tried them. It was a racketeering charge, but it went on for over a year at trial and they won their case. They were all acquitted," explains Buccino. "They did a HBO special on it. They didn't have the evidence on them, but later on when we flipped Tumac, he said one of the jurors were blood. We turned that information over to the FBI and they ended up arresting the juror. I believe he did time. One juror doesn't make it an acquittal, you know what I mean."

THE BOSS TURNS RAT

Tumac, the old school gangster, was tired. With the feds and state police hounding him relentlessly and his name on a hit list, he was getting sick of the gangster life. Law enforcement was in disbelief that the Jersey mobsters beat the feds, but the state was already preparing another case against them. It was a race to see who would get the Jersey crew first, law enforcement or Gaspipe.

Old, overweight, and suffering from medical problems, Tumac considered doing the unthinkable. He would turn rat and betray his mafia oaths and all that he stood for. It was a big step for the career gangster to even be considering that option, but the thing that really turned him was when he found out that Gaspipe and Little Vic had given a hitman a photo of his wife and put a contract out on her. To Tumac that was crossing the line. It was one thing to green light him, but his wife? Where was the honor in that?

It seems that Amuso and Gaspipe really messed up their mafia careers by first taking on Tumac with the "whack Jersey" order and then putting a hit out on his wife. Enough was enough, Tumac decided.

He was going to turn against the organization that he had devoted his life to. Tumac broke with the Mafia and turned snitch. He went straight to his childhood friend, Bob Buccino, to make the deal.

Gaspipe had Tumac in a corner and the only way Tumac could get out was by becoming something he detested. He had one escape from his predicament, life in prison or death, and he used his wild card. Gaspipe should have killed him while he had the chance. And he wasn't the only one. Casso and Amuso had ratched up the climate of fear so drastically in their reign as bosses of the family that they had three Lucchese capos turning on them: D'Arco, Pete Chiodo and Tumac.

"They cooperated, they gave up all those homicides," Buccino says. "And Tumac was too smart. When he was in Florida and he was tried, he came out with Alzheimer disease defense, so they didn't prosecute him. When he comes back to New Jersey and we convict him under first-degree racketeering he wants to cooperate and I met with him and I said, Tumac, we can't use you, because in Florida you said you had Alzheimer disease, so how could we use your information?

"He goes, 'I was taking a shower and I slipped and fell and hit my head and I no longer have old timer's disease.' He's funny. He was smart enough. He gave us the businesses that he had penetrated. One was ECD Wiring in Hillside. The state got a lot of money out of it. He really knew he could not testify in a criminal case against other people, but on the civil end, giving the state money makes them happy. He was smart enough to do that, so he really didn't do much time either."

Whack Jersey never became a reality because everyone ended up turning on Amuso and Gaspipe, and Gaspipe even turned snitch himself. Though he lied to the feds so much they reneged on their deal with him. He sits in ADX Florence, the Bureau of Prisons supermax facility—a fitting place for the vicious mob enforcer. In essence, the legend of Whack Jersey has become more pop culture legend than real fact.

"What's most intriguing about Amuso's 'Whack Jersey' order due to Tumac's refusal to share his NJ-FLA rackets with Lucchese crime family administrators, is that the edict's portrayal in pop culture far exceeds its impact in real life," said Scott Burnstein, who runs *gangsterreport.com*. "*The Sopranos* TV show depicted a 'Whack Jersey' storyline in its pivotal final season, where top members of protagonist Tony Soprano's New Jersey mob crew were targeted for murder by fictional New York mafia don, Phil Leotardo. The storyline was inspired by Amuso's desire to off Tumac's whole Jersey faction. But unlike in the show, where the Soprano crime family is thrown into chaos, in real life, nothing happened and nobody was harmed. Instead, in an ending more realistic than 'made-for-film' conclusions shown in *The Godfather* movies, everyone went to prison. Pretty fitting if you ask me."

LUCCHESE FAMILY HIERARCHY

ANTONIO "TONY DUCKS" CORAL
IMPRISONED BOSS

Old time mafia boss who went to prison for 100 years on the infamous Commission Case. He handpicked Little Vic and Gaspipe to run the Lucchese and was good friends with Tumac from the New Jersey faction.

ANTHONY "BUDDY" LUONGO
MURDERED ACTING BOSS

Short lived boss of the Lucchese crime family allegedly killed by his protege Little Vic on orders from Tony Ducks who felt that Buddy was trying to isolate him from his crew after his imprisonment.

VITTORIO "LITTLE VIC" AMUSO
BOSS

Protege of Buddy Luongo, but he killed the acting boss on orders from imprisoned boss Tony Ducks Corallo. He was the boss of the Lucchese Crime family and was called the "Deadly Don" by United States Attorney Charles Rose. He created chaos during his reign as boss and let his underboss Gaspipe run rampant killing friend and foe alike.

ANTHONY "GASPIPE" CASSO
UNDERBOSS

Gaspipe was Little Vic's partner in crime and is regarded as a homicidal maniac in mob and law enforcement circles. As underboss of the New York faction he killed at will and when he got busted he told the feds he wanted to cooperate but he lied so much the feds didn't hour his cooperation agreement and sentenced him to life.

ALPONSE "LITTLE AL" D'ARCO
NEW YORK CAPO

Little Al was known as the Professor and became acting boss of the Lucchese Crime Family when Little Vic and Gaspipe went into hiding due to federal racketeering charges being filed. He became the first acting boss to become a government witness.

PETER "FAT PETE" CHIODO
NEW YORK CAPO

The son of a mobster Fat Pete was a capo in the Lucchese crime family. He was involved in the Windows case and plead guilty. Little Vic and Gaspipe thought he was going to snitch so they put a hit on him and he ended up snitching on them.

ANTHONY "TUMAC" ACCETTURO
NEW JERSEY CAPO

He was an old school mobster from New Jersey who was good friends with Tony Ducks, but when Little Vic and Gaspipe took power he refused to pay them more taxes and that started the whole Whack Jersey fiasco.

MICHAEL PERNA
NEW JERSEY CONSIGLIERE

He was the consigliere of the New Jersey faction. The whole Jersey crew was taken to trial by the feds and won in the mid-80's. There was a book about it called, *The Boys From New Jersey*.

MICHAEL TACCETTA
NEW JERSEY ENFORCER

Known as "Mike T" or "Mad Dog", the 5-foot-7, 300 pound enforcer was a protege of Tumac and was extremely loyal to him. He was a part of mob royalty as his father was reputedly a made man and his cousin was Michael Perna, the consigliere of the New Jersey faction.

GIACOMO "FAT JACK" DINORSCIO
NEW JERSEY SOLDIER

Known as Fat Jack, he was the mobster who decided to represent himself when he feds took the New Jersey crew to trial for racketeering charges. Vin Diesel portrayed him in the film *Find Me Guilty*.

ANTHONY ACCETTURO, JR.
NEW JERSEY SOLDIER

The son of Tumac who was also a made guy. When the Whack Jersey order came down he went into hiding with his father and helped to run the rackets in Florida.

11

WILLIE FALCON & SAL MAGLUTA
MIAMI'S O.G. COCAINE COWBOYS

From a drug baron, to a prisoner of the War on Drugs, to a possible political refugee, the man known as Willie Falcon lived a charmed and dangerous life. Existing and operating on the perimeters of the law, while flaunting the attributes of his ill-gotten gains, the Cuban-born Falcon made billions with his partner, Sal Magluta. After dropping out of high school, Falcon shot straight to the top of the cocaine world from his base in Miami during the 1980's. At the peak of the *Miami Vice*-era he became the go-to smuggler for the Colombian cartels. He was a cocaine kingpin who was the biggest drug dealer in the biggest drug dealing city in the world.

NOVICES IN THE TRADE

Back in 1979, Willie Falcon and Sal Magluta were nobodies. The duo were simple Cuban immigrants in Miami, dropouts from Miami High. Outsiders basically, but Americanized enough that they weren't above pursuing the American dream in Miami's criminal underworld. They started their drug dealing escapades as small-time dope slingers. From the beginning, Falcon acted as the point man while Sal was the negotiator, the brains behind the face. Falcon was a big hit, both in athletics, he was a high school track star, and with the ladies, who really couldn't resist him. He was a flashy cocaine playboy who raced boats.

Always at the center of the party, Falcon engaged the crowd while Sal, who was known for handling business, took stock of the players. Falcon, a Don Juan, macho man-type acted as the ambassador for the duo, as they climbed the hierarchy of Miami's cocaine underworld. It was a vicious battleground that announced its presence to the world with the 1979 Dadeland Massacre. Falcon and his partner were solid businessmen, not the type to steal or rip people off, but when it came to money they weren't afraid to get their hands dirty. Their Tony Montana-act was more a sign of the times than outright criminality.

"We pretty much had a failed state on our hands in South Florida," says Roben Farzad, the author of *Hotel Scarface: Where Cocaine Cowboys Partied and Plotted to Control Miami*. "If you look at the cover of *Time* magazine's 'Paradise Lost' issue in November of '81, this place went from a sleepy terminus on the sunbelt to the murder capital of America. From the outside, growing up and listening to Nancy Reagan, George Bush, and the drug task force you'd think that all these cocaine dealers were monsters, but I found a lot of these guys are very eloquent."

Just from being around the drug game and in its central hub, Falcon and Sal ended up with an offer they couldn't refuse. An old acquaintance basically got stuck with a lot of coke and asked the boys to help unload it on the black market. They were in the game at a high level instantly—a dream come true for the two wanna-be Scarface's! By the late 1970's, more and more Cubans were partnering up with Colombians in the drug trade.

Falcon graduated to working directly with Colombia suppliers and his fortune was made. Through some contacts he knew at a local bank, he was able to leverage those financial connections to grow his drug empire. Moving from the small-time to the big-time, Falcon was on his way to becoming a very rich and powerful man. At only 24-years-old, Falcon dealt directly with infamous drug lords like Pablo Escobar and Griselda Blanco.

"Falcon started dealing cocaine in the mid-1970's," explains Scott Deitche, the author of *The Silent Don: The Criminal World of Santo Trafficante Jr.*. "At that time, a new wave of younger Cuban gangsters were moving in to replace the older generation *bolita* bankers and drug kingpins, many of whom came over in 1959 after Castro took over Cuba. In Miami, these early Cuban gangsters worked closely with *mafioso*, like Tampa boss Santo Trafficante Jr.," and the Colombians who were controlling the coke trade.

THE MUTINY: COCAINE CENTRAL

In the late-70's and early-80's, Miami was the murder and drug capital of the world, and the Mutiny, an exclusive hotel and club at Sailboat Bay, just south of downtown Miami in Coconut Grove, was where the cocaine cowboys partied and schemed. Its floors were full of drug traffickers, gangsters, informants, and criminals of all types who came to make deals, look for business, and trade information. Falcon and Sal were the stars of the scene, holding court at the hotel as they reigned supreme. They acted as overlords of both the bloody cocaine-charged underworld and the star-studded Mutiny environment that catered to celebrities and musicians.

"If you're a kingpin at this club and you see Stevie Nicks walk in, you see Led Zeppelin walk in, some of the biggest personalities, you don't want to go fawning like a little kid at a Beatles' concert," Farzad relates. "You want to be like, 'I'll send a bottle to his table.' It was very much everybody understood why everybody else was there. For the most part they didn't shoot at each other there or bust one another there."

The drug lords were the main attraction despite the who's who of athletes, celebrities, and musicians that frequented the luxurious hotel. They conducted their illicit business in the open with shadowy spy-type figures and criminal types, making million dollar drug deals and putting hits on rivals—basically using the Mutiny as headquarters for Miami's burgeoning cocaine trade.

"Between the cops and the drug lords it was kind of treated as a free trade zone," Farzad says. "Like we know why you're here, you know why we're here, let's not create a scene here. The criminals held nothing personal against those cops. The cop's job was to chase them. The criminal's job was to evade them and corrupt them. That lasted until Miami became this paroxysm, this explosion of murder and bloodlust."

The hotel was truly elegant and very popular among international jet-setters, globetrotting spies, and criminals galore. The Mutiny was a classy establishment with an edgy reputation, hosting Cuban killers, CIA affiliates, informants, shady bankers, Colombian drug lords, and secret agent types. The epitome of what the decadent-70's and capitalistic-80's represented in the cocaine boomtown that Miami became. It was America at its criminally finest.

The hotel catered to Latin America's *nouveau riche* and was home to the members only, Mutiny Club. Members carried gold winking pirate cards signifying their importance to the world. It was a club of outlaws and wanna-be's who reveled in the hotel's exclusiveness. The atmosphere at the Mutiny was said to have rivaled Studio 54's at its height and some saw the hotel as a de-facto Playboy Mansion for Miami. No matter the hotel's seedy clientele, it was known as one of the top destinations in the world. The affluent and wealthy flocked to the highly sought after spot.

"The owner himself told me you could be in some place like Cartagena or Panama and see people flash the license plate on the front of their bulletproof Benz or Rolls Royce's, the winking pirate logo, the gold license plate, you started seeing that all across South America and Europe," said Farzad.

By the mid-1980's, the duo, dubbed *Los Muchachos*, built an empire founded on cocaine, which included real estate, racing boats, exotic cars, and legitimate businesses to clean the millions of dirty dollars. The offshore powerboat racing circuit was a magnet for drug smugglers in the late-70's and 80's. Many of the biggest smugglers were also champion racers, akin to how NASCAR was formed out of the Prohibition-era drivers who evaded the law.

"The racing boats weren't just for fun in the sun either; it was a clever hidden in plain sight scheme," explains Christian Cipollini, the author of *Lucky Luciano: Mysterious Tales of a Gangland Legend*. Racing boats were often used to run dope from the Bahamas to Florida, therefore making racing boats part of their legitimate endeavors was a smart way to perhaps throw off any suspicion of why they owned so many racing boats." In South Florida, Falcon and Malguta raced under the "Team Seahawk" name.

"Falcon also raced under the name 'Team Cougar,'" Deitche said. "Some boats, like a twenty-six foot racing boat that was for sale on Craigslist a few years back, were built specifically for Falcon. Avid participants in the sport, Magluta won a number of national championships and Falcon won a Florida Keys offshore race in the mid-1980's." The *Muchachos* were avid practitioners of the sport.

One of Falcon's speedboats was named, *Rum and Coke*. That was his favorite drink too and he'd tip the waitresses at the Mutiny one hundred dollars each when they brought him his drink. Willie Falcon and Sal Magluta were the biggest cocaine dealers in Miami, which was the cocaine capital of America, with a direct line to some of the biggest figures in the Medellin cartel.

SMUGGLERS EXTRAORDINAIRE

"Magluta and Falcon, aka *Los Muchachos or* The Boys, were the living breathing manifestation of what a film like *Scarface* or a show like *Miami Vice* was built upon. Two Cuban immigrants in Miami that quickly begin to live the American underworld dream," said Cipollini. "According to one of the prosecutors at the time, Willie Falcon and Sal Magluta were the reigning 'Kings of Cocaine' in Miami and responsible for importing 75 tons of the high priced powder in the United States from the late 1970's up to the time of their arrest in 1991."

With a fleet of speed boats carrying cocaine from the Bahamas to Florida that the Coast Guard couldn't catch, the *Muchachos* controlled a huge conglomerate. It was a cocaine enterprise that rivaled the top corporations in the world, if not surpassing them due to the sheer enormity of their cash flow. With excess money they assembled fleets of planes and boats, an assemblage that fed America's monstrous cocaine habit, flooding the country in the 1980's with Colombian *yayo*. With large sums of cash available, greedy banks enabled the drug lords by laundering their money through dummy corporations in offshore accounts.

"The most ostentatious thing they could do was just order cases and cases of *Dom Pérignon* and pour it into a hot tub and jump in naked with groupies," Farzad said. "It was the most democratizing thing, cash. A rags to riches Cuban or Venezuelan, who would not get time of day at this exclusive club, got in, because once you're a coke kingpin, once you have that kind of money, all sorts of women would sleep with you, all sorts of celebs would party with you. These guys rubbed shoulders with Crosby, Stills, Nash and Young, Fleetwood Mac, The Cars, and more. That cash was the ultimate equalizer."

Falcon and Sal kept a whole floor at the Mutiny to themselves. They would throw wild parties with tons of women, who got high on cocaine and drunk on champagne, doing whatever the drug lords wanted. The Boys were royalty at the hotel, living out the rock star dream. *Los Muchachos* used the hotel as a business office, to entertain, and most importantly, to party.

"The flashiness was the Cubans and the gringo hanger-ons," Farzad relates. "The Colombians, when they did go to the Mutiny, were not flashy people. They were much more businesslike and it was life or death for them. Dealers would throw a lot of cash around and make it abundantly clear to everybody that money was no object. They'd have a shit ton of *Dom Pérignon* and *Perrier-Jouët* on the table, paying cash and tipping the waiter two hundred dollars."

LENGTHY LEGAL PROCEEDINGS

Los Muchachos thought they could buy their way out of anything. It was America, right? In a capitalistic nation money rules the roost. But it wasn't always true, as Falcon and Sal found out. With operations in multiple states they were solidifying their empire and bringing in mad cash. The two were paying bribes where they had to, avoiding costly beefs, and moving product in quantity to keep the price low. And the belief that money could solve any and all problems was very prevalent in the Cuban community.

"A cop told me that these guys were snorting more up their nose in one night than he made in a year, even with overtime," Farzad says. "When you have that kind of cash you can corrupt cops and even buy judges. The Miami Police Department had a horrific time with recruitment and attention, because you had so many prominent cops, law enforcement, and justice officials that were dirty. They saw the money and they couldn't resist it."

In pre-communist Cuba, everything was for sale. It was a kleptocracy, and that kind of spirit carried on very much so into the Mutiny. The prevailing attitude was that you could buy justice. You could buy yourself out of a hit and run or a rape charge, or even a murder. The Cubans at the Mutiny thought the same way. They thought that money made you untouchable in America and in Falcon's case, it did for a while, until the government decided it was time to get them out of the way.

"It was one of the most high profile drug cases in Florida history," Dietche says. "While the prosecution thought they had a strong case, the jury came back with acquittals on all charges. It later came out that Falcon and Magluta had bribed three of the jurors, including the foreman, who got 500,000 dollars. The jury foreman was actually convicted of taking the bribe in 1999 and sent to prison."

Indicted in 1991, the pair was acquitted in 1996. *Los Muchachos* had unlimited funds to fight the feds. They would use their billions to buy their freedom if necessary. But the feds re-indicted on gun and money laundering charges after the acquittals. The proceedings got ugly as defense lawyers accused the prosecution of having a personal agenda in regards to Falcon and Sal. Over a thirteen year period, 2.1 billion in property was seized from *Los Muchachos*. The feds weren't even making a dent in their operation.

"Falcon and Magluta were in prison on lesser charges for brief stints in the late 90's but were put on trial again in the early 2000's," says Dietche. "Magluta was convicted in 2002 of money laundering related to drug trafficking activities. He was sentenced to 205 years in prison. He was sixty-two at the time." Falcon ended up with a sweetheart deal, pleading out for only twenty calendars. Lucky, considering his partner got in effect, a life sentence. The feds suspected that the *Muchachos* were ordering hits from their jail cells, trying to eliminate potential witnesses, but those allegations were hard to prove since Falcon and Sal were never in that part of the game. They prided themselves as gentleman gangsters.

THE AFTERMATH

Falcon pled guilty to laundering money used to finance corruption at his 1996 drug trial. Falcon told the court that he used cocaine profits to pay off jurors and witnesses. The judge was initially reluctant to accept the twenty year sentence for the drug kingpin, but she finally relented, and even called Falcon a gentleman in court. Falcon did his twenty years in federal prison and was released in 2017, only to be swooped up by immigration officials who wanted to deport him back to Cuba. But given the current political landscape in the country that would be tantamount to sending Falcon to his death.

"During their reign as cocaine cowboys, Falcon and Magluta sent money to anti-Castro paramilitary groups and were also alleged to have been involved with funding CIA-backed anti-Castro efforts in the 1980's," explains Dietche. "There are even links between associates of Falcon and Magluta and infamous anti-Castro figures like Luis Posada Carriles, CIA asset and veteran of the Bay of PIgs invasion, and Watergate burglar Frank Sturgis. Posada Carriles and Sturgis were once part of the CIA's 'Operation 40', a 60's-era anti-Castro paramilitary group that also included Mafioso Johnny Roselli."

With changes during the Obama administration opening diplomatic relations with Cuba, as well as ending the wet foot/dry foot policy, giving Cubans who landed on US soil a path to citizenship, there's been an opening for immigration officials to deport violent Cuban felons. This is something the US was unable to do when diplomatic relations were non-existent. Falcon is a permanent resident, but not a US citizen. Since he was convicted of a felony he can be deported back to his home country, in this case Cuba. It's unclear whether the current Castro regime would even take him back. They would have to agree for it to happen.

"Falcon got out of jail in June," Farzad said. "His brother was caught after being on the lam for twenty-five years and effectively gave himself up in May. I believe it was so the government doesn't take revenge on his brother, maybe he fell on his sword, but the point is the government is trying to deport him right now to Cuba. Which is almost like a death sentence for a person who left Cuba as a young child, who left Castro, who was an anti-communist activist, and a doper. It's amazing to me that the Willie and Sal story continues to dominate the headlines in Miami."

Through documentaries like *Cocaine Cowboys* putting a spotlight on the era, cocaine gangster's like Willie Falcon have come into vogue. Today, their stories remain relevant in culture and drug lore. "Look how heavy *Miami Vice* is in syndication. Look how many times *Scarface* has been re-released. Look how much it influenced *Breaking Bad*," Farzad says. "I think Saddam Hussein named his front company Tony Montana Enterprises or something. This is a pop culture totem and we have a lot of evidence that it was heavily influenced by this club and the dopers there.

"You see the size and textures of all these people, who you were led to believe were just coke-headed monsters. But it works both ways.

They wanted nothing to do with the film *Scarface* when it was filmed in '82 and '83 in Miami, but now that the film has kind of created a life of its own, been quoted on *Sports Center*, and it's been re-released a thousand times, a lot of these guys want to come forward and say, 'you know what, I think that was based on me, man.'" And most of the Miami drug dealers that have been depicted in film are based on the cocaine gangster, Willie Falcon, a legend in the chronicles of the dope game.

CRIME BY THE NUMBERS

75 TONS
The amount of cocaine that federal prosecutors said Falcon and Magluta moved into Miami.

$2.1 BILLION
The feds seized over 2 billion worth of properties, money, and cocaine from Falcon's organization over 13 years.

24-YEARS-OLD
The age that Willie Falcon got into the cocaine game big-time.

2017
The year that Willie Falcon got out of prison, but instead of going free he was seized by the INS for deportation.

20 YEARS
The sweetheart deal that Falcon got after fighting federal prosecutors for close to a decade.

1980's
Virtually the entire pro speed boat racing circuit was comprised of wholesale drug dealers and smugglers in the eighties.

$17 MILLION
This was how much the Mutiny hotel was sold for in 1985 after law enforcement pressure shut it down.

16 COUNTS
Willie Falcon and Sal Magluta went to trial in 1996 on a 16 count indictment and got acquitted of all charges.

$500K
The amount that Willie Falcon paid the jury foremen in the 1996 trial to make sure the jury didn't convict.

COCAINE COWBOY SHOOTOUTS

When the Medellin cartel was flooding Miami with cocaine in the late-70's and early-80's, a lot of beefs erupted between the Colombian's and their associates. With all the money available guys weren't taking any shorts. They wanted theirs and they would get it by any means necessary. Legend holds that Griselda Blanco aka "The Black Widow", invented the motorcycle drive-by to surprise and dispatch rivals. The vicious cocaine queen did as she wanted, killing randomly and wantonly. Luckily, Falcon and Magluta never got in her way. As two of the cartel's biggest smugglers they were very valuable to the higher-ups like Pablo Escobar.

The violence that surrounded the cocaine cowboys was emphasized to the nation in the Dadeland Massacre. This vicious assault and shootout happened in the middle of the day at a trendy mall, proving that the cocaine cowboys only cared about money. If you messed with their money or their territory, then you were dealt with. Everything was life of death for them. They lived the life that Hollywood dramatized. A hail of bullets and a motorcycle speeding away announced the presence of the cocaine cowboys and what they were trying to accomplish.

FREEDOM DENIED

Willie Falcon thought he was getting out in 2017, but the feds had other ideas. Falcon is a permanent resident in the US, but he made an error back in the day that is currently the source of his immigration troubles. He never completed the naturalization process. Prior to the current relationship between the United States and Cuba, most Cubans who served time in American prisons were permitted to remain in the country after jail. The current situation however is not stacked in favor of Falcon, because the US labels him a 'convicted felon' who is technically not a US citizen, and, Cuba now considers taking back people on a case by case basis. An interesting side note is that Falcon's brother, who had been in hiding for the past two decades, was just picked up by federal marshals in April 2017, living under an assumed name in Kissimmee, just outside Orlando. Now he is in federal prison and Willie is most likely going to end up in a Cuban jail, if he is not killed outright.

12

PAVLE "PUNCH" STANIMIROVIC
LEGACY OF THE PINK PANTHERS

The infamous Pink Panthers are notorious for their *Mission Impossible*-type heists and the Riviera locations where they ply their trade that seem to mirror the settings of the comedic Inspector Clouseau's crime capers of the same name. Neither low-level criminals or mafia gun-thugs, these gentlemen thieves defy criminal stereotypes. There has been much speculation as to where they started, who founded the group, and how many members they have, but up until now it has been a mystery.

All law enforcement knows is that the crew, which has been making headlines with daring robberies all over the world for the last two decades, are made up of Serbians, Bosnians, Croatians, and Montenegrins, all from the former Yugoslavia. The true origin of the Serbian Pink Panthers is a question that can only be answered by a genuine Pink Panther. And the fact of matter is the group didn't originate in Serbia. It all started in New York City on 47th street in Manhattan.

"Punch" Pavle Stanimirović was the youngest and highest-ranking member of what some called the American Serbian Mafia, what the FBI called their imaginary super gang, the YACS, and what the international media now calls the Pink Panthers. Born in New York, raised in Swiss boarding schools, and son of Serbian Mafia godfather, Vojislav Stanimirović, Punch is gangster royalty. He's a true gentleman bandit and safe cracker extraordinaire.

THE BEGINNING OF A LEGEND

"Everything started with my father escaping the former Yugoslavia," Punch recalls. "My father is such a great and charming person with so much love. He's one of the most generous people I've ever seen and the last true gentleman thief." Mr. Stan, as he's known, was a journalist by day, who was married to an artistic and beautiful model, his third wife, Branka. But he also had friends like master thief, Alex "Texas" Karalanovic, who helped Mr. Stan become the greatest diamond thief in New York City.

"No one spent money like my pops," Punch says. "He was the first true flexer in this game, a true OG that earned the respect of the mob, even John Gotti. He's a saint for thieves who was deeply embedded in the trade buying up all the stolen diamonds from European and American thieves. He's a big-time poker player who loved to watch boxing, play chess, and speaks four languages fluently."

Mr. Stan was also the orchestrator of the famed Vizcaya Museum Heist. On March 22, 1971, the Vizcaya was infiltrated and more than $1.5 million's worth of historical artwork and silver was stolen by three individuals from New York City. It was a daring robbery that set the precedent for the Pink Panthers of the future. A notorious legacy started right before Punch was born.

"According to Branka, Punch's mother, the famous museum heist begins with nothing more than a delightful opportunity for a romantic sun-drenched celebration of her husband's birthday," says Burl Barer, who wrote *The Saint: A Complete History in Print, Radio, Television, and Film*. The book about Punch, focuses on Simon Templar, the character Val Kilmer played in *The Saint* and *Stealing Manhattan*.

Ambassador John H. Taylor asked Mr. Stan to do him a favor: pick up Taylor's new Rolls Royce in Florida at the Vizcaya Museum and Gardens and bring it up to Manhattan. The Vizcaya was a famous national historic site "that was the winter residence of industrialist James Deering. It was designed as a palatial Italian Villa on tropical Biscayne Bay and Deering filled it with European art, state of the art technology, and surrounded it with beautiful gardens," Barer says.

"Two first class tickets to Ft Lauderdale Airport were purchased by Mr. Taylor and they flew down. Branka was excited to go away with Stan for his birthday. It was to be just the two of them alone together in lovely Florida at the glorious, enchanting Vizcaya, followed by a pleasant drive up the coast in Mr. Taylor's Rolls Royce. Branka was one happy passenger until they were about to retrieve their luggage."

When Karalanovic pulled up to pick them up at the terminal, Branka knew it was trouble. Branka figured the romantic vacation she hoped for wasn't in the cards, but she had no idea she would be participating in one of the grandest heists of the century. By the end of their stay, two Louie Vuitton suitcases of valuables would end up in the Rolls Royce they were driving back to New York City.

On March 25, 1971, the three jewel thieves were arrested in New York City after Mr. Stan's Manhattan apartment was raided by the NYPD. The cops recovered two-hundred fifty thousand dollars of the loot and charged the trio with suspicion of possession of stolen property. One of the items was was a priceless silver bowl that had once been the property of Napoleon Bonaparte. Cops didn't even know what they had uncovered and the majority of the Vizcaya booty was never recovered.

THE RISE OF THE YACS

Punch was born in 1972 and his father started tutoring his son in the methods of robbery at a young age before sending him off to a Swiss boarding school. Mr. Stan had determined that his son would be a master safecracker and he made sure the boy had all the tutelage he would need to succeed in the trade and to blend into finer society.

"I grew up in this criminal network and was the first American Pink Panther," Punch recalls. "My father controlled it all with close associates from the beginning. I started at sixteen and it wasn't until I got involved in the 1990's that the alarm companies were infiltrated and made us millions. That's what I brought to the table. We have been operating since the 1960's and it was huge, but NYC is where it was born."

Before they were known as the Pink Panthers, the loose confederation of burglars and gentlemen thieves were known as the YACS, who the *New York Times* called "a well-organized, highly disciplined group of commercial safe burglars" of Yugoslavian, Albanian, Croatian and Serbian descent who were linked to hundreds of heists around the country.

"I was born directly under and grew up in this criminal organization that the feds placed all in one group and labeled with the name YACS," Punch explains. "Every Pink Panther heist anywhere in the world uses methods, techniques, and ideas created either by my father or me. The infamous twenty-six seconds or less smash and grab was one of my contributions, but one my father did not endorse."

In the 1990's, the NY Metro area was hit real hard by the YACS. They could steal an ATM out of a bank lobby in under a minute and shift the focus of their operations from super markets, to banks, to jewelry stores at the drop of a dime. The YACS would plan for every possible outcome, even the possibility of being arrested. They operated under aliases, had passports in different names, and spoke multiple languages.

Extensive surveillance would be done before the robbers entered a store on the weekend or in the middle of the night. Punch even recalls setting off alarm systems on purpose to see how long it would take the police to respond. With lookouts watching nearby, the YACS would pry open safes and ATMs with crow bars or sledge hammers. They would monitor police scanners and use walkie-talkies to communicate. When caught the YACS wouldn't cooperate with law enforcement, refusing to give police any information.

"I served more prison time than anyone else in our sophisticated crew because I was the only American citizen," says Punch, who did sixteen years inside the belly of the beast. "The rest were all deported. And that's exactly how it became famous and mainstream in London, England around 2003 when the Pink Panthers became known. A few pissed off soldiers from the former Yugoslavia Republic gave a green light to steal in Europe and linked up with The Engineer and others like Bruno Sulak and Stiv, who've become legends in Europe."

Punch says that despite the news reports of the Pink Panthers numbering over five hundred, there were only six original members. The rest were hired hands and most times they didn't even know who hired them, instructed them, trained them, or told them exactly what to do and how to do it. He claims that The Engineer was the head honcho in Europe and was the one who started the Panthers robbery spree in the early 2000's that stretched from Dubai, Paris, Tokyo, and London.

THE GREATEST LIVING SAFECRACKER

"My first score was a gem heist that I brought to my father at only sixteen," Punch says. "I'd been preparing for this since around seven-years-old, but really my entire life. I was ready to do this and the next day I was officially rich and had my own money. I did this India Star Company, a Gem distributor. This was in 1989. It was a piece of cake and I popped my cherry. I knew what I was going to be doing for the rest of my life and it was exciting as fuck. The safe was a punch vault.

"That's how I got my name Punch, for this specific safe door that I can get into in less than sixteen seconds. I was like an Olympian and burned through 47th Street in the Diamond District in New York City, stealing hundreds of millions of dollars worth of jewels. I was born rich so I didn't do it for the money. It was a challenge and a big game. There was nothing like it in the world. It was an exciting life without a single boring day."

Punch learned how to crack a safe from The Moth. They would practice drilling open different types of safes in a warehouse in Hoboken, New Jersey. Seeing how quick they could get it done by timing everything. Punch says it's all about the planning and looking for strategic soft spots in the security detail. He would find those flaws and expose them. He says many of the guys that have worked for the Pink Panthers didn't even know who they were working for and that there were only a handful of guys that were the shot callers behind the heists.

Punch says the Balkan Wars, which broke up the former Yugoslavia in 1991, supplied him and the other brains in the organization with an endless supply of soldiers. These weren't criminals or gangsters, but disciplined men who were ready to follow directions explicitly. These soldiers didn't know how to burglarize diamond stores, but they learned quick and followed orders. But the number one rule, handed down by Mr. Stan and followed by Punch, was that no one gets hurt in the robberies.

"Any scum can pull the trigger or hurt someone for money," Punch relates. "But not one person ever got hurt when we stole things. It was like being James Bond and my father never got caught. We robbed luxury watch stores, jewelry and diamond stores, high-end clothing stores, whatever we wanted. In the 1990's we were stealing Manhattan."

Punch ended up doing sixteen years in prison for his crimes, mostly in upstate New York, but he was in the feds also. By 1994 he was serving time and he would do several bids before he decided to retire in 2012. He never cooperated with authorities and held his head high in prison, despite doing time at violent prisons upstate and at Rikers. A lot of his cohorts were arrested and did state time in New York and the feds, but when they were released they returned to Europe, which was how the Pink Panther legend was born.

MISSION IMPOSSIBLE-TYPE HEISTS

Punch committed hundreds of heists that netted him duffel bags of precious and semi-precious gem stones like emeralds, sapphire, rubies, and diamonds. His criminal activity included the infamous Regency Hotel heist in Manhattan in 1992 where 36 out of 150 safety deposit boxes were robbed, while his cohorts in the Pink Panthers have gone on to orchestrate some Hollywood movie-type banditry in Europe.

From the 2013 Carlton Intercontinental Hotel heist during the Cannes Film Festival, to the robbery at the upscale Wafi Mall in Dubai in 2008, to London jewelry heist that put them on the map in 2003, the crew has used daring, subterfuge, speed, and precision planning to carry on the methods begun by Mr. Stan and Punch in New York City. Playing the role of gentlemen thieves to perfection and stealing hundreds of millions of dollars worth of valuables.

"Today we are retired people who are left with a crazy true story," says Punch. "I have no regrets. It was justified to me because I got this special thing inside me that makes me do things that I'm not supposed to do. You might see 'Danger! Do Not Enter,' but I see 'explore the shit out of it.'" Punch has been crime-free since 2003, but still applauds his cohorts' exploits. He has watched from the sideline in America as the thing his father started has taken on a life of its own.

KIM KARDASHIAN GETS ROBBED

In 2016, Kim Kardashian was attending Paris Fashion Week in France when she was tied up, held at gunpoint, and robbed of $9 million in jewelry at the *Hotel de Pourtales* in Paris. Speculation in the media ran rampant as to who was behind the heist and it was widely believed that the Pink Panthers were the culprits. The well planned, nonviolent, and high profile robbery fit the profile of the infamous jewel thieves and they were known to base their operations out of Paris.

The robbers, who were dressed a police officers, gained entry through the concierge who was waylaid, handcuffed, and left off the entryway. The culprits were in and out very quickly, getting what they came for before jumping on bikes and riding into the Paris night. Eventually seventeen suspects were arrested for the robbery with ten being indicted on criminal charges in France. A man dubbed "Omar the Old" was said to be the mastermind of the robbery. The jewelry was never recovered and none of the suspects were linked to the Pink Panthers.

CRIME BY THE NUMBERS

£90 MILLION
A robbery of diamonds, jewels, and gems at the Carlton Intercontinental Hotel in Cannes, France in 2013.

£8 MILLION
The heist of Graff jewelers in Dubai where thieves drove cars into Wafi Mall in 2008.

2008
Four gang members dress as women and break into France's Harry Winston Jewelers.

$65 MILLION
A 2009 heist of an exclusive London jewelry store.

£23 MILLION
Theft of diamonds from jewelers in Mayfair, London where loot was hidden in ice cream.

£17 MILLION
Comtesse de Vendome, a 125 carat necklace encrusted with 116 diamonds stolen in Japan in 2004.

£1 MILLION
Diamond specialist Graf in London had diamonds stolen in 2005.

2005
A jewelry store in Saint-Tropez was robbed and culprits escaped on a speed boat.

380 ROBBERIES
The Panthers are responsible for over 380 robberies across 35 countries value of over 334 million Euros.

13

CASH MONEY BROTHERS
EVEN MIKE TYSON WAS FAIR GAME

In the early 1990's, a group of teens from Lafayette Gardens projects took these lines to heart. They started an organized crime ring that sold narcotics and dubbed themselves Cash Money Brothers (CMB) after the 1980's urban film, *New Jack City*, which depicted the drug culture in New York City during the crack era. The gang was headed by brothers Damion "World" Hardy and Myron "Wise" Hardy, a charismatic pair that held court in the projects like ghetto royalty between 1991 and 2004.

DO OR DIE BED-STUY

"I grew up in Brooklyn, New York in a section labeled 'Do or Die Bed-Stuy," says James "Popsie" Sessoms, a founding member of Cash Money Brothers. "When I was growing up it was none of this lame shit like what's going on in the streets now—it was real out there. In my hood it was a lot of thoroughbred street legends. I used to like their style, so I emulated them."

Popsie was down with the CMB crew from day one. He grew up with World and Wise. They were soldiers in street life, solidified by their camaraderie and the gangster ideals that they embodied. Growing up in Brooklyn wasn't easy, but the youngsters held each other down. They lived the lifestyle that Jay-Z and Biggie Smalls rapped about. They were the kings of the projects.

"Back in the days it was gangs, but nowadays the gangs out there are more ruthless," says Eric "E-Bay" Moore, a man described in court records as CMB's hitman. "It went from fighting and stabbing to now people are getting shot up every day out there. Niggas is hustling on every block trying to be the next kingpin. Soon as a nigga gets some money they start flossing, so they might be a victim to somebody from a rival projects. It's always something to get into out there, good or bad, day or night, it's never a dull moment."

The streets of Brooklyn were off the hook, but this was the environment that these young gangsters were born and bred in. They didn't take any shorts and they definitely didn't have any picks. They stuck their chests out and had a chip on their shoulders because there was a sort of pride that kids had coming up in Bed-Stuy. Hip-hop artist Lil' Kim, who would play a part in this story, summed it up best:

> We get it on where we live. /
> You better have a pass when you cross that bridge. /
> Welcome to Brooklyn.

"The streets in BK was crazy, nigga's was either selling drugs, robbing, extorting, or doing scams," recalls Popsie. "My friends started selling drugs and getting money. They was popping the bottles and had all the bitches around them. They were driving, had all the fly gear and jewelry. There was crazy guns so we would have numerous shootouts, violating anybody who came in our circumference."

The crew held it down by any means necessary, but when you're in the narcotics business nothing ever lasts. The rap songs and videos make it seem like it's the American dream, but they're walking off the video set at the end of the day. In Do or Die Bed-Stuy, life was more like *Grand Theft Auto*, but in real life there's no reset button. And when the bullets started flying and the bodies started dropping, the feds took notice. CMB started beefing with rival crews and that was the beginning of their end.

THE BEGINNING OF THE END

On July 19, 2005, Roslynn Mauskopf, United States Attorney for the Eastern District of New York, announced the filing of federal racketeering and narcotics charges against Damion "World" Hardy and twelve additional leaders, members and associates of the Cash Money Brothers. According to the feds, CMB were a violent Brooklyn street gang responsible for five murders, widespread crack distribution, the attempted murder of a witness, the kidnapping and attempted robbery of a drug dealer, assault, and illegal firearms possession.

The charges and arrests followed an eighteen month joint ICE, FBI and NYPD investigation coordinated by the US Attorney's office as part of an ongoing initiative to eliminate violent street gangs that erode the quality of life in many of the district's neighborhoods.

As the investigation into CMB heated up, their charismatic leader was very visible in the hip-hop world dating rap vixen Lil' Kim. World was also suspected of trading shots outside the DoubleTree, a New Jersey hotel, with 50 Cent and his entourage in September 2003. New York police also said that World had confronted 50 Cent earlier that year outside radio station Hot 97 after 50 Cent insulted Lil' Kim on air.

"I have seen the statements Lil' Kim made when the government interviewed her concerning her relationship with World," Popsie says. "She stated that she had never heard of no gang called CMB and she had no knowledge of World selling any drugs. Kim kept it one hundred percent and told the truth, that World was focusing on getting in the music industry and that she had no knowledge of none of the things the government alleged he was involved in."

But the indictment told another story. "The arrests announced today strike a devastating blow to a drug gang responsible for spreading fear and violence in one of our communities," stated US Attorney Mauskopf. "When gangs flood our streets with drugs, assassinate rivals, attempt to murder witnesses and endanger the lives of innocent residents, we will mobilize all resources available, including federal prosecution, through the RICO statute. This case is the latest of several successful joint investigations that demonstrate our commitment to protect public housing from gang violence. We are determined to return control of these communities to their rightful law-abiding residents."

The government's investigation revealed that for more than ten years, CMB members, led by Damion Hardy, controlled narcotics trafficking in the Lafayette Gardens Houses in the Bedford-Stuyvesant section of Brooklyn through violence and intimidation directed against their drug trafficking competitors, innocent civilians and potential witnesses.

Hardy, Eric "E-Bay" Moore, Dwayne "Thor" Myers, James "Popsie" Sessoms, Kenwayne "Stro" Jones, Robert "Troub" Footman, Carl "Big Jim" Davis, James "Jimbo" Farrior, Lamont "Sambo" Johnson, Zareh "Puff" Sarkissian, Abubakr Raheem, D'Jebara "DJ" McMillian, and Isheen "Sha" Campbell were charged with conspiring between 1991 and August 2004 to distribute crack cocaine using apartments they controlled in Lafayette Gardens to buy, cook, and store their drugs.

"This case is another example of the continuing resolve of the FBI and our partners to reign in gang violence," agent Mark Mershon said. "The lethal combination of gangs, guns, and drugs can terrorize neighborhoods and victimize innocent people. Our purpose fundamentally, is to secure for all New Yorkers the right to be safe and out of harm's way in their own neighborhoods, whether they live on Park Avenue or in public housing."

"The feds had been fishing around trying to inquire about us, but World was trying to get in the music business," Popsie says. "But things spiraled outta control once two people who used to affiliate with World, Edward 'Taz' Cooke, and Allen 'Boo' Bryant, got locked up at JFK with eight kilos of cocaine. They started snitching on anyone they could, just to get home."

THE MUSIC BUSINESS & 50 CENT BEEF

As the story of CMB became public a lot of other factors involving the hip-hop world, Brooklyn's street culture and the execution of rival gang members came to the forefront. A lot of big names in the entertainment business, including Mike Tyson, Lil Kim, and 50 Cent, were connected to the case and to CMB's charismatic and notorious leader World, in some form or fashion.

The tale that emerged was one of intrigue, betrayal, and murder. The story was ripe with all the elements of a Hollywood blockbuster, well suited for the big screen, a Teri Woods hood novel, or a big budget Quentin Tarantino film. Throughout the 1990's the government claimed that Ivory "Peanut" Davis was one of CMB's drug dealing rivals in Lafayette Gardens. On June 12, 1999, Davis' nephew, Rumel Davis, shot and killed World's brother Myron "Wise" Hardy during a so-called turf dispute while World was locked up in the state.

When World got out he investigated the circumstances of his brother's death and the feds alleged that World and the other members of CMB retaliated by conspiring to murder Peanut and four of his associates. World, E-Bay, and Puff were charged with the murder of Darryl "Homicide" Baum on June 10, 2000. This is the same Homicide rapper 50 Cent accused of shooting him nine times earlier that same year in May. 50 Cent also implied in his song *Many Men* that Hommo was killed in retaliation for shooting him.

Homicide was a Brooklyn stick-up kid and gun thug who counted boxer Mike Tyson as a close friend and employer. He was even living at Mike Tyson's home when he was murdered. The feds concluded that World targeted Homicide because of his association with Peanut. They alleged E-Bay shot Homicide in the back of the head at the corner of Quincy Street and Marcy Avenue and fled in a get-away car driven by Puff. The feds implicated World, E-Bay, and Abubakr Raheem in several other murders relating to this beef.

On July 25, 2003, Homicide's brother, Tyrone "T-Rock" Baum, who the feds alleged World believed was seeking to avenge his brother's murder, was killed. On World's order, Thor and Raheem located T-Rock by a construction site at Reid Avenue and Hancock Street in Brooklyn where T-Rock was shot three times in the head.

"It was a lot of murders they felt we were involved in, but they never had no proof we were. Then once Taz and Boo got locked up they started feeding the government lies to get their selves out of a jam," Popsie says. The feds base a lot of their cases off of cooperator testimony. They don't need hard evidence to prove conspiracy cases.

"When they got locked up in 2004, Taz started snitching on me because he thought I was crazy and wouldn't do no time," E-Bay relates. "There was no ongoing RICO organization, but when Taz got locked up, he told the feds we were all under World, which was a lie. The feds are alleging that I killed people for World. It isn't much I can say now, but these allegations are bullshit."

The indictment detailed events that seemed to come straight out of a gangsta rap video. Numerous newspaper headlines connected the CMB and in particular World to famous figures in the worlds of entertainment and hip-hop. "Lil' Kim's Ex and Gang Indicted," the *New York Daily News* headline read. "Tyson in 50 G Hit-Man

Deal, Trial is Told," another *New York Daily News* headline read on June 13, 2008.

Plus with the connection to 50 Cent and his alleged shooter, Homicide, the innuendos and hype didn't stop in the streets or on the Internet. In Abubakr Raheem's trial it came out that after Homicide was killed, Mike Tyson and another Brooklyn thug Muhammad Nur, who was close to Homicide, contributed fifty thousand dollars each to the bounty on the heads of CMB leaders World and Taz.

"Why would Mike Tyson put a hit out on Taz and World?" Assistant US Attorney James Loonam asked CMB turncoat Dwayne "Thor" Meyers. "He was close friends with Homicide," the snitch answered. Tyson dedicated his thirty-eight second whipping of heavyweight Lou Savarese in 2000 to Homicide, who had been shot dead two weeks earlier.

In 50 Cent's song *Many Men*, he references Homicides murder implying that he had a hand in it:

> *Almost shot me, three weeks later he got shot down /*
> *Now it's clear that I'm here for a real reason /*
> *'Cause he got hit like I got hit, but he ain't fucking breathing.*

But 50 Cent ain't no killer, he's a rapper and the only affiliation he has with CMB and World is that he got punked out by them due to his beef with Lil' Kim, which World promptly handled like a gangsta, not a rapper.

It also came out that when World learned of the 50,000 dollar bounty Tyson had offered to have CMB members killed, World planned a retaliation. The plot was later abandoned. Tyson denied links to the murder plot and was never charged for anything, but New York's tabloid news ran with the story. World sat in the hole, in 24-7 lockdown for some years before he was finally tried in 2015 as Brooklyn prosecutors tried to put the death penalty on him and E-Bay.

And in sleazy tabloid fashion the *New York Daily News* headlined their article announcing "Death Penalty Trial Looming for Lil' Kim's Ex," with photos of World and Lil' Kim splashed across the page. But with the trial seemingly nearing, more twists in the case emerged. World's lawyer claimed his client underwent a religious conversion, legally changing his name to Isa Ibn Jibril. He was also mentally ill, the lawyer said.

"I was never supposed to be in prison," World says. "Everybody knows the federal government has to catch or observe a person committing a crime to arrest them. This applies especially to narcotics because it is a transaction, whereas with most other crimes the victim files the complaint with law enforcement."

To the feds though it didn't matter. With their overzealous prosecutors and cooperator testimony they have a 99.5 percent conviction rate. As different people on the case like Popsie pled guilty and received thirty-five year sentences, World and E-Bay awaited trial.

"They think World and us were ruthless people and once they say we were affiliated with Lil' Kim, they think she is ruthless also," E-Bay says. "The media know Lil' Kim, Mike Tyson, 50 Cent, and Jay-Z came from the streets. And right around Lafayette Gardens they grew up or hung around, so one way or another they believe we are connected to them in a negative way or a positive one. But they are gonna feed off the negative since that's what sells newspapers."

Zakia Baum, sister of Darryl and Tyrone Baum, the brothers who World had killed, said at sentencing, "I'm not going to sit here and pour my heart out to either World or E-Bay because I know they don't care. I feel you are an incredibly dangerous, selfish, vicious, and insecure souls who killed because it empowered you."

After a three week trial, World and E-Bay were convicted of six murders and running a drug organization out of Lafayette Gardens. They were both sentenced to life in prison. Everyone else on the case is in prison too with sentencing ranging from thirty-five years to life. The only ones who are home are the ones who turned on their comrades, betrayed the street code and testified for the government.

Popsie offers his own reasons why World was arrested and convicted. "They didn't want nobody that was on the bottom to rise to the top and make it, because that's the life they wish for," says Popsie. "If they really believed we were that notorious they would have got us off the streets with physical evidence, not a bunch of half-truths from snitches. People probably felt if World got in the music industry that he would either be the next Jay-Z and they didn't want him to be that."

STUCK IN THE HOLE

Damion "World" Hardy was in the hole for most of the eleven years he was in jail awaiting trial. He was shuffled back and forth between the federal holding facilities in New York and the federal prison medical unit in Springfield, Missouri, as the feds tried to determine if he was competent to stand trial. In 2007, he was diagnosed and treated for schizophrenia and a judge ordered him incompetent to stand trial. But in 2011, BOP officials started forcibly medicating World in an attempt to make him competent enough for court.

Prison officials reported that World was a terror behind bars. He belted a guard with a sock full of batteries, stabbed an inmate in the head with a sharpened comb, frequently threw an unknown liquid substance at staff members, and resisted guards who were trying to subdue him. According to one report, prison guards once confiscated a toothpaste tube from his cell which had been emptied and refilled with feces and urine which World intended to fire at guards.

"They had World in the box because he had codefendants or someone who was trying to cooperate on him on every floor in MDC," says Popsie. "When I was in MDC, I asked the CO's several times to bring him down to the floor I was on so we can fight our case together, but they refused to. They try their divide and conquer routine, so people think everyone is cooperating against each other."

"They were mentally trying to break World in the box on twenty three and one, with little food and no sunlight," Popsie relates. "He was not complying with them or doing what they wanted, so they were trying to break him by any means necessary, but you can't break the unbreakable. On the outside it may look like World had a good life fucking with a rap star, driving exotic cars with money out the ass, but in the blink of an eye the feds took his life away from him and he was wearing an orange jumper, socks, drawers and sneakers and he's stuck in the hole."

World is now serving his life sentence on the mainline at USP Hazleton, a federal prison in West Virginia, that is known for its violent inmates.

DARRYL "HOMICIDE" BAUM

Homicide was a legendary stick up kid whose name resonated in Brooklyn and New York street culture. He earned the nickname "Homicide" at the age of twelve for being a vicious knockout artist. He would walk up to a person and knock them out with one punch and then rob them for whatever he wanted: sneakers, jewelry, coat, or money. As he got older, his crimes got more brazen and he developed a notorious reputation around Brooklyn spending numerous years in and out of jail on various charges.

Homicide and Mike Tyson met as juveniles while they were both serving time in Spofford Juvenile Center, a correctional facility for young offenders locked in the Hunts Point section of the Bronx. Sharing a lengthy arrest history (Tyson had been arrested 38 times by the age of thirteen) the two became fast friends. As Tyson went on to boxing glory Homicide stayed in the streets and eventually graduated to real prison.

When he finally emerged in the late 90's, Tyson bought his friend a Rolex, a brand new Mercedes Benz, and gave him cash. He also employed Homicide as one of his security detail. But Homicide was still in the streets and allied himself with Peanut, the dude that Cash Money and World was beefing with for control of the drug spots at Lafayette Gardens. Peanut felt that Homicide's fearsome reputation would tilt the scales in his favor. Homicide was infamous and everyone knew that having him on your team could only make you stronger.

But World realized this too and after he took out Peanut, Homicide was the next to go. Homicide was already a street legend and had a lot of notoriety from being in Mike Tyson's camp, but once 50 Cent accused him of being the one who shot him on his track "Many Men" on *Get Rich or Die Tryin'*, Homicide became a part of hip-hop's lyrical lore. But he never got the chance to answer 50 Cent's accusations because he was already dead.

HOW THE FEDS BUILD CASES

According to the streets, when feds get a new case they construct it based on the lies, half-truths, and insinuations perpetrated by rats, cooperators, and snitches. It doesn't matter if what the witnesses are saying out of their mouths is true or not. The feds just roll with it. There is no investigation or nothing substantial going on. The US attorneys just rely on what their snitches are saying. The cooperator's words become the universal truth that prosecutors base their case off of. And in reality, the snitches are just saying whatever it is they think the feds want to hear, so they can get out of whatever jam they have managed to get themselves into. Whatever happened to the saying, if you are willing to do the crime, be willing to do the time?

These big multi-layered RICO act cases that the US attorneys crank out have become more a matter of the feds getting their snitches stories to fit the indictments they have concocted, and less a practice of justice or looking for the truth. There have been numerous cases that show how the US government works. They are using statutes made to convict mafia families and Colombian drug lords on inner-city drug crews, who are usually more unorganized chaos than organized crime. The feds have a tendency to identify the ultimate target of their probe before the investigation into their affairs has even started. If someone's name is ringing in the street then they are a target. This is especially true in regards to the feds' tough on crime policies as they apply to their war on minorities. With black people accounting for 15 percent of the US population, but 50 percent of the prison population, some may ask, "How can those numbers be justified?"

But the feds don't act alone putting cases on people; the snitches play along, doing whatever it takes to get that time cut. They say one thing in their proffers to get people indicted, but once they get on the stand they change the story up, doing whatever the prosecutor wants them to do so they can get that 5k1 or Rule 35 sentence reduction motion. Nobody is willing to do that twenty year sentence even for their so-called man. In the streets it's every man for himself because the feds don't play.

When dudes get busted, they talk about "death before dishonor" but when it comes down to it, if they want to get that time cut, they take the dishonorable route of becoming informants. The prosecutors are the same way; they don't care what they have to do to get their convictions. They have no sense of honor and justice or right and wrong. They will literally do whatever it takes. On the streets, the attorney profession is considered a pit of snakes and sharks.

Maxims like "death before dishonor" and "stop snitching" don't exist in the drug game and criminal underworld anymore, except in very rare cases. They are ideals of the past, held up in memory and supposedly cherished, but not honored in the present day. Most dudes in the streets are playing a dirty game. When that indictment comes down it's literally every man for himself. It's like the buffet, whoever is first in line gets the best deal.

14

THE KANSAS CITY MOB
THE CASINO SKIM THAT MADE MILLIONS

The Kansas City mob is a traditional old school Sicilian mafia or *La Cosa Nostra* that came from Sicilian immigrants in the early 1900's and modernized during Prohibition. In the 1930's, they made a lot of money in bootlegging and were heavily intertwined and connected to the KC political boss, Tom Pendergast. They advanced each other's causes in exchange for help at election time. It was a case of one hand washes another. This cabal basically ruled KC until 1939 when a "Clean Sweep" movement shook up the state and local government. Tom Pendergast went to jail for tax evasion, but the mob stayed in business—pulling the strings from the shadows.

The Kansas City mob has historically been involved in large scale thefts from truck lines, jewelry, and fur stores. They ran a few "protected" card games in the back of bars and inside a few private residences. They did a little loansharking and ended up "busting out" a few businesses. When strip clubs became more fashionable and popular, mob members started a couple of high end "gentlemen's clubs." But, the main source of *La Cosa Nostra's* money was from Las Vegas by the early 1970's.

CONTROLLING THE TEAMSTERS FUND

"Kansas City mob boss Nick Civella had compromised and put in his pocket Roy Lee Williams who rose to power in the Teamsters in Kansas City, and was made the Director of the Central States Teamster Conference in Chicago, and as such had a seat on the board of the Teamster pension fund," explains William Ouseley, who retired as Supervisor of the Organized Crime Squad, Kansas City FBI Field Division after a 25 year career. "Civella controlled Williams' votes on loans, many for Vegas properties, the fund considered. Other fund members were controlled by mob bosses in Chicago, Milwaukee, and Cleveland."

With mob control of the fund loans, those applying for loans to purchase Las Vegas hotels and casinos had to be sponsored by one of those crime families. In return for getting the loan approved there was normally a kickback and management of the casino had to be turned over to people working for the mob so that the money being generated could be skimmed from the casinos. The skim proceeds were then shared among the four crime families.

Besides controlling a vote on the fund, it turned out Civella played a very prominent role in the conspiracy as he was well respected by the Chicago crime family who had the final say, and was highly respected by organized crime elements operating in Vegas. In this manner the mob gained control of the Stardust, Freemont, Hacienda, and Marina hotel-casinos owned by a San Diego businessman named Allen Glick.

"During the late 1940's into the 1970's, the KC Mob created a relationship with powerful local Teamster's Union officials," says Gary Jenkins, who was assigned to the Kansas City Police Department's Intelligence Unit from 1976 to 1984 as a detective and spent years investigating the mob. "The Union officials used mob muscle to intimidate any opposition from within the union and truck lines that resisted their efforts to obtain a better contract."

In Kansas City, this started with the mob helping to intimidate rivals of their supported candidate in a union election. They intimidated trucking company executives to help get better contracts. Because of these past activities, mob guys were given jobs on the docks and they set up thefts. They kicked back money from these thefts to union leaders and kept these leaders in power. Later, the mob was allowed to influence who was able to borrow Teamster pension fund money. They then kicked back to the Teamster officials. There were no innocent parties to this unholy alliance, both the mob and the upper level Teamsters officials made money off the backs of the rank and file.

"The KC Mob teamed up with Chicago, Milwaukee, and Cleveland mob families and manipulated the Central States Teamster's pension fund to make loans to persons wanting to buy into the Vegas casino scene," says Jenkins. "In one case, they made a 62 million dollar loan to a 32 year-old real estate developer named Allen Glick. He bought the Stardust and three other smaller casinos but he was forced to hire Frank 'Lefty' Rosenthal, the Robert DeNiro character Ace Rothstein in Hollywood mob movie *Casino*, to run the operation. Lefty set up a stream of skim income from casino gaming receipts back to Chicago."

Nevada casino owners and gaming officials had already created an "anything goes" atmosphere in Vegas. The early casino and owners came out of the illegal gambling business and they were already connected to the mob. By the 1960's, Nevada gaming officials became more sophisticated and started to tighten up on the industry. For example, they created the "Black Book" or a book that listed professional gaming cheaters and other professional criminals that were banned from the casinos.

THE CASINO SKIM

As incomes in the US and particularly southern California increased, gambling moved from a small industry into a big money business with major corporations wanting to build Vegas hotels and get into the gaming industry. The Mob used their influence over the Teamsters' Union pension fund to ensure certain people obtained those loans to buy casinos and hotels. Once that happened, they demanded a kickback in the form of skim from the cash receipts. This was done by the mob forcing the new owners to place their associates in positions of power where they selected the employees who counted the money. These employees would then skim off a percentage for the Mob.

"They shared that with the Kansas City, Milwaukee, and Cleveland Families," says Jenkins. "This was done by having key employees inside the count room. The cash was brought from the tables, uncounted, and deposited inside this secure room. The count room employees then set aside a percentage of that cash and then counted the rest. This was the money sent back to Chicago. We don't know exactly how much this was."

Independent of this scheme, Civella gained control of the Tropicana Hotel and Casino when a former Kansas City resident sought Civella's help in getting a Teamster Fund loan for the

Tropicana, which was a deep financial problem. Civella shared the stolen skimmed money with Chicago as a show of respect.

"In the Tropicana operation, the courier was intercepted with two month's skim and that total was 80,000 dollars," explains Jenkins. "This was a separate skimming operation set up by Nicholas "Nick" Civella, the Artie Piscano character in *Casino*, head of the KC Mob family. Because he did not need the help of Cleveland or Milwaukee to establish his control of the Tropicana count room, he did not have to share with them. The Kansas City family was given the job of management of the skimming operation."

At this time, the skimming operation meant the midwest mobs had a regular stream of cash income. This money was used to grow mob power by making political contributions and keeping people in government on a regular payroll. Casino money was being directed to certain politicians in order to acquire influence. This movement into manipulating corporate entities educated mob members into more sophisticated scams and they were watching the stock market and attempting to cash in on inside casino information.

"Those of us working organized crime long knew of the situation in Vegas with the skim," says William Ouseley. "I also was well aware of Civella's interests in Vegas and had reason to believe he was getting money from there. His control of Roy Williams was also well known, as was the fact the Teamster pension fund was akin to a mob bank financing Vegas properties, and the Teamster Union was mob infiltrated. However, doing anything about it was another matter. So it took a break and the ability to capitalize on it by reason of having as an investigative tool legal electronic surveillance."

PROBLEMS FOR THE KANSAS CITY MOB

The 1970's was a very tumultuous time in the Kansas City underworld. The Civella mob's authority was challenged by the independent Spero brothers, who blamed Nick Civella for ordering another of their sibling's murder. The rackets in the city's then burgeoning River Quay neighborhood, a cluster of bars, nightclubs, and restaurants on the waterfront, were being fought over in a nasty skirmish that raged between Civella. Civella's street boss William

"Willie the Rat" Cammisano, and mob soldier David Bonadonna, whose son Freddy was the main property developer behind the River Quay resurgence and made a loose alliance with the Speros.

"Kansas City was a city losing its downtown core and white folks were moving out to the suburbs, like most major cities," explains Gary Jenkins. "The KC mob and their associates were moving into that void and trying to upgrade their old strip clubs to discos and moving into the newly created entertainment district close to downtown. This area was called the River Quay and it was a lot like the East Village in New York City or the French Quarter in New Orleans."

Bodies fell, including David Bonadonna's, a hit total that listed in the double digits, and within a few short years, as the 1980's approached, the River Quay district was in shambles, practically completely abandoned. The Speros would all be killed and Cammisano sent to prison for extortion based partially on Freddy Bonadonna's testimony in court. It was a chaotic time that attracted a lot of law enforcement attention in Kansas City.

"The River Quay murders were part of a dispute between Willie Cammisano and a man named Fred Bonadonna," explains Jenkins. "Fred's father, David Bonnadonna was part of Willie's crew. Fred was an influential bar owner in the River Quay organization and he was warning the other business owners and the Kansas City liquor control officials that mob guys were wanting to get liquor licenses in this area and they should be kept out. He also had a bunch of unused city parking leased and he was charging parking fees at night."

Willie the Rat thought he should get a piece of that action. When Fred refused to cooperate with Willie, his father David was killed. A friend of David's named Sonny Bowen then killed a Civella associate named John "Johnny Green" Amaro in retaliation. Sonny bragged about that killing. Sonny Bowen was soon killed in retribution for that killing because it had been done in Civella's home neighborhood.

At the same time, another small criminal organization led by a young mobster named Carl Spero wanted to move in on some of the Civella's rackets, enacting a street tax on the strip clubs and fencing operations. But the Speros were quickly rubbed out. He and his brothers Mike and Joe Spero were all killed by the Civellas. All these murders drew the law enforcement heat that led to the uncovering of the skim.

THE GANGLAND WIRE

"Interestingly and maybe a little bit ironically, an FBI bug planted in a local mobbed-up KC restaurant looking for information on murders spawning from the River Quay war sprouted the initial intelligence regarding the midwest mob's Las Vegas casino skim," says Scott Burnstein, an attorney, journalist, and organized crime historian who wrote *Motor City Mafia*. "This intelligence discovery was parlayed into the legendary 'Operation Strawman I' and then 'Operation Strawman II', the pair of federal racketeering cases that broke the mafia's hold over Vegas."

Law enforcement officials Gary Jenkins and William Ouseley both played pivotal roles in the operation that ended the mob's control of the casino skim.

"The Strawman case was initiated in 1978 in Kansas City as the result of an FBI hidden microphone in a mob frequented restaurant, wherein the acting crime family boss and the street boss were discussing their interest in ongoing events at Vegas casinos," explains William Ouseley. "This led to expanded electronic surveillance here, in Las Vegas, Milwaukee, Chicago. Kansas City was the lead FBI office in this case."

A hidden mic in a Kansas City bar caught Tuffy DeLuna and Cork Civella talking about Vegas casinos, Teamster money, making payments, and naming prominent Vegas casino persons. One night, as they discussed this subject generally, Tuffy made a statement that he had to "get to a phone." This led to the wiretapping of several pay phones and monitoring agents started hearing Tuffy DeLuna talking to a Vegas mole named Joe Agosto about specifics. Later, these conversations led agents to place a hidden microphone inside a house where Nick Civella, Tuffy DeLuna, Carl Civella, Joe Agosto, and Carl Thomas talked very specifically about how to skim money from a casino.

"The skimming had been going on as long as the state of Nevada had been taxing the profits," says Jenkins. "Part of the reason to skim was to avoid the gaming taxes. In the early 1970's, the midwest mob obtained sole control of the Vegas area, the skimming became more organized and sophisticated."

Allen Glick obtained a 62 million dollar loan to buy the Stardust, the Marina, the Hacienda and the Fremont hotel casinos. His mob handlers were told to hire Frank "Lefty" Rosenthal, the Chicago mob associate and gambler. Lefty set up underlings to skim the money. One of the schemes was uncovered by a gaming official named Dennis Gomes. He caught them using a secret switch to alter the weight when they weighed coins from the slot machines. The extra coins were then changed into cash and transported back to Chicago. A man named George Jay Vandermark (John Namce in *Casino*) was the manager of the slot operation. Vandermark disappeared after this discovery and has never been found. Lefty was allegedly controlled by Joseph "Joey Doves" Aiuppa (Remo Gaggi in *Casino*) out of Chicago.

"I was assigned to the KCPD Intelligence Unit," recalls Jenkins. "I was developing my own sources and informants into the mob. I was also assigned to surveillance crews to follow these guys around. For example, if we had a hidden mic inside a place, or a tap on a bank of pay phones, a physical surveillance had to verify that a named target was inside the place with the hidden mic or where the pay phones were located before they could turn on these devices. I got into the Intelligence Unit because that is the place where we had freedom to work on the top criminals in the city. I liked investigating the Mob because they were smart and a real challenge to my investigative skills. I liked putting the pieces of a criminal organization in place to make sense to me and others."

A man named Carl Thomas was employed at the Stardust for a while and later inside the Tropicana. He was a long time casino executive that seemed to be clean. He set up a scheme where he staffed the cash count room with trusted underlings and they skimmed off the cash directly before it was counted. Thomas was overheard by FBI agents on a hidden microphone bragging about stealing from the Circus Circus casino when he was younger and made a statement to Nick Civella and Tuffy DeLuna how he "loved taking money outta these joints."

"We know at least 40,000 dollars was taken monthly from the Tropicana alone," explains Jenkins. "They were getting other five figure payments monthly from the Chicago Mob, and that was coming from the Stardust."

Thomas was charged in the Strawman case and he became a witness against the mob bosses. He was in witness protection for a while and later came back and tried to get hired in a Colorado casino during the 1990's. He was denied a license and has since died in a suspicious traffic accident in the Las Vegas area. Another Tropicana employee was a man named Joe Agosto. He was a Sicilian born guy who had a relationship with Nick Civella. It is unknown how he became connected to Civella. He had made himself a valued employee at the Tropicana and worked with Carl Thomas to set up the skim. He also became a government witness and died of natural causes before the trials were over.

THE STRAWMAN CASE

"The Strawman case was the culmination of a long journey," says William Ouseley. "To be a part of a case that not only saw the demise of the Civella organization, but to topple other notable mob bosses and family members in other cities, for all intents and purposes end mob rule in Las Vegas, and result in the cleanup of the corrupt Teamster pension fund, was the highpoint of my career.

"I spent over twenty years working the Civella crime family. I saw it when it was riding high and law enforcement was struggling to make inroads. *La Cosa Nostra* families were formidable entities with a long history of operating in America. We were eventually successful because the FBI was committed long term to its eradication, and its various organized crime squads were manned by dedicated, innovative, and motivated agents." When he retired, Ouseley wrote a book about his investigation into Nick Civella's crew: *Mobsters in Our Midst: The Kansas City Crime Family*.

Kansas City was the locale of two major trials in this case. The first had to do with the Tropicana. Nick Civella died in March 1983, prior to any trials. His brother Carl was sentenced to thirty years. He died in prison. Carl DeLuna, the street boss, got thirty years. He is deceased. Charles Moretina, a key family member, got twenty years. He is deceased. Carl Caruso was the skim courier who transported the stolen money to Kansas City. He received three years probation and is now deceased also.

In the second trial that had to do with the Stardust and other properties, Carl Civella got ten years to run concurrently with the Tropicana sentence. Carl DeLuna got sixteen years to run concurrently with the Tropicana sentence. Pete Tamburello, Nick Civella's driver and confidant received five years on a guilty plea. He is deceased. Of note, other defendants in this trial included the Chicago boss, Joe Aiuppa, the Chicago underboss, Jack Cerone, and two family Capos, Joe Lombardo and Angelo LaPietra. Also Milwaukee boss Frank Balistrieri and Cleveland mob figure Milton Rickman received substantial sentences.

"When it comes to *La Cosa Nostra*, the crime families are structured to protect the top leadership, and its more important members," explains William Ouseley. "They operate behind the scenes and are not involved in the day to day mob criminal activities. The codes the members and associates abide by, loyalty, silence, need to know and fear on the part of those who do business with the mob or know things about the mob, all make prosecutions difficult. So of course the top leadership, boss, underboss, consiglieri, captains of crews, will always be difficult.

"Considering that, the big guys are normally the hardest to bring down, however, as has been proven in Kansas City, and around the country, having the laws to work with and the proper tools, such as legal electronic surveillance, in the end, no one is immune." That's the backstory to the film *Casino* and how the FBI ended the skim that was making the midwest mafia family millions.

A WIRETAP INADVERTENTLY LEARNS OF THE CASINO SKIM

Two of the Kansas City Mafia's main players were heard talking about the casino on a wiretap that was meant to discover info on the River Quay murders.

As law enforcement in Kansas City was investigating the violent and ghastly River Quay murders they inadvertently found out about the casino skim being generated from the Las Vegas casinos that the Mafia controlled. Imagine their surprise as Tuffy DeLuna and Cork Civella handed them the makings of one of the biggest cases against the mob ever. The event has been immortalized in the movie *Casino*.

Carl "Tuffy" Deluna (the Artie Piscano character in *Casino*) was the "Underboss." Tuffy was the guy who took care of hits and other street activities when necessary. For example, when a rival group threatened the Civella rule, Tuffy organized and led a small crew of hit men to attack and kill one man isolated in a public place (a bar) and shortly after caught three brothers (the Spero brothers) inside another bar and led a three man team to kill them. They killed one and wounded the other two. He was the person assigned to travel to Las Vegas to tell Allen Glick, partner in the Stardust casino operation, that he must sell the casino. Tuffy is his nickname because he was tough. He died a natural death after release from prison a few years ago.

Nick Civella's brother, Carl "Cork" Civella was his adviser and held a slightly lesser position. Cork was named this because he had an explosive temper. He once took his penis out in the hallway of the courthouse and shook it at some newspaper reporters. He was a loose cannon and held almost as much power in the mob as his brother Nick did. He died while still in prison for the skimming case.

MONEY, MONEY, MONEY

The Mafia/Teamster connection was generating tons of money for everyone associated with the skim.

At the Casino trial in 1985 in Kansas City, Angel A. Lonardo, one of the highest ranking mafia members to turn government witness, testified that the mob was skimming up to two million dollars a year from the Stardust and Fremont casinos that Allen Glick operated after securing the 62.7 million dollar Teamster loans. The Teamster officials involved were getting payments of 1,500 dollars a month, the Cleveland mob was getting 40,000 dollars, Kansas City and Chicago were getting even more. Nick Civella, the Kansas City Mob boss also had a separate skim set up at the Tropicana that generated forty thousand in additional funds a month for his family. The mafia families from Chicago, Kansas City, Milwaukee and Cleveland who orchestrated the skim through their Teamster connections were getting rich. In the 1970's, two million dollars was a lot of money.

15

VORY V ZAKONE "THIEVES IN LAW"
RUSSIAN GANGS OF NEW YORK

The Russian Mafia has a mystique and mystery all its own that rivals that of the Italian Mafia in popular culture. When the iron curtain fell, a new type of gangster was unleashed on the world as the *Vory v Zakone* (Thieves in Law) seized power in Russia and beyond. The group began sending their representatives far and wide to secure and control their criminal rackets. Far beyond the typical mainstays of drugs, extortion, murder, heists, and gambling, the Russians moved into fraud, the cyber world, gasoline scams, and even chocolate.

From their base in New York City, the Russians have gained a foothold in the criminal underworld juxtaposing techniques and ideals forged in the gulags with modern business principles to create the type of gangster that thrives both in the real and online worlds that our society has created. The Russian gangs of New York are entrenched in America running scams, extorting people, working with the Italian Mafia, and going about their activities like they are regular business men. To the Russians, crime, politics, and business all intertwine and where they intersect the Russian Mafia reigns supreme.

BRIGHTON BEACH STRONGHOLD

Brighton Beach, at the end of the subway line in New York City, is a well-known stronghold for the Russian Mafia. Right next to Coney Island and with a high number of Russian immigrants, it's the perfect breeding ground for organized crime and the *Vory*. The insular community has been a center of Russian Mafia activity since the 1970's, spawning infamous crime bosses like Evsei Agron, Vyacheslav Ivankov, and Marat Balagula. These men held the same regard in their communities as John Gotti did on Mulberry Street in Little Italy.

With scores of members and a reputation for challenging *La Cosa Nostra* for dominance on the Eastern Seaboard, the Russian Mafia has engaged in the typical crimes: prostitution, drugs, extortion, and murder, creating a criminal culture based on the edicts of the *Vory*, who formed in the harsh environs of the Soviet Union gulags during the Stalin era. But they've also ventured into health care and tax fraud, getting money anyway they can. The ways and means don't matter to the Russians, only the end result.

"To the Russians, police in the US are Mickey Mouse," suggests Palve "Punch" Stanimirovic, a Serbian-American founder of the Pink Panthers, a bold and daring jewel heist crew. Punch grew up in New York City, the son of an infamous Serbian gangster who did time with the Russian crime groups. "The *Vory* are the godfathers of Russian crime. Very respected just like the Mafia Dons in the US."

Centering their activities in the busy Brighton Beach neighborhood with its Old World charm and panache, the Russian gangs came to dominate crime in Brooklyn after the fall of the Soviet Union as the *Vory* and other gangsters made their way to America. There they formed *brigadas*, independent but interlocking criminal groups whose main priority and function was to get money by any means necessary. Little Odessa, as it was known, was 95 percent Russian and the criminals dominated the area in the 90's.

"It was all different groups, no one answers to one guy," recalls a Russian gangster from the era. "But some guys get more respect because of how they are." And typically those were the *Vory* gangsters. What they lacked in education, they made up with charisma and brute force. Vodka, steroids, and cocaine fueled the gangsters of Brighton Beach. Parties on 300 foot yachts in Sheepshead Bay where alcohol, drugs, and sleazy women were commonplace. The gangsters broadcasted their wealth by sporting Armani suits and wearing Rolex watches.

THE FIRST RUSSIAN DON

Evsei Agron was the first notable Russian don in Brighton Beach. The Leningrad-born *Vor* was the most feared man in Little Odessa. He arrived in Brooklyn in 1975 and set up shop. A master extortionist, thief, and killer, he organized the Russian gangs and acted as a protector and guarantor of good behavior in the criminal underworld. Agron was a defender of honor among thieves mentality born in the gulag. He held court in the Russian baths in East Village, dispensing justice, discipline, and orders with a brigada of gun thugs at his beck and call.

"They had their own distinctive culture," explains Mark Galeotti, author of *The Vory: Russia's Super Mafia*. "Just as we know that *The Godfather* actually shaped how the New York Mafia thought of themselves, and how more recently *The Sopranos* has had a powerful impact on the self image of New Jersey gangsters. We know too that both domestic and foreign gangster movies, gangster clichés, and pop culture idioms worked their way into how the Russians thought of gangsters."

Agron wanted to be the boss, but the Russians didn't like bosses. If they came from the Soviet Union, US law enforcement put everyone under the same umbrella, but that wasn't necessarily the way things were. In January 1984, Agron was shot in an assassination attempt, but the shooters failed. Agron told cops not to worry about it; he would take care of it. But in May of 1985, Agron was shot again and killed. His bodyguard, Boris Nayfeld was uncharacteristically absent. Some thought the Italian Mafia was to blame.

Agron had been working with the Genovese family and even though they were making loads of money there was friction between the Russian and Italian mobsters. The Italians lived under the radar and avoided attracting attention, but the Russians flaunted their wealth, lived in the limelight, and partied all the time. They earned money from old-fashioned jewelry heists, to credit card fraud, to counterfeiting, to bootlegged gasoline. "The Russians don't have the same codes as the Italians," said David Amoruso, who runs *Gangsters Inc.*. "The Italians don't kill civilians, not even the family members of mobsters who flipped. The Russians don't have these rules."

CHALLENGING THE MAFIA

"In the pioneering years of Russian organized crime, Russians kicked up more than half their earnings to their Italian superiors," Gary "Gunz" Govich wrote in his book, *Career Criminal: My Life in the Russian Mob Until the Day I Died*. But in the years to follow the tables would turn and the Russian Mafia would start calling the shots. The relationship with the Italian Mafia has remained steady, but the parameters of that relationship changed as the Russians started spreading their wings.

If you beat a Russian with a bat they would come back with a knife. If you stabbed them with a knife and you would get the heaters. Disrespect one of their associates and face the penalty. That was their creed. In the late 80's and early 90's, law enforcement in New York attributed sixty-five homicides to the Russians criminal activities. *New York Magazine* quoted a member of the Italian Mafia: "We Italians will kill you, but the Russians are crazy; they'll kill your whole family."

The Russians didn't have any respect for anyone and weren't afraid of the consequences. They felt that the crime groups and law enforcement in America were "pussycats." Their M.O. was plug one of us and you better murder us all. From violent crime on the street to drug dealing to more complex schemes, the Russians were gung-ho when it came to crime. The *Vory* had thrived in a system of oppression and to them America was easy pickings.

Using fear, deception, and treachery, the career criminals from the *Vory* oversaw multimillion dollar criminal enterprises. It was a true old-boy's club, an exclusive brotherhood that brought in loads of cash from their criminal exploits that flooded and revitalized Brighton Beach. The gangsters would be at the local coffee shops drinking warm vodka from teacups, wearing velour warm-ups, and sporting platinum watches and chains.

To them, the Italian Mafia were just players in the local criminal underworld. To an organization like the *Vory*, that was truly international in scope, they meant little in the big scheme of things. The Italians were minor pawns in a global game of chess. Where money, infamy, and fortune denoted the trappings of success and glory in the annals of gangster lore represented everlasting fame.

GANGSTER ROYALTY COMES TO BRIGHTON BEACH

An enigma, Vyacheslav "Yaponchik" Ivankov, lived and died with an air of mystery. He came up in the Cold War era where it was not uncommon for people in the Eastern Block to exploit the black market that thrived under Soviet rule. Once the Iron Curtain fell, the power vacuum propelled would-be gangsters into full fledged organized crime lords and numerous gangs rose to international levels.

Yaponchik, which meant "Little Japanese," arrived in the United States in the early 90's to establish a strong Russian mob presence in Brooklyn and to organize all the brigada's under one rule. A fabled *Vory* overlord who demanded fealty and handled disputes by murdering the offending parties, Yaponchik turned an assortment of loosely organized crime groups into a nationwide entity that took orders from Moscow.

"He was like a negotiator," the Russian gangster from the era says. "If you had problems with another crew you need somebody to squash the beef. He was known worldwide. He made an impact in a very short period of time. Very violent and very respected. Everyone was scared of him." Yaponchik was known for ordering the killing of a Russian boxer in Brighton Beach in broad daylight. He didn't give a fuck.

"People don't know what they are capable of," the Russian gangster says. "By the time they find the body the assassin is already back in Moscow. In the early 90's a lot of people were getting killed. He was a tough guy. A shot caller and everyone complied. He did extortion himself. He would do a robbery himself and he has hundreds of guys under him.

"He doesn't have to do a thing but he does. You would never see a mafia don like Paul Castellano do that." But by 1995, Yaponchik caught a case for extortion and ended up in federal prison for nine years before being deported back to Russia to face murder charges, which he beat. He ended up being killed himself by a sniper as he tried to solve a dispute between two gangsters.

STATE OF THE MOB TODAY

"The Thieves-in-Law is a Eurasian crime syndicate that has been linked to a long list of illicit activity across the globe," said John Smith, director of the Treasury's Office of Foreign Assets Control. "Treasury is designating the Thieves-in-Law as part of a broader strategy to disrupt the financial infrastructure of transnational criminal organizations that pose a threat to the United States and our allies."

Designated a "Transnational Criminal Organization" by the US Treasury, the *Vory* are a high priority for US law enforcement. As a "TCO," the Thieves-in-Law joined notorious criminal organizations such as Japan's *Yakuza*, Mexico's *Los Zetas* cartel, Italy's *Camorra*, and Central America's MS-13 as enemies of the state.

Marat Balagula is the latest Russian gangster to set up and ply his trade from Brighton Beach. Law enforcement accused him of amassing over six-hundred million from bootleg gasoline after arriving from Odessa. Wiretaps determined that Balagula was "the power broker at the center" according to AUSA John P. Pucci of the Eastern District of Pennsylvania. In addition to the gasoline scam, Balagula's criminal schemes included counterfeiting currency, bank, and corporate checks.

"He was into gasoline schemes—the biggest in US history," the Russian gangster says. "He was making so much money he paid the Genovese family four million for protection. They guarded him from every angle." Balagula also operated a drug ring, an illegal gambling establishment, a credit card scheme, cigarette smuggling operation, gun-running, fencing of stolen jewelry, and kidnap-for-hire. His crew even orchestrated the heist of ten thousand pounds of chocolate.

"Of all the cases I've ever worked, I've never seen a case that wild: casinos, cyber, kidnappings, chocolates," recalls John Penza, an FBI agent who specializes in organized crime. "Nothing was off the table." In Brighton Beach, the Russian gangs of New York still rule the criminal underworld. Working with the Italian Mafia in an everlasting tug-of-war where only money and violence reign king.

STRAIGHT OUTTA THE GULAG

The Vory v Zakone were born and bred in the harsh environs of the Soviet Union's gulags.

The title, *vor* for short, translates to "thief in law," a Soviet term that denotes the highest rank in Russian organized crime. Formed in the Stalin-era gulags, the fierce and anti-establishment *Vory* go back to the late 19th century—a hard man culture that has taken over Russian organized crime. Covered in tattoos that signify rank, the *Vory* are intelligent thugs who prey on society like sharks in a feeding frenzy. A 1920's Vor and a 1950's *Vor* could read each other's tattoos perfectly, no problem.

"A lot of the Russian tattoos were designed to be visible," says Mark Galeotti, author of *The Vory: Russia's Super Mafia*. "It's really obvious things like the barb wire across the forehead—a basic way of saying I am not one of you." One of the purposes of the tattoos, apart from just sort of showing how hard you are, was to basically giving the finger to conventional society. But the new model *Vor* doesn't want to stand out, he wants to be able to pass in respectable society, and go abroad without problems. That sense of physically demonstrating that you're an outsider has disappeared.

INFAMOUS RUSSIAN VORY IN NEW YORK

Boris Nayfeld — Active from 1970's to 2010's

Released from his third prison sentence in New York. Bodyguard to Russian Don, Evsei Agron. In the 1970's, Nayfeld betrayed his boss and partnered with Marat Balagula. He is rumored to have white eyes and be possessed by the devil. He's a life long criminal and has been in the news saying he just wants to go home to Russia.

Monya Elson — Active from 1970's to Present

After several stints in US prisons, now living in Israel. A convicted extortionist and murderer, Elson was beefing with Nayfeld and his crew. Elson would drive all trough Brighton Beach with his girl like Bonnie and Clyde. He had an ex-KGB as his bodyguard. His name used to ring bells, but now he's considered a snitch.

Armen Ghazaryan — Active from 1980's to Present

Is currently living overseas. An Armenian gangster—who came to the US in 1996—that was the ringleader of a massive Medicare fraud case. His contacts within the Russian Mafia and *Vory* enabled him to oversee the fraud case.

Boris Komin —Active from the 1940's to Present

Currently Living in the United States. The oldest thief-in-law in the United States at 91 he is also the boss now. He was one of the first *Vory* to move to the US in the 1970's. He stays in the shadows and has tremendous power.

Razhden Shulaya — Active from 1970's to Present

Currently under indictment in the US and facing 65 years, Shulaya has been involved in everything from forgery, counterfeiting, bribery, gambling, drugs, extortion, and hacking. He is currently indicted for attempting to break into a casino, transportation and sale of stolen goods, and using fake documents.

Oleg Korotayev — Active from 1970's to 1990's, killed in 1994

Known as a gangster athlete, Korotayev served as a foot soldier for the Russian Mafia before deciding he deserved a bigger piece of the pie. He got mixed up with the wrong *Vor* and was killed for it.

16

RICHARD "THE ICEMAN" KUKLINSKI
THE PSYCHO MAFIA HITMAN

In the 1970's, locals said that New Jersey had way more mafia guys than New York. Jersey was infested with mob activity as a litany of associates, hangers on and wanna-be's emulated what they'd seen in *The Godfather* movie. It was death before dishonor and the criminal underworld was ripe with gangland antics, making it easy for guys with violent tendencies like Richard "The Iceman" Kuklinski to not only get into the life, but thrive. Being that the FBI wasn't really focused on the mob back then, and when they were it was the big names, killers like The Iceman had a sort of free reign, the proverbial license to kill, and in cold blooded fashion he carved a niche for himself in the East Coast's mafiadom.

"I think the type most often described as cold-blooded is a psychopathic or sociopathic personality, someone who has no remorse, no feelings or guilt, empathy, or any aversion to violence," explains criminal psychologist Stephen J. Giannangelo, a retired state of Illinois criminal investigator, and author of *The Psychopathology of Serial Murder: A Theory of Violence* and *Real-Life Monsters: A Psychological Examination of the Serial Murderer*. These people, like Kuklinski, have often had violence in their childhoods so extreme that it's normal and is the only way they know how to deal with anything. This makes them more equipped for the job as a hitman.

However, the predatory nature of a psychopath, the cold-bloodedness acts in concert with a certain amount of patience and manipulativeness, and often intelligence, that makes them good at what they do. A successful hit man is someone who can do it for thirty years like Kuklinski, rather than someone caught in the early stages of their careers.

By the 1980's, Kuklinski was one of the most feared hitmen in the State of New Jersey and nobody could control him. He was a loose cannon who did what he wanted and killed at will. If someone disrespected him they were dead plain and simple. He took hits by the dozens, but he also killed for the pure enjoyment of it. He was just a violent, violent guy.

"I think Kuklinski is one of the few hit men that I would say crossed over into the realm of a full-blown serial killer," says Giannangelo. "Researchers and FBI nowadays include many multiple murder offenders in their statistics as serial murderers without much regard for motivation. But some, mainly those more oriented towards the psychological angle of study, still look at serial killers as those who kill for a reason, a need. Kuklinski continued to kill for far more reasons than a guy who was paid well and lived the good life; he killed because he loved it."

And he was under the radar for a long time until he made a crucial error. Kuklinski killed Louis Masgay and kept his body frozen in a freezer for two years. He finally decided to dump the body in Rockland County, New York. Masgay was wrapped in plastic bags and was still wearing the clothes he had on when he disappeared, two years earlier. When police found the body, Masgay looked like he was only dead for a week. The deep freeze masked the time of death and that was how The Iceman got his name—but things didn't work out as planned.

"When they did the autopsy they indicated reversal decomposition that began externally rather than internally and they found ice crystals in the tissues when the body was discovered in August or September, which is hot," says Dominick Polifrone, the retired ATF Agent who worked undercover and brought Kuklinski to justice. "He made the cops look like jerks. He told me, 'Dom, you know I wrapped him up and I had him in there for two years in the freezer and he didn't even decompose, he looked like he died yesterday and he had the same clothes on for two years.'"

HITMAN OR PSYCHOPATH?

"He's like the Jolly Green Giant. He wore these tinged orange glasses," Polifrone says. "But he's a big, big man." Keeping bodies in the freezer was something straight out of Jeffrey Dahmer's playbook—pretty scary. Most mafia guys just want to make money. They don't want to kill people and get bloody. They don't like murder, it's a last resort. But in organized crime guys like The Iceman were very useful.

"I think he got enjoyment out of killing," said Ed Scarpo from *Cosa Nostra News*. "For most mafia guys it's just about pushing a button or pulling a trigger. They don't think about it. It's just what they have to do. Usually they don't even know the guy. They don't even know why he's the guy getting killed or who wants it done. But Kuklinski liked to get his hands dirty. He liked to feel the guy die."

Kuklinski was a full blown psychopath, actually more accurately a sociopath if we are to believe he was just a product of a horrific upbringing of poverty, violence, and abuse. "A child living in a household of violence normalizes it and even thrives in it," Giannangelo muses. "Of course, without testing, we will not know what Kuklinski's genetics might be, or if there were other biological factors regarding his development.

"Regarding how he said in the HBO specials, that he felt nothing when he killed, he didn't feel anything. Ted Bundy and Jeffrey Dahmer needed alcohol to commit many of their murders. Kuklinski had no such inhibitions to overcome. He enthusiastically tortured animals as a child and as found significant by researchers of human to animal violence, he enjoyed the torture of animals normally regarded as pets like dogs and cats indicating a non-empathetic, sadistic, impulse-driven need for violence that precludes any feelings to disregard.

"I'd compare that to gang activity of today, where many kids are a product of their environments, where poverty and powerlessness is a breeding ground for extreme measures to escape such a life. The rewards that can come with gang activity, or in Kuklinski's heyday, organized crime life, can be voluminous: money, status, power, women. It's not hard to see how some people could eventually justify that this life is forced on them, that it's their only way to survive or succeed, and that they are convinced their circumstances are not their fault.

"It depends on the individual. A person I described as a product of their environment can compartmentalize and justify their actions. They can be narcissistic, immature, and believe their own excuses. It is possible they could reflect on the damage to peoples' lives. A psychopath or a sociopath however, could adapt, even thrive in this life with little difficulty and no distress to their sensibilities.

There's still a narcissism and a disdain for those who live a lawful life consistent with that personality that is compatible with murder for hire. In these cases I see no toll on that sort of mind."

TAKING DOWN THE ICEMAN

"I was called to stop by the Bergen County Prosecutor's Office in New Jersey where I met these individuals who were working on a case involving this individual by the name of Richard Kuklinski," Polifrone says. "Kuklinski was meeting individuals in Bergen County and Hudson County New Jersey areas and then they would be disappearing, but they also alleged that there was poison involved and he liked to use pure cyanide."

Polifrone was an undercover ATF agent who was good at his job and had a ton of experience. Been Country prosecutors knew that Kuklinski was a killer but they couldn't prove it. He was just too good at his job, but so was Polifrone. He infiltrated a wise guy joint in Patterson, New Jersey and started making inroads there, becoming known as the guy who could acquire anything. With the federal government at his back, Polifrone could be anyone he wanted to be.

"They had been investigating him for several years and they had a lot of circumstantial evidence, but no direct evidence," Polifrone says. "There were a lot of cracks in the case. They wanted to charge him for the particular murders and they needed an undercover agent with a lot of experience to find out details. They had information that these guys met Kuklinski and then disappeared, but there were no eyewitnesses or anything to what took place.

"I started hanging out at The Store in Paterson, New Jersey where all the bad guys were. It was just like the movie *Goodfellas*, where all the bad guys would come in and they'd do their business and they had a lot of different schemes that were going on and where they'd plan their next heist. They'd also do large hijackings of trucks and they would distribute the booty all over the place. It took me about fifteen months to get in and Kuklinski was not hanging out at this store, because he felt that a lot of people were onto him, meaning the police.

"Word was getting out that I could get anything. And after hanging out at the location for over a year the telephone rings one morning and this guy picks it up and says Dom, it's the big guy, he wants to know if he can meet with you at the Dunkin' Donuts in Paterson, New Jersey. When I got there he wore these tinged glasses and when I talked to him it was like he was reaching out to grab my soul and control me.

"He says to me, 'Can you get pure cyanide?' I couldn't believe how he was starting the conversation off. I said, 'Yeah, I can get pure cyanide'. I knew he also killed his main guy, that supplied him with the pure cyanide and word was out there that I can get anything. So he felt comfortable when I told him 'yeah', but that it wasn't easy.

"Later on Kuklinski calls me. We met at the Vince Lombardi service station. I go over a lot of scenarios that took place on how these people were found dead. For instance, we were talking about how we murdered people. I said, 'Rich, I kill people with guns. I don't understand this cyanide stuff.' He says, 'Listen, you put this pure cyanide on food or in an inhaler where they breathe it in and he squeezes it. They breathe that in and there's no antidote. By the time they find out what it is, they're dead.' He says, 'this is nice and easy.' He says, 'these police don't know what they're doing.' He says, 'where there's smoke there's fire, but he puts a lot of smoke in front of it and they can't get him.' We started talking about how we each killed people and he was telling me very detailed stuff.

"They went to trial with this. Kuklinski pled guilty and then he was serving two life terms. His wife and kids were in the courtroom, but once they heard the undercover tapes it was too late they couldn't believe how he was talking and how he would murder people. I remember the judge asking him why he did it and he said it was strictly business."

LEADING THE DOUBLE LIFE

"They had information regarding Kuklinski that he was associated with organized crime people and he lived in an affluent area in Bergen County, New Jersey," Polifrone says. "He had a wife and two children and he had a lot of different organized crime connections that left many police departments in several states with empty leads for close to over a decade."

Leading a double life, one at home with his family as a typical suburban husband and father, and the criminal side where he would meet Roy DeMeo at the Gemini Lounge in Brooklyn for business purposes. The Gemini Lounge was the mafia club in Flatlands where DeMeo and his crew would cut up bodies. Jerry Capeci immortalized the crew in the book, *Murder Machine*.

"Roy DeMeo killed sixty-four people himself," Polifrone says. "He was a made guy and had his own crew. DeMeo winds up dead later on and some people think Kuklinski did it. But he was an associate of all these people; they would call him out to do all these contract hits and to him it was strictly just business, you know, a day's work." He was masking his day job from his family who thought he was a businessman working the money markets.

"Some people could say that Kuklinski exhibited doubling, a psychological process where an individual can live two entirely different and seemingly conflicting lives separate from one another," Giannangelo explains. "This was a theory made popular by Robert Lifton regarding Nazi-era Doctors. But Kuklinski, in my opinion, simply was participating in the compartmentalized parts of his life. His position as a vicious, high status, feared hitman who was able to enjoy the violence, success, and respect his business brought him was one major part of his life.

"The other part was his home life, where he could be the loving and protective father, who also exhibited power and violence and control. He needed to extend the intelligence he exhibited in avoiding law enforcement in the meticulous manner he did for as long as he did. I can't imagine the duplicity was all that difficult for him. This sort of dual life isn't particularly unheard of with a psychopathic serial murderer. Dennis Rader, the BTK Killer, had no issues living a similar double life. His family was who he would die for.

"A prototypical sociopath is going to be highly defensive of his status, how he is perceived, almost to the point of paranoia. This drives a lot of his pathological need for control. He was known for an extreme aversion for public embarrassment and any hint of disrespect. The defense of his family is partially because he cares for them, but is just as much driven by how he is viewed, and how anyone could dare threaten someone in his circle. It should be noted that Kuklinski did seem to have a genuine concern for the effect the exposure of his criminal life had on his family, not unlike the BTK Killer and Albert DeSalvo, among others."

CRIMINAL CELEBRITY

"For as long as any of us can remember, people have been engrossed in stories of crime and violence," says Giannangelo. "Whether it's Jack the Ripper or Bonnie and Clyde or the Manson family, tales of crime and murder and death keep people gripped to books, magazines, TV shows and films. The stories about true crime, I think, fascinates us all the most, as you feel like you could be a part of many of these stories.

"How many movies has Hollywood made about the Mafia and organized crime? About serial killers? Both subjects are absolute gold at the box office when done well like *The Godfather, Goodfellas,* and *Silence of the Lambs*. Even average stories will make an awful lot of people sit and watch another television documentary or movie. I never have an empty seat in my classes about criminal psychology and serial murder. And many are students with majors that have nothing to do with the subject. They just love this stuff.

"Kuklinski's story is an amazing combination of both of these favorite genres. A man with a classic horrible home life, grows to have a successful career in the mafia as a professional hitman and takes it to the level of a full blown serial killer. It seems Kuklinski's enjoyment in being interviewed and appearing in the media belies a love for the fame and status reflective of his mindset, not unlike some high-profile serial killers." But others think Kuklinski might have been coached and even question the credibility of his claims.

"I think Kuklinski was mostly going for the media attention because in the first HBO special he didn't talk about the mob, just killing people, but in the next episode he started getting more specific and mentioning the mob and Roy Demeo," says Ed Scarpo from *Cosa Nostra News*. "I wouldn't be surprised if the producers talked to him about how the mafia stuff was really popular and told him to drop names. Because in the first show he doesn't mention the Mafia.

"To me Kuklinski is mostly a media invention. Those shows were really popular on HBO. In my time covering *Cosa Nostra*

News, whenever someone mentions Kuklinski I think they're full of shit. One guy tried to tell that Kuklinski was there when they killed Tommy DeSimone, the Joe Pesci character in *Goodfellas*."

TRUTH OR TALL TALES?

"It's not uncommon for psychopathic killers to brag and exaggerate their kills," explains Giannangelo. "These are pathologically narcissistic individuals, who, once in a position to confess, lose nothing in claiming a higher status. Then there's killers like Henry Lee Lucas who claimed hundreds of kills that were later discounted.

"But Lucas went on field trips and ate restaurant food eagerly provided by investigators trying to solve cold cases. Murderers have many reasons to lie about their inflated victim totals. I'm not sure if Kuklinski exaggerated anything, but he certainly would have legitimate motivations for people to believe he was the most fearsome executioner alive, both in his professional life and as a criminal celebrity."

It was Phillip Carlo's book *The Iceman* that gave Kuklinski relevance in pop culture, but nothing was corroborated. Carlo just took what Kuklinski told him in the interviews as God's honest truth. He wrote the story based on Kuklinski's words and gave a lot of false credibility. Not to say that he wasn't a hitman that took contracts from the mob, but his actual associations and how close he was to the Mafia and Roy DeMeo in particular has been questioned.

"Jerry Capeci wrote *Murder Machine*, the book on Roy DeMeo's crew," Scarpo says. "It was a major research piece, he talked to everybody involved with the case. Capeci does this whole book and talks to five hundred to one thousand sources, he had full access to the FBI and DEA files. Kuklinski's name is not mentioned once in that book.

There was some truth to what Kuklinski said. He had mob connections. I've heard that there was a single surveillance photo of him outside the Gemini Lounge where DeMeo was, but he was probably just trying to get a gun or something."

As his criminal celebrity and fame rose it seemed that Kuklinski claimed he was in on every unsolved murder. Investigators eager to close cases, let him confess and HBO producers, eager for viewers, let Kuklinski tell his story the way he wanted to, embellishing his relationship with the Mafia and who he killed.

"I doubt he killed DeMeo," muses Scarpo. "That was a mafia thing. That was the Gambino's that killed Roy DeMeo." And Dominick Polifrone, the undercover ATF agent who finally collared Kuklinski doesn't believe his high body count either.

"I don't believe he killed over a hundred people," Polifrone says. "I'd go as far as ten, fifteen people maybe—that's about it."

The Iceman killed to practice and hone his skills before he embarked on his storied career as a mafia hitman.

"He supposedly killed a lot of people, not as part of organized crime, but more as the classic serial killer," Ed Scarpo from *Cosa Nostra News* says. "He would get in fights at bars and wait outside and kill the guy when he came out. They would find bodies but they never knew who did the killing. On one of the HBO specials they did some research and they found cases that matched his stories.

"In one he was driving on the highway somewhere in New Jersey and a carload of young guys started messing with him. Kuklinski forced them off the road and shot and killed them all. The HBO people found an unsolved murder that matched that description. Like three or four guys all killed. Laid out next to the highway and no one ever knew what happened to these guys."

Kuklinski was a big man and most people were afraid of him. They called him big guy and he was this massive dude that used to wear these crazy orange tinged glasses. He was into porn and killing people. He fit in perfectly with the organized crime world. He had a rough upbringing and found that he enjoyed making other people feel pain.

"His mother and father abused him tremendously and one day he found his oats. I think it was at a pool hall or something, where he beat somebody to death with a cue stick later on—he was feeling his oats," Polifrone explains. "He got into pornography. He started making big bucks, starting hanging around with the wise guys making more money and then he started doing more contract hits and he was feeling good, but he was getting sloppy too.

"He could never be a made guy, because he wasn't a true Italian. He murdered a couple of people, shooting them in the back of the head, another one he shot in the back of the head and put him in the trunk of the car. He was still alive so Kuklinski grabbed the tire iron and beat him to death."

METHODS OF MURDER

Most Mafia hitman were strictly gun types. They liked to get in close and pull the trigger to commit murder, but Kuklinski was very inventive in the ways he would kill people.

Kuklinski told Polifrone, the undercover ATF agent, that if someone wanted to make a statement or make the hit look dirty, it wasn't a problem. He would cut the guy's tongue off, stick it in his ass, or put a parakeet in their mouth. He could do it nice and clean with a little cyanide where people would think the person had a heart attack. He put some people in barrels. When rigor mortis set in he would cut the limbs so he could stuff them in the barrel.

FEEDING VICTIM TO THE RATS

Kuklinski once allegedly put a guy in a cage and filmed a rat eating him, a torturous and painful death. It seemed the Iceman enjoyed the torment of his victims.

DEATH BY HANGING

Kuklinski once hung someone by using his body. He put a rope around their neck and jerked it over his shoulder. He was standing up hunched over and he was so tall he hung the dude and strangled him using his body like a gallows.

CYANIDE WITH YOUR HAMBURGER

Polifrone says that Kuklinski told him they gave one victim hamburgers topped with cyanide. They watched the victim eat the hamburgers and watched his eyes roll back.

OLD FASHIONED KILLING

Kuklinski wasn't above shooting a victim with a .38 caliber and stuffing them in a barrel. This was a well practiced organized crime tactic.

STRANGULATION AND SUFFOCATION

As a big man Kuklinski used his size to his advantage. It was nothing for him to strangle a victim and leave them in a motel room in New York or even just suffocate them with whatever was at hand.

17

BAC GUAI
CHINATOWN'S WHITE DEVIL

They called the big, crazy, white Irish kid, Bac Guai, which translated to "White Devil". From a homeless kid to second-in-command of a Chinese gang, Willis worked himself up through the ranks of *Ping On*, one of the most violent Chinese gangs in Boston. After paying his dues by going to prison for the gang, Willis reinvented himself as an Oxycontin kingpin. Capitalizing on the opioid craze that swept the nation in the early 2000's. He generated millions of dollars for himself before getting busted by the feds in 2011.

"At seventeen, eighteen, there's nothing anyone could tell me," Willis recalls. "I was angry at the world. I was gonna do what I was gonna do and that's it. My mother died when I was a kid, my father left when I was three. The people who raised me were from another world. This was about the struggle of not having parents, the struggle of having to prove yourself on a daily basis, to learn a new culture. I think Boston's Chinatown is a small Chinatown, but I think it's a close knit community. There would be different factions of people that we might have problems with, but it's not like you're a Blood or a Crip, it's an organization."

PING ON IN BOSTON'S VIOLENT CHINATOWN

Ping On came to power in Boston's Chinatown in the 1970's. The gang was founded by Stephen "Sky Dragon" Tse, a Chinese national who was affiliated with 14K, a powerful mainland China Triad where new members drank their own blood mixed with the blood of a beheaded chicken as a part of the initiation ritual. In the 1980's and 90's, *Ping On* was the most fierce gang in Chinatown, wreaking havoc at their whim with violence as their lovely mistress. Sky Dragon ran his illicit gangland empire from the Kung Fu restaurant on Tyler Street, playing the role of "Dai Lo" or big brother of the gang.

"I think he liked me because I was white, I was bigger," Willis says. "He felt it was a novelty to have a white guy who could speak broken Chinese and have someone who didn't typically grow up in Chinatown. My story is different from others, not saying that I'm better or worse, it's just the way that I lived that allowed me to assimilate into a culture where they didn't accept outsiders. When I was young, you didn't go to Chinatown, you didn't belong there if you weren't Chinese."

But in Chinatown, they treated Willis like a brother or a son. The gangsters gave him money, clothes, and a place to live. More importantly they let the troubled young man become a part of something that was bigger than himself. The *tongs* and the gangs that supported their criminal activity had been around in Chinese culture for thousands of years. Willis embraced his adopted culture and learned to speak the language fluently, opening up doors for him in the gang.

"When I spoke Chinese, I spoke with a Chinese accent," Willis says. "People respected me, people talked to me, and treated me well because of that. I grew in the ranks from being a kid and knowing nothing, to knowing ten words of Chinese, to speaking fluent Chinese, to basically having my own group of people, my own group of guys. I wasn't asking for money anymore, but giving money back."

During his formative years in the gang, a young John Willis was literally dodging bullets as he played bodyguard for the gang's overlords. Chinatown erupted in violence between 1988 and 1992, resulting in two-dozen gangland slayings. In January 1991, the warfare reached a crescendo with the gory Tyler Street Massacre, where five people were executed in an after-hours gambling den run by the *Ping On* organization. Within six minutes of arrival, the gunmen shot six of the seven men in the Tyler Street basement in the head, execution-style, one by one as they begged for mercy.

"It was a very violent Chinatown," Willis remembers. "There were a lot of murders, a lot of stabbings, a lot of gunfights. You had to be aware of your surroundings, because if you weren't, then you'd end up dead. We had radios just like the police. We had different protocols. You were here from a certain time to a certain time, and then other guys would show up, and it was almost like punching a clock. This is your job today. You stay in the parking lot, park the cars. If you have a problem with the guys from New York, you're watching for the New York plates."

Shortly after the Tyler Street killings, a crew of gunmen pulled up and shot a *Ping On* associate standing right next to Willis when they were out collecting money. When the gunman pointed the pistol at Willis and pulled the trigger, the gun jammed. With the killing spiraling out of control, Sky Dragon took off for Hong Kong, leaving his gang to take care of his business interests. As the warfare intensified, *Ping On* continued to operate, fighting to gain control of Chinatown.

"At that time, there were different things going on in Chinatown," Willis says. "Power struggles, fights, murders, the building of an organization from where we were standing. It went basically full battle mode. You're scared, but you're not scared." Under Willis' direction, gang members would track down rivals and brutally beat them down. When asked about participating in any murders or gangland hits, Willis says, "I've never been convicted of killing anybody."

THE WHITE DEVIL BECOMES KINGPIN

As Willis advanced in the organization by proving his loyalty he'd be farmed out to affiliated Chinese gangs in different cities. This tactic worked both ways. When the drama got thick, his boss would call in guys from California or New York to handle things. If there was a situation in New York, Willis might be sent down there to take care of it. A lot of the gangs were connected through the *tongs* back in China and the American-based organizations used their soldiers interchangeably.

"When I went to New York City, or San Francisco, or somewhere, and I got there, these people didn't look at me like, 'Hey, he's a white guy,' they looked at me as, 'Hey that's John. He's from Boston. He's our people,'" recalls Willis. "They looked out for me. So I always kinda keep that in mind. I'm white, but I look after the guys that are Asian. Let's face it, they're not big people, it's not like they're running things, especially if they're not gangsters." Even though John was white he felt safe within the confines of his new adopted culture, despite the violence and dangers all around.

"You learned through that culture that you come up a certain way and whatever you derive, you take care of your people, your brothers, your family," Willis explains. "That's how I came up. At that time in my life, it was more about learning the culture and dealing with my people. I'm the type of person that if you're my brother, you're my brother." But with all the heat the feds were doing a lot of surveillance in Chinatown.

"The feds would just sit there all day. They'd switch, different guys would come in, they weren't fooling anybody. We knew. One kid's job would be to keep an eye on them, where are they, or who are they, what are they doing? They'd follow us back to Chinatown. They'd park in Chinatown at the end, over near the gate. We went about our daily business. We knew they were there; they knew we were here." Eventually things started to change in Chinatown and after several short bids in state prison Willis decided to branch out from the gang.

"Times change, people start telling. And the culture was not what the culture used to be because they got away from the way things were supposed to be," Willis says. "From China there was a pecking order. People started complaining so much about gangsters being on the streets that they lost sight of the jobs that gangsters had protecting the people walking around with all the money to the gambling houses, the old ladies walking around with their food and their purses.

"As far as the drug side of things, I didn't do that in Chinatown. My boss never wanted to sell drugs. He'd tell you straight up, 'Don't sell drugs, brings too many problems' and that's the way it was when I was a kid. I just followed what he said, but then as you grow older you step outside, and you do what you do to make money."

US Attorney Timothy Moran called John Willis "the kingpin, organizer, and leader of a vast conspiracy." The feds said Bac Guai parlayed his Asian mob contacts into a position as an oxycontin kingpin that sold over 260,000 pills in two years, generating over four million dollars in profits trafficking pills from Florida to the Northeast. Willis used the cash he made to buy a fleet of sports cars, oceanfront property in South Florida, speedboats, and strip clubs.

"The money was really good and I was young. I started selling drugs when I was 22-years-old," Willis recalls. "Twenty-two years old buying houses, cars and boats. The money influenced my decisions. I never did it in Chinatown. Never did it around any of my people. You invest money, you do different things. Do you want to get involved with importing thousands of pounds from Canada? Or do you wanna get in hundreds of pounds from California? Or do you wanna do pills? Is it drugs or prostitution? I had different investments."

Willis kept his ear to the streets as a drug dealer. "What's going on in the streets? What does the street want?" he mused. "The street wants pills, you go and get the pills. At one point it was commercial marijuana. Then it went to British Columbia and then it went to the high end stuff out of California. So you change with the times, you roll with it. We all work to make money. We all work to survive. We all look for a better life. We all become slaves to our money. Even multi-multi-millionaires, they live a certain way and then if they don't keep that income up, they go bankrupt. They fail. They lose.

"I made all the decisions. I just dictated and got people to do what they were supposed to do. My whole feeling is, because of the way I was raised, if you take care of somebody and you treat them the right way, then they're going to be honorable and do the right thing. And that's what I got out of the Chinese culture. But people don't see it that way. As far as American people, I'd say."

THE FEDS SWOOP IN

FBI agent Scott O'Donnell said he'd "never seen" a white guy in the Chinese Mafia before Willis. The federal investigation into Willis' drug dealing affairs resulted in the seizure of a 38 foot speed boat, 13 firearms, over 480,000 in cash, approximately 12,000 oxycodone pills, and numerous luxury vehicles. Willis was also into illegal gambling and prostitution operations, as well as loan sharking and extortion activities. The feds were doing stings on Asian whorehouses in Boston when Willis showed up on surveillance. The feds abandoned their stings and Willis became their focus.

"Mr. Willis and his associates are an example of the opportunistic nature of organized crime groups whose members share a common bond of victimizing their communities through drug dealing, illegal gambling, extortion, and exploitation of women in their quest for illegal profits," said Vincent Lisi, special agent in charge of the FBI's Boston

Division. "The methodical nature and duration of this investigation reflects the focus of the Boston Organized Crime Task Force to secure justice for the victims and to make the community safer."

Bac Guai's journey started in Dorchester and ended in federal prison, but he makes no excuses. "They see an American that is involved in this culture that nobody's involved in," Willis explains. "There's unanswered murders, different things. Nobody wants to talk to them. They hear about these guns. My name comes up. They come see me and I tell them I don't know what they're talking about. They feel that's a slap in the face. That's how this all started. The amount of money they seize from people. There should be no budget, no deficit, no nothing.

"Whatever the feds write about me, that's their interpretation of me. My interpretation of me is a person who's about his people, about the culture that he grew into and that's why I feel that my story is not just a gangster story. It's a story of survival. It's a story of camaraderie. It's not a drug dealer story; it's the story of a way of life, an organization. I don't think white people anywhere in the Asian culture are accepted the way I was or am. I'm grateful for that."

In 2013, Willis was convicted on federal drug and money laundering charges. He pleaded guilty out of love and loyalty to his girlfriend so that the feds wouldn't make her life any harder. He also agreed to forfeit 2 million dollars and several vehicles, boats and pieces of real estate as part of his plea deal. He was sentenced to twenty years and is now serving his time at Federal Correctional Institution Danbury, a low security prison in Connecticut.

"Twenty years in federal prison is well-deserved for Mr. Willis, a career criminal and the mastermind behind this organization," says US Attorney Carmen M. Ortiz. "Not only did this investigation expose a world of illegal gambling, prostitution, and extortion, but also revealed a significant oxycodone distribution operation. This case significantly disrupted the flow of this highly addictive, dangerous heroin substitute, which has been responsible for numerous deaths in Massachusetts."

Bac Guai takes his incarceration in stride. He's been in situations where people got murdered, situations where rival gangsters pointed their guns at him, ready to kill him only to have their guns jam. Willis has been involved in Chinese culture for so long that he considers himself Chinese. "All these things are part of the story, the struggle, the acceptance, the way of life," he says. "Do I look at myself as white? Yeah, I'm white, my DNA says I'm Caucasian. But, at the end of the day, my wife's Vietnamese, my daughter's mixed.

"I'm never going to walk away from my people. They took care of me in my life. That's kind of a vow that you make, you never ever walk away from the people that took care of you and care about you. Always honor your people. Honor your friends, your family. Respect and give loyalty to your brothers that haven't written you off. I'm not gonna change, not in that aspect." As he sits in his prison cell doing hard time in the federal penitentiary, Willis reflects on his life, who he is and what he's done, and surprisingly he's okay with it.

"This part of my life is more about the pain, the struggle that we all go through," he muses. "People think it's fun and games, and this is what you learnt, and this is what you did, and this is who you are. Survival is what we do every day. They've taken my freedom already. The things that scare me are the time away from my family. 'Cause time doesn't stop. Sure, I'm an American, but now I just say to people, inside I'm white, but outside, I'm Chinese."

WHITE DEVIL ON THE BIG SCREEN

Boston based entertainment lawyer and literary manager Matthew Valentinas, who represents John Willis, says that the book based on his client's life entitled *White Devil* by Bob Halloran has been optioned to Sony Pictures International Television and 3 Arts Entertainment by KV Media Inc. as the basis for a potential television series. Robert Kamen (*Taken*, *The Karate Kid*) is writing the script.

Valentinas states, "John's story is perfect for the screen. His personal character combined with his amazing life experience is something that's never been seen before in the gangster genre. His story is very relatable and has wide international appeal. We've received a lot of interest from Canada, China, Italy, Germany, and India. It's only a matter of time before the entire world is very familiar with the story of the White Devil."

18

WHITEY BULGER
HE PLAYED THE FEDS ... AND LOST

The world of federal gangland informants is a shadowy one that exists in subterfuge and seemingly has no rhyme or reason. Criminals play both sides of the fence in a twisted game of self-indulgence, often pleasing both their law enforcement handlers and cohorts in the streets in a double agent role. And when the indictments come out they disappear, reemerging later to testify in court, before being whisked into the witness protection program. That is the theory of a snitches existence. But it doesn't always work that way.

Because in reality, the odds are stacked against anyone working with the law as they strive to uphold their reputation in the underworld, while at the same time snitching on the men they are breaking bread and doing dirt with. Betraying the code of *omertà* gets a criminal branded with all types of labels, like a rat or a snitch, or as they call them in Boston, a "tout."

THE TOUT

Getting a jacket as a tout can ruin a gangster's criminal career before it even begins. It's a death knell to whatever street dreams they harbor. Touts are ostracized from the underworld hierarchy or even worse, killed for their betrayal of the street code. To be branded a snitch is tantamount to career suicide in the world of criminals. It's the worst thing that can happen to a potential gangster.

"Touts are the lowest form of life," relates a Boston mobster doing time in the feds and remaining anonymous as he goes through an appeals process. "No real man would sell out to avoid jail. You just do your time and get on with it. Anyway, it's character building in the long run."

But some men make the decision to forego the unspoken death before dishonor vow that pervades criminal life. They choose to betray their comrades and work with the feds. Minimizing their own exploits and putting cases on others shifts their culpability. Some are brazen enough to do it while still active in what they call "the life" or "the game". They strategically play both sides as they attempt to stay one move ahead of everyone else. It's a dangerous game they've initiated as they hover between cops and robbers.

Because in the criminal underworld there's only one rule: no snitching. When a gangster breaks the code it can lead to death, but it can also lead to the destruction of his legacy in the chronicles of gangster lore. Gangsters are romanticized in our culture but informants are despised. Becoming an informant, or a tout as they say in Boston, is a serious no-no for members of the Irish gangs that hold sway in the city.

But that didn't stop Whitey Bulger, the Irish mob boss who ruled the Irish enclaves of Boston for more than two decades. He's been immortalized in print and in film, but to those in his hometown, he's nothing more than a rat. The lowest of the low, criminal scum that has no morals. In the case of Whitey Bulger, there was no honor among thieves.

"Whitey Bulger had a long run and was king of Boston's criminal underworld for a long time," the Boston mobster says. "But he was leading a secret life. He was having his cake and eating it too. Making money, committing murders and basically doing whatever the fuck he wanted to do. While at the same time working for the FBI and feeding them information on *La Cosa Nostra*." Whitey was snitching on his competition in order to build up his own criminal empire.

"And the thing was, no one ever suspected this of Whitey," the mobster says. "He was beyond reproach. The people in Boston were terrified of him, both criminals and citizens. Everyone knew not to cross Whitey Bulger. No one ever thought he was a snitch. He carried it so hard that he was seen as the ultimate gangster." Bulger was a symbol of what the street code stood for, enforcing it at will on whoever dared to betray it.

Whitey grew up in a housing project in South Boston and was busted early in his criminal career. He was sentenced to twenty years in federal prison and even served time at the infamous Alcatraz. Whitey wasn't anyone special back then, just another Irish hooligan brought into a life of crime by circumstances, but he would become the boss of bosses in Beantown.

After that case, everyone in the town figured he was the consummate stand up guy, but it turns out he was ratting even back then. FBI and prison records show that Whitey began cooperating with law enforcement from the jump. "Bulger, after his apprehension, cooperated with this bureau," states a July 1956 FBI report. Bulger copped to what he did and informed the FBI who his accomplices were in two bank jobs they were suspected in.

But from the start, Bulger didn't want it on paper and he would never sign anything or testify in court. He felt this was his best defense against being labeled as a tout. As long as there was no proof, in his mind he didn't do it. He was playing all sides against the middle. "He made these oral admissions but insisted that it not be put in writing," said Dick Lehr, who wrote *Black Mass*, the book that the movie is based on. No paperwork to muddy his trail.

SOUTH BOSTON EXPLODES WITH VIOLENCE

"He rose to the top of a vicious underworld and managed to get away with it," says David Amorso from *gangsterinc.com*. "That's why people are so mesmerized by his story. Bulger was a violent gangster who rose to the top by all means necessary. Along the way, he broke all the rules of both the legitimate and underworld. Even manipulating the FBI—a true outlaw."

After serving nine years of the twenty he was sentenced to, he got out, went home to Boston, and set about to make his name in the city's rackets. He is alleged to have killed forty people in his lifetime, starting with the bloody Boston gang wars of the 1960's when many Southie gangsters were gunned down in the streets and seedy bars of the town, as rivals perpetuated a life and death struggle to be crowned king of Boston's underworld. But Whitey wasn't playing fair.

"He was a cheater," the Boston mobster says. "He was vicious and smart and cunning and had all the factors he needed to thrive but he took it one step further. He wanted to hedge his bets, so to speak. He wanted to ensure he would always be on the winning side."

As he was making inroads with the notorious Winter Hill Gang, he also formed a partnership with Steve "The Rifleman" Flemmi, another rising criminal who had mafia connections. The duo would blow sky high in the criminal ranks, becoming an outlaw Batman and Robin that clattered the streets of Boston like a raging tsunami. But not all things were what they seemed.

Not even ten years into his re-emergence into the criminal ranks Whitey became an FBI informant again. With Flemmi by his side in the snitch game he formed another important relationship with FBI agent John Connolly. The agent made Bulger his top-echelon informant in 1975. Due to Connolly's protection, Bulger was able to make big power moves in the criminal underworld, unmolested by law enforcement.

"Whitey could do as he pleased because he was protected by the FBI," the mobster explains. "Everyone kind of knew what was up but no one could prove it, but people were definitely talking about it. Because how else was everyone getting busted and Whitey never went to jail? He was like the Teflon Don. But the world knows now; it's because he was a tout."

FBI agent John Connolly and his immediate supervisor John Morris developed Bulger as their office's prize informant. They sold him to the FBI as a top source of valuable information on the Italian Mafia, who the FBI had their sites on. But other law enforcement agencies, including the Massachusetts State Police, didn't like the relationship Bulger had with the FBI. They were questioning the legitimacy of it even back then.

As the criminal stature of Whitey Bulger rose in the streets, so did his desire to protect his illegal rackets. He would protect them at all costs, resorting to murder, snitching, or whatever it was he had to do. On the streets he was known as a shrewd intimidator who played the thugs, drug dealers, street figures, local toughs and gangsters of Boston with equal aplomb. In the game of chess that Whitey was playing no one could fathom what his next move would be. He kept everyone off balance and the FBI in his back pocket.

SNITCH STATUS DEBATED

The legitimacy of his cooperation with the government has sparked debate and been called into questions by many quarters. It's become a convoluted picture of juxtapositions as the public decides who was really playing who. Many think that Whitey, who was a master manipulator, never gave up anything to the government and in fact used them for information to his advantage. The world wants to see everything in black and white, but sometimes that's not always the case.

"Whitey is claiming that he paid the government cash and gifts in exchange for information and protection," says Mark Silverman, a Boston mob associate and author of *Rogue Mobster*. "He claims that he gave them 'shit and got gold in return.' I've never been around any high level gangsters who didn't have contacts inside the circles of law enforcement. A rat testifies. He gets up on the stand and points the finger at the friends who cared for him his entire life."

And despite all the criticisms of Whitey, he has never done that. But the questions about Whitey being an informant remain. His 700 page FBI file and informant card gives proof that Bulger provided information on murders, drug deals, armed robberies, and criminal fugitives that led to several arrests. He also snitched on the Mafia and rival gangs, protecting only those in his inner enclave of the Winter Hill gang.

But at his latest trial, after his capture after sixteen years on the FBI's Most Wanted list, even an FBI agent questioned his legitimacy as a rat. "He said he would never testify," said Robert Fitzpatrick, a former agent who wrote the book, *Betrayal*, about his time in the FBI with John Connolly. "You can't have the head of a gang as an informant, because then you're validating the gang, you're actually part of the management process if you will."

Fitzpatrick knew that Whitey was not a legitimate snitch because as he said, "The worst thing for an Irish guy in Boston is to be a tout." Whitey's reputation was important to him and being labeled a snitch or tout was not something he could abide. He would kill to protect his secrets and he was so brutal to informants that no one would ever suspect. But usually it's the person that goes the hardest against something that has something that has the most to hide—the perfect ploy in Whitey's case. But still there are doubters.

"I think he has an irresistible narrative," said Joe Berlinger, whose documentary, *Whitey: The United States of America vs. James J. Bulger*, gives viewers an up-close look at Bulger's life story and his 2013 trial. "Here's a guy who was on top of Boston's criminal empire for twenty-five years, not even charged with so much as a traffic ticket. Whitey rises to the top of Boston's underworld, and he has a life of crime, extorting and killing his way to the top."

Whitey's M.O. is not in question. It's a given fact that he lied, cheated, and stole his way to the top of the criminal hierarchy. Nothing was out of bounds for Whitey. No crime was beyond him and killing was just another routine motion for him, a tool at his disposal. "Whitey was the devil, pure and simple," the Boston mobster says. "He had no honor, he had no scruples or morals. No loyalty. Why is he held up as a man of honor in pop culture amazes me. He is no John Gotti." But to his admirers he is the classic Irish gangster. That's why Berlinger made a film about him.

"A point permeating the film is the relationship between the notorious mobster and the FBI. The agency has long maintained that Bulger was their informant; but Bulger, who has been perversely heralded by some who said he did more good than bad for his South Boston community as the Robin Hood of Southie, claims that the reverse was true," Berlinger said. But Southie doesn't claim snitches, no matter their iconic status.

"He had an unusual relationship with the FBI," Berlinger explains. "The conventional narrative is he was an informant, and while he was an informant he was eliminating his rivals and, at the right moment, when the heat was on and he was about to be indicted, his friends in the FBI tip him off, and he goes on the lam." That is the accepted story, but just as Whitey has his detractors, he has his supporters. The filmmaker being one.

"What my movie tries to explore is some of the claims of the defense that Bulger, in fact, was not an informant, that there was evidence that demonstrates the relationship was much more corrupt," Berlinger said. And when it's pointed out that John Connolly and the FBI had hundreds of pages of documented paperwork outlining Bulger's informant status he said, "It's full of information that's not unique, where there are duplicative sources, sometimes from other informant files. The very definition of an informant file is one that is replete with unique information that directly leads to a prosecution."

The film also airs a sequence with the aforementioned FBI agent, Bob Fitzpatrick, who went to interview Bulger at his house to legitimize him as an FBI source for Connolly. "[Bulger] told me, 'I'm not an informant. I pay them for information—not the other way around,'" Fitzpatrick said in the film. "At that point, I made a mental reservation, 'What am I doing here? What's going on here?'" It seems Whitey made a lot of people feel like that.

Was it because he was playing the game on a level that most people can't even comprehend? It's no secret that he was successful at what he was doing for a long time. But in the end, he lost, so what's the difference? He will spend the rest of his days in a prison cell, but is that enough for a man who allegedly killed forty people? At eighty something, he is in his twilight years, so in reality he is not paying that high a price. Only his legacy remains and few names have resonated more or been better associated with Boston than Bulger's.

BULGER'S ARREST SHOCKS BOSTON

"Whitey is notorious for many reasons, he did time at Alcatraz, survived the Irish gang wars, corrupted J. Edgar Hoover's supposedly incorruptible FBI, became a Robin Hood figure to a South Boston neighborhood reeling from the school busing crisis of 1970," says George Hassett, the author of *Gangsters of Boston*. "But most important is the fact that his brother happened to be the most powerful man in Massachusetts for many years, State Senate President Bill Bulger. That's just an accident of birth. Whitey is not a criminal mastermind, just a bully who understood how to manipulate others."

For all his accolades he was a very well insulated and protected gangster. With Connolly on one side and his brother on the other, it's no wonder he lasted as long as he did as Boston's reigning kingpin of crime. "Whitey Bulger was better protected than any criminal," the Boston mobster says. "With the FBI on his right and a senator on his left he was untouchable. Or at least he thought he was. But karma's a bitch and what you reap, you sow. So I say rot in hell, Whitey."

Bulger's history as the leader of the Winter Hill Gang, an Irish crime family that grew out of his Southie neighborhood in Boston, is well known, as is his role as a top echelon FBI informant, who operated with lawless impunity for twenty years, under the protection of his FBI handler, Agent Connolly. The result was free reign for Bulger and top associate Stephen "The Rifleman" Flemmi.

They manipulated Boston's underworld to suit their own purposes and advance their own criminal enterprise ahead of *La Cosa Nostra's*, the feds often turning a blind eye and even encouraging the murders of rival mafia and recognized crime figures.

But when he was finally captured in 2011 and hauled back to Boston, people speculated about what card he might have up his sleeve to get out of the jam he was in. The Whitey mystique and mythology resonated thoroughly and everyone in Boston figured he had an ace in the deck and was about to pull it out. The charges were stacked against him but if there was an out, Whitey would find it.

"When Whitey was first captured, many people in Boston compared it to the Red Sox winning the World Series in 2004," Hassett says. "We couldn't believe it happened. We figured he was dead or the FBI didn't want to find him. The bombing of the Boston Marathon obviously is the big local story now, but Whitey's court appearances were still news." The media and the public were salivating at witnessing his last and greatest trick on the biggest stage of all.

"People were wondering, who can Whitey give up in the FBI? The Boston police? The state police?" Hassett says. "If he does have law enforcement corruption to reveal, most of it would be barred by the statute of limitation. If Whitey told all, could he solve any of Boston's gangland mysteries such as the Black Francis Massacre? The art heist of a Rembrandt painting at The Isabella Stewart Gardner Museum on Huntington Avenue?"

In fact Whitey didn't say much at his trial accept to mutter, "I'm not a fucking informant," when the litany of witnesses, mostly former comrades turned snitch themselves, described his relationship with law enforcement officials. "It was a great show," Hassett says about the trial that captivated Boston's and the nation's attention. Whitey's infamy was on the big stage and he didn't disappoint, posing question on top of question about his alleged cooperation with the government.

But in the end he lost and is now doing life in prison. He was able to escape his fate his whole life, but now he's paying for his crimes. Because regardless if he was a snitch or not, he was a violent and brutal criminal who turned Boston's gangland into a killing field for over two decades. He will live on in notoriety as Hollywood glorifies his legend, making him a gangster icon in the process.

Despite his jacket as a snitch, Whitey will forever be mentioned in the same breath as Al Capone, Pablo Escobar, and John Gotti, the other gangster legends of the twenty first century. That much is certain. Locked away in federal prison, the elderly Bulger has been the toast of Boston and highlight of local talk radio shows and Hollywood alumni. As he serves his time, documentaries and films like *Black Mas*s keep his name alive, romanticize his legend and add to his mythology. But to some it's a wasted effort, because in reality who wants to glorify a snitch?

POP CULTURE'S OBSESSION WITH WHITEY BULGER

The legend of Whitey Bulger has been immortalized in print, film and multimedia. Upon his return to Boston after being a fugitive for sixteen years the media couldn't get enough of him. First there was *The Departed*, which based the Jack Nicholson character off of Whitey Bulger and now there is *Black Mass*, the Johnny Depp vehicle, where he plays the celebrated Irish gangster. It's been a while since Hollywood put out a good true crime film, this might be it. Johnny Depp looks the part as Whitey Bulger and seems to have nailed this role. There's a chance this movie can go down as a classic in the genre with *The Godfather* movies, *Goodfellas,* and *Scarface.*

It's a fact that a lot of people don't like the fact that Whitey Bulger is a snitch but it seems like a lot of the best movies are based on criminals that were snitches in real life or turn into snitches during the movie. Look at *New Jack City, Blow, Donnie Brasco,* and *American Gangster.* A lot of hardcore dudes and guys in the pen serving life don't respect Whitey and rightly so. You don't portray the death before dishonor ethos when you don't really follow it, but that is the mindset in the streets. In entertainment it's a different perspective and people just want to be entertained and celebrate the mythology of a guy like Whitey. If you locked Martin Scorsese, Quentin Tarantino, and Francis Ford Coppola in the same room, it's debatable if they could come up with anything as entertaining as the real life story of Whitey Bulger. With all the twists and turns his real life is definitely stranger than fiction. And his story has generated tons of interest.

In fact everyone related to Whitey is cashing in. Numerous books by his former cohorts in crimes have appeared, including *Rat Bastards* by John "Red" Shea, *Brutal* by Kevin Weeks, *Hitman* by Howie Carr (the story of Johnny Martorano), *A Criminal and an Irishman* by Patrick Nee, and *Street Soldier* by Edward Mackenzie. The only ones without books out are Stephen "The Rifleman" Flemmi and Whitey himself. But plenty have chronicled their underworld escapades and more are soon to come. Some journalists have made a career of covering Whitey. Dick Lehr and Gerard O'Neill have written not one, but two volumes on Whitey's criminal exploits: *Black Mass* and *Whitey*. *Boston Globe* reporters Keven Cullen and Shelly Murphy, who worked under O'Neill at the paper also have a book, *Whitey Bulger: America's Most Wanted Gangster*. And there have been many others and will most likely be many more, as Whitey Bulger has remained a vivid figure and gangster icon in popular culture. John "Red" Shea, who is actually one of the only solid guys from Whitey's crew is involved in a documentary film, *Whitey Bulger: The Making of a Monster*, which Dick Lehr was also instrumental in. Plus don't forget the Joel Berlinger film, *Whitey: United States of America v. James J. Bulger*. Just like outlaw heroes from Billy the Kid to John Gotti and all those in between Whitey has been immortalized.

THEY TESTIFIED AGAINST WHITEY BULGER

When Whitey Bulger went to trial on June 12, 2013 for 32 counts of racketeering, money laundering, extortion, and weapons charges, including his complicity in 19 murders, the witnesses ready to testify against him were all his former cohorts and comrades in arms. All Bulger's partners in crime, including Patrick Nee, Kevin Weeks and John Martorano, who all authored best-selling books about their true crime exploits with Bulger and the Irish mob, testified against him. Flemmi, Bulger's former informant-in-crime, also testified against his former boss. Flemmi remains imprisoned for 10 murders, in a little know Witness Protection Program for prisoners, while Weeks and Martorano are both free after serving their sentences. Martorano admitted murdering 20 people and spent 12 years behind bars. Weeks admitted to helping Bulger and Flemmi kill five people. The feds gave out massive deals to amass more evidence against Whitey.

Not only did they have books out detailing their lives in crime with Whitey, but now they were trying to bury him under the jail. "I don't think the witnesses who've written books ever thought Whitey would be caught. The defense will use their own words against them now. It will raise many issues of witness credibility," Silverman says. "The Stevie and Whitey reunion will be a show down. A war of words with a Machiavellian undertone." The trial was all that and more. Some called it the Trial of the Century. "Departments such as the state police and DEA who tried to get Whitey and failed, due to Whitey's corrupt team of FBI agents, were eager, in their more honest moments, to see not only Whitey punished, but the FBI exposed. The FBI undermined investigations into Whitey for years, to the point where witnesses were killed," Hassett tells *Real Crime*. "It was one final reunion for the gang. The only one not there was the only one who didn't turn informant—the cop, FBI agent John Connolly." A twist of fate if there ever was one. But Connolly was Southie to the core, he didn't turn like everyone else involved with Whitey. But Whitey turned himself so how can a rat call a rat a rat?

Concerning that, David from *gangstersinc.com* says, "He played the same game and lost, so he can't start complaining now. I think it serves him right to have so many of his former crew members look him in the eyes as they share all their secrets. If we know one thing about Whitey, it's that he had no code of honor whatsoever. He was looking out for himself. Everyone else could go fuck themselves. I don't see it as a problem that all his cohorts have out books. At least they have a script to go by for the trial. It would be nice if they donated the proceeds to their victims, but I doubt that will happen. As far as breaking the code of silence, they already did that. Most of them anyway. So a book is the logical next step. Especially if there is a market. And after *The Departed* and *Black Mass*, there is a huge market for books about gangsters in Boston." So the glorification of the legend of Whitey Bulger will continue, snitch or no snitch. On August 12, 2013, he was found guilty on 31 counts, including both racketeering charges, and was found to have been involved in 11 murders. He is currently serving life in the feds.

19

PETER "BIG PETE" JAMES
GODFATHER OF THE CHICAGO OUTLAWS

Peter "Big Pete" James always wanted to be an Outlaw. When he first got involved with the Motorcycle Club in the mid-90's, they were involved in a vicious war with the Hells Angels, who were encroaching on Outlaw territory in Chicago and trying to gain a foothold in the city. A series of bombings, fights, and shootings ensued and a lot of the Outlaws that Big Pete came in under were sent to prison for their actions in the war. With the Outlaw leadership in Chicago decimated, Big Pete stepped up to the plate.

He had witnessed the devastation the war wrought to his club firsthand. And despite the bloodshed, the Hells Angels were still there. Big Pete realized they weren't going anywhere. He understood what his predecessors were trying to do, but he decided he would combat the problem with a different strategy. Big Pete was practical after all, and as the Chicago Outlaw's new boss he wanted to leave his mark on the club.

Founded in the city in 1935, the club couldn't dispel the Hells Angels because there was no unity. It was every chapter for itself and Big Pete sought to change that. He was on a mission to unite all the splintered Outlaw factions under one banner. At the same time he wanted to consolidate his power base and hold the city of Chicago, insulating himself as he solidified the Outlaws rackets. Because to Big Pete it wasn't about the individual riches he could accrue or the infamy he could achieve from his position. It was about unifying the club and being the boss of Chicago.

NOT YOUR TYPICAL BIKER

"I knew where I was going from the time I was in the eighth grade," Big Pete says. "When I was in college I was coming down the highway and two bikes came up behind me really fast and then they moved out, went around me, and it was a really cool thing to see. I read their vests and it said, "Outlaws". I kind of kept that in the back of my mind and as time went on I organized my own club. But I always wanted to be an Outlaw. I was an outlaw personally inside and I wanted to be at the top of the food chain."

Big Pete was a gangster from the jump. He used to sell contraband soda on the school bus and he knew that graduating from high school, going to college, and joining a fraternity would come back to help him later in life. Not a typical route for a biker, but Big Pete was a new age biker with old school values. He was groomed by some serious One Percenters and for him everything was pretty calculated. He knew he had leadership skills, but the thing that really made him decide his fate was when he got out of college and went to a job interview.

"I had to do a couple of aptitude tests and I sat down with the guy about a week later," recalls Big Pete. "He told me that he really liked me, but that he couldn't hire me. I was like, why not? He said because you scored off the charts for being a risk taker and you're not going to listen to anybody. And that's kind of been the whole way my life has gone. I decided then that I was strictly going to be an entrepreneur and I'll do whatever it takes to get whatever I want. that's what I did."

In college, Big Pete was a driver for his roommate's dad, a bankruptcy lawyer. All day long Big Pete would drive him around to see clients and along the route had access to this brilliant mind. He wasn't going to sit up there and listen to the music. Big Pete started asking questions and learning. He liked to get into other people's heads to see how things work. Knowledge about how people succeed was paramount to Big Pete.

"If you don't teach me something then there's no reason for me to talk to you," Big Pete relates. "I know that sounds cold, but I can look out the window and see what the weather's like. I don't like to make small talk. If you're here to teach me something great. Not to say I won't talk sports and stuff like that but I'm not one for idle conversation. If I have to ask myself why am I talking to this guy, then I'm wasting my time."

Big Pete equates it to a salesman going into the office and giving a great sales speech to the secretary. She can't make decisions, so why would he waste his time with her? He learned from a great salesman that he shouldn't talk to people that can't make decisions. It's a waste of time. Big Pete stresses that you have to talk to the guy that can make a decision if you want to succeed in life. Don't waste your breath until you're in front of that guy. This was the philosophy that Big Pete lived by and it served him well.

BORN TO BE BOSS

"Everybody makes the joke that he's playing checkers while I play chess, but in chess you have to lose pieces to win the game," Big Pete says. "You have to sacrifice pieces, but if you play the Chinese game called *Go*, you just take territory. How easy is it to take territory if I have a club that belongs to my confederation? I didn't have to give up anything. The only thing I had to do was to make sure the clubs didn't start beefing between themselves. It took a little while, like a couple of years, but eventually it got to the point, where if there was an argument or disagreement, I would sit down and monitor the meeting and we'd come to a conclusion that led to everyone being happy."

Big Pete saw the long view and recognized early on that if could unite all the various Outlaw cliques into one group, they would be unstoppable in Chicago. It was a force that couldn't be easily displaced. He realized that if he was going to be the boss, he'd have to be able to play politics in the criminal underworld. To Big Pete it was like being a rock star, you had to cross genres. "If you're a country musician you can be really successful," he says. "But to be the megastar you have to get to the people that like rock-n-roll, you have to get to the people from other genres to buy your songs."

Big Pete prescribes to the theory that when you're a boss you can't isolate yourself. "You have to be able to move within the different criminal groups and you have to have their respect or they'll say who's this, how did he get here?" the Outlaw biker says. "And it doesn't take long. You might get a seat at the table because of where you come from, like you're here because you're an Outlaw, but when you open your mouth you'll find out if you get to come to that table again. There's a fine point and a finesse point that a lot of people don't understand and that's how it goes."

Being a boss was something that Big Pete had in mind since he was a kid. He didn't know what he would be the boss of, that came later, but he knew that he would be a boss in Chicago. That was his dream, that was his goal, that was his destiny so to speak. And he fulfilled it to a degree. He'll admit that he was close to his eventual goal but was thwarted by cancer before he could see all his life's work come to fruition.

"I was close," Big Pete admits. "If I wouldn't have gotten cancer I would have pulled it off. We only got so far because some clubs were better at doing things than other clubs. But if we had another three years we could have refined the talent. Clubs were starting up and each one bought different values. Being a leader, you can't set people up to fail. If you're good at something, that's what the leader needs to find out."

Big Pete took his position seriously and studied the classics which helped him refine his leadership skills. "Most people that are leaders read Machiavelli and the prince is a pretty cool guy, but for myself I preferred Sun Tzu, *The Art of War*," Big Pete relates. "The title is kind of a misnomer, because what he says and what he teaches are philosophies that you can use in everyday life. They work. And as a leader if you don't understand these qualities or have them in you, you will fail. Look around. I can name you off more failures than successes.

"Guys out there who thought they could do this, thought they could do that. But there's an old saying, if you don't know history then you're bound to repeat it. Well that's an old one and everybody kind of chuckles, but most times it's true. If you don't understand why something is then you're hit. I used to look at things like if I'm the smartest guy in the room then I'm in the wrong room. I don't want to be the smartest guy in the room. I want to walk in the room and learn from somebody and I always did that."

ALLIED TO THE MAFIA

"There was always work supplying dancers to the strip joints," Big Pete says of the MC's relationship with Chicago's Mafia. "But you got to look at it like this, the Outlaws started in Chicago in 1935 and there was a natural progression toward each other as time went on. Now those guys back in the 30's and 40's, they weren't looking at things the same way. But then when the 60's came along, more entrepreneurial guys started looking into becoming part of motorcycle clubs and that kind of started it rolling. There were guys who had chop shops, guys who ran gambling."

Being that Chicago is Al Capone territory, outsiders would think that Big Pete idolized the Syndicate's gangster legend, but Big Pete holds another Chicago mobster in high-esteem. "One of my heroes is Tony Accardo," Big Pete says. "Accardo did it all. He took over the unions, he took over Vegas, and he never spent a day in jail. There are things that you can learn from guys like Tony Accardo. Technically he made Al Capone look like a drugstore wise guy.

"Money and things are nice, but the goal is the accomplishment. You don't need to be out there all flashy, traveling around the world. I drove late model cars. I didn't always have the flashiest bike with new paint jobs. When there were nationals or big parties, I didn't go around those parties. I didn't want to become famous among other Outlaws, because I had everything I wanted. I had the city of Chicago. That was my goal. Once you reach your goal you stop."

Working with the Mafia was nothing new for the Outlaws, but Big Pete made sure that he had the right connections that would benefit his club. "It's funny because it goes in ebbs and flows," he relates. "It all depends on who's calling the shots, where they came from, what they believe in, and how you reach out to each other. Usually it's between mutual friends, but if you don't have those mutual friends, no one is going to talk to you. No one is going to say, hey guy what do you think about this?

"It's a difficult thing to explain to someone who doesn't live in Chicago, but there's no other city that has the reputation of Chicago. I mean think about it, who's the most famous gangster out there: Al Capone. He's from Chicago. And his spirit is still in the blood of the people here. That's just how it works. In Chicago a favor is worth more than money. If you have a favor from a mob guy or an outfit guy or even a politician, you can do more with those favors then if a guy walks in with money.

"Now don't get me wrong, nobody's going to turn down money, but those favors, if you got them lined up in your pocket, or you've done things to get favors that you can call on, you're in a good position. Because there's still that honor out there. When people give you favors they'll honor them. But it works both ways. You can't just be running your mouth."

PEOPLE IN THE CLUB CHANGED

In the 90's, when Big Pete first joined the Outlaws, the bikers wearing the patch were stone cold gangsters. They lived by the gangster code. Not too many of them had nine-to-five jobs and they walked around with money in their pocket. Now, Big Pete says bikers have regular jobs and don't have any money. It's not so much the Outlaws, because the core values are still there, he stresses. It's the people and how times have changed.

"The rules and the beliefs are the same for the club," Big Pete says. "But because of the newer people that came in things have changed. If you focus on 1995 to 2015, that's a twenty year span, and the difference between those guys that took on the Angels in the 1995 versus the guys that were around when I finally left and had my falling out with is night and day."

With Big Pete being diagnosed with cancer he fell short of growing and strengthening the club even more as he wanted. He also fell out of sorts with his immediate subordinates who decided that they knew best and didn't have to listen to Big Pete anymore. There was an incident where a member of the club was disciplined and the men under Big Pete wanted to do it in public, at a function, in full view of the bikers family and even kids. Big Pete wholeheartedly disagreed. He told them it was the wrong move. But they defied him and did what they wanted anyhow.

"I believe in the saying, honor among thieves," Big Pete says. "If we're all going to be thieves, then we have to have some honor amongst ourselves. It doesn't matter what anyone else says or does. I know there are laws and rules, but I look at those like nothing more than suggestions. If I don't like them or don't believe in them, then I don't follow them.

"But there has to be honor amongst the thieves and I don't even mean that we're all thieves. It's an old saying from a long time ago. You have to have a certain amount of honor. You do not do things in front of a family. You do not do shit in front of kids. That is a fucking no-no. Whatever you want to do to the individual, which I thought was a bad idea in this case, you can't break the honor amongst thieves.

"You don't have the same type of dude that says hey you know what, these are what our beliefs are. This is what we are going to do. Those guys are gone. And I think the other thing that helped change that is just society itself. Coming through the 90's, when all the sentencing changed with longer prison terms and no parole, it changed guys' mentality. I remember a defense attorney telling me, because there were some times when there were close calls, times have changed. It used to be that guys got three, five, or seven years and everybody was stand-up, but with fifteen to thirty years, that really tested guys that didn't want to take those risks anymore."

With the stress the cancer was putting on Big Pete's body, he found he didn't have the strength to fight his brothers, so he walked away. Twenty years invested in the club and then he just left them to their own devices. But Big Pete has fond memories of his time with the club that he documented in his book, *The Last Chicago Boss: My Life With The Chicago Outlaws Motorcycle Club*, a memoir on his life and times with the M.C..

"I will say this, I had certain guys that I did certain things with," relates Big Pete of his criminal activities. "But we also had a scholarship fund, we had picnics, every summer there was a big one for all the clubs, we had an all club ride. This was like some unheard of shit. People would look at me like, 'what?' At times I would catch heat. I didn't have a boss in Chicago, but I had bosses in the club and they were like, 'What are you up to?' I would explain it to them. Sometimes they would shake their head, but they were like, 'You live there. You must know what you're doing. Go ahead. Good luck.' That's how that played out."

The dream of a united Outlaw Nation didn't pan out for Big Pete, but he's well respected for accomplishing what he did. Taking the M.C. in a different direction, solidifying the club's power base in Chicago, and holding the city with a steady hand during his twenty year reign. Big Pete says writing the book was a bittersweet process. It's frowned on by the Motorcyle Club, but Big Pete felt he was pushed into writing his story. He felt that the ideals which he and the club stood for in Chicago were being tarnished. He felt he was justified to tell his story—the true story of an Outlaw boss.

THE LINE UP

The Outlaws stormed down the highway like Viking marauders on steel steeds, always in tight formation, like fighter jets on a mission.

When Big Pete and his crew headed out on a run, they would form themselves up on the highway in a tight formation that placed bikers up and down the line according to stature. As the boss Big Pete rode at the head of the caravan next to his road captain. Traveling two abreast, the bikers would never break the speed limit—the sound of their engines attracting enough attention and scrutiny. On a run, Big Pete and his crew wouldn't carry any guns or drugs or anything like that. It wasn't if they'd get pulled over, it was when. Precautions were taken and all contraband items were stashed in the crash truck ,which some prospects usually drove. By sticking to this rigid formation on their runs Big Pete and his club could get to where they were going without any arrests.

WHO'S THE TOP DOG?

In the world of outlaw motorcycle clubs The Outlaws rank high in hierarchy with the other notable clubs like the Hells Angels, Mongols, and Bandidos, but they absorbed smaller clubs to increase their numbers.

SUPPORT CLUBS (OUTLAW SUPPORTERS)
Twisted Image M.C. led by Coyote
Loyal Order M.C. led by Papa Joe

After the success of shows like *The Sons of Anarchy*, Big Pete says there was a big jump in guys showing up at the Outlaws club house wanting to be sanctioned to fly their colors in Chicago. Groups of bikers would come in and pay their respect to Chicago's boss, looking to form alliances, so they could ride Chicago's street bearing their patch.

SATELLITE CLUBS (OUTLAW AFFILIATES)
Crossroads M.C. & New Attitude M.C.

Big Pete had clubs that were affiliated with the Outlaw Nation in Chicago. He was the guy who politicked with all the different MC's, getting everyone to cooperate for the betterment of the whole. The affiliates could be hard to work with, but Big Pete was focused to keep all the clubs under the Outlaw banner.

REGIONAL CLUBS (OUTLAW ALLIES)
The Fugarwe Tribe M.C. led by Gator
The Brothers Rising M.C. led by Gypsy

These clubs were very loyal to the Outlaws and had been allies with them for some time. Some even prospected as whole clubs for the Outlaws. Big Pete had very good relationships with these M.C.'s who backed the Outlaws on any and whatever subject.

LARGER ONE PERCENT CLUBS (OUTLAWS M.C.)

The Outlaws were founded in Chicago, and as one of the national big four One Percenter outlaw bike groups, they were at the top of the hierarchy. Big Pete did business with *mafioso*, politicians, and business owners, helping to transform the Outlaws into an international brand.

HOW BIG PETE BECAME BOSS

Big Pete joined the Outlaws in the early 1990's and shortly thereafter he was thrust into a position as boss of Chicago.

BOSSES BEING JAILED

When the Outlaws and Hells Angels became embroiled in a vicious territorial beef in Chicago in 1995, Big Pete was on the scene. As the retaliatory bombings, assaults, and shootings went tit-for-tat, Big Pete watched as all his mentors in the club and Chicago Outlaw leaders were incarcerated. This left leaving a power vacuum in the M.C., which Big Pete stepped up to fill.

THE ANGEL HUNTS

While negotiating for a truce with the Hells Angles, the first act of his tenure at Outlaw boss, Big Pete initiated Angel hunts, Where armed and ready for battle Outlaws would cruise around the city looking for Angels to jump. This helped turned the tide and forced the Angels into an agreement that Big Pete dictated.

THAT MAFIA ATTITUDE

Big Pete grew up knowing that he would be the boss of something. He studied organized crime types like Tony Accardo, amazed at how they engaged in the rackets, but never got their hands dirty, or got arrested and put in prison. Big Pete modeled himself after *mafioso* like Accardo. Knowing that that mafia attitude would help him when he became Outlaw boss.

20

POP CULTURE
HOW POP CULTURE KILLED THE MOB

Pop culture has embraced gangster themes since gangsters became newsworthy in the early twentieth century. Like anything else in life that intrigues us, perhaps frightens us, or romanticizes us, the concept of this mysterious subculture or organization called "the Mafia" piques curiosity, and that in turn draws interest, which then draws in profit-potential. Movies are a staple of pop culture trends, basically gauged on what's hot at the time and it seems themes with real life and even fictional mobsters are always a pretty safe bet for theatres to fill some seats. But has this trend in pop culture whacked the Mob and their criminal aspirations?

In its broadest sense, American culture from 1950's through the 1970's certainly set the Mob up for its fall from glory. The emergence of mass produced print media, televised organized crime hearings, a flood of books—especially inside accounts—and film adaptations has had a destructive impact on the way the Mob handled their business. From 1929's St. Valentine's Day Massacre to John Gotti's courtship with the media in the 1980's, mobsters have became a regular staple in national and even worldwide headlines. It created a lasting fanbase that worships the so-called men of honor.

THE MAFIA INVADES POP CULTURE

"Pop culture popularized the Mob, but law enforcement more than anything else killed the Mafia that once ruled so many aspects of life in New York including the Javits Center, the Fulton Fish Market, the concrete industry, the Garment District, the construction unions, and garbage carting," explains Larry McShane, the author of *Chin: The Life and Crimes of Mafia Boss Vincent Gigante*. "Breaking up those lucrative cartels made the Mob less appealing. So did the steady incarceration of mob bosses. If you're a capo, making money with a good crew, why give up the money for the headaches and near certain FBI scrutiny? Being the boss in 2017 is a long way from being the boss in 1967."

The decline of the Mafia started with the decrease in numbers of street hardened young men who were willing to risk their lives and freedom for loyalty to the outfit. Many fathers who grew up in that life steered their sons away from a life of crime. Some even got their kids into law school. A combination of factors including new anti-racketeering laws, task forces that targeted the Mob, tougher drug trafficking penalties, loss of control of the unions, and the witness security program brought a tremendous assault against the American Mafia and it was documented in the newspapers everyday.

"The attempted murder of Frank Costello in the 1950's was front page tabloid news," McShane says. "And the *Daily News* of my youth was rife with tales of Don Vito Genovese and Tommy 'Three Finger Brown' Lucchese, long before the FBI was making the Mob a priority. Things changed more within the FBI after Hoover left, with the formation of specific squads to pursue the five families. But the New York press corps for sure helped cast the bosses into the spotlight. Think about New York news anchor John Miller putting John Gotti on the nightly news."

Through that success, police and gangster stories were sold in every form of media and when the films on mobsters became big hits, it was over. Certainly there were gangster and racketeer films that preceded it, but *The Godfather* was hugely successful, as was Mario Puzo's book initially. The film combined the violence of this secretive criminal organization rooted in Sicily with beautiful elements of Italian culture such as family, food, opera, and Roman Catholicism. This juxtaposition produced an irresistible masterpiece of story that mesmerized audiences.

"When I was a boy it was *Adam 12* and *Dragnet* on TV, then *Hill Street Blues*. Then *The Sopranos* and *Boardwalk Empire*, and on and on." Rick Porrello, who wrote *Kill the Irishman—Danny Greene and the War that Crippled the Mafia*, tells *Real Crime*. "I can no longer keep track of all the crime related TV and cable series. And here we are online talking about it. Why the attraction? Human beings seem hardwired for drama. But more than that, we have a curiosity about the far reaches of society. Most of us are somewhere in the middle. We're fascinated to learn about the extremes. Violent serial criminals and secret crime society members on one hand, and wealthy and powerful celebs on the other." But once the *mafioso* had a taste of pop culture they were infatuated.

MOBSTERS CRAVING NOTORIETY

"They had already become part of popular culture thanks to Prohibition," said David Amoruso, founder of *Gangsters Inc.*, a website that covers organized crime. "They were everyone's favorite friend during those days as they supplied a popular demand. When newspapers reported on them it made the public aware of who was behind not only the murders, but who supplied the booze, the broads, and the fun bars with great entertainment."

Pop culture didn't create the Mob's problems, but the media in general certainly helped perpetuate the fascination and closer examination. Despite trying to be a secret society, the Mob gave the media plenty of material over the last century, and that kind of exposure not only sells the news, it firmly places the subject matter into the collective pop culture psyche. The public's fascination with organized crime certainly added to the many elements that bring law enforcement attention.

"The early Black Hand that preyed on its own people in the very early twentieth century were arguably one of the most secretive, though not entirely," explains Christian Cipollini, the author of *Lucky Luciano: Mysterious Tales of a Gangland Legend*. "The next wave of up and coming mobsters, circa the late 1920's, opted for ousting old school ideology and those who refused to get with the times, and joined forces with Jewish and other ethnic gangs.

"Then following the violent *coup de tat* in the early 1930's, the original five mafia families of New York were established. What was a good idea at the time later became plagued again with inter-family wars, and definitely more attention from law enforcement as more and more showboat mobsters would garner attention to organized crime. Not everybody liked staying in the shadows, some of them loved the limelight."

Many mob bosses had big egos. And no doubt there were egged on by Hollywood. It wasn't enough to just know they were mob bosses. They needed validation. Having their photos in newspaper and magazine articles or being covered on the evening news gave them celebrity status. The media coverage satisfied their huge egos. Those who courted the media spotlight made themselves easier and more attractive targets for ambitious investigators who had their own desires for validation and recognition.

"Going back to Murder Inc. in the 1930's, before the world even knew that notorious name, guys like Harry 'Pittsburgh Phil' Strauss and Martin 'Buggsy' Goldstein knew exactly how they wanted to be viewed," Cipollini says. "In 1935, while in a Brooklyn police station answering questions regarding a recent murder, a reporter walked in and mentioned to Goldstein that his name was number six on the top ten public enemies of New York. Goldstein fired back, 'That's a lousy rating. I've worked hard and hope to get a better rating than that.' While some mob guys preferred to be low key, plenty of others loved the attention that likely made them want to live up to their public image even more."

The idea of the Mob was to pretend that it never existed. As mobsters started getting courted by the media and becoming household names, it increased their risk of being caught for their illegal ventures. Becoming enamored with the attention mobsters bought into their own celebrity and started thinking of themselves as public figures. Bad news for a criminal that's supposed to be operating in the shadow world where nobody knows who they are. The Americanization of the Mafia turned them into criminal superstars who dressed to impress, gave reporters clever soundbites, and flaunted their wealth and status.

BECOMING HOUSEHOLD NAMES

"The notion of bad versus good has always intrigued the public," says Chris Chiarmonte, who runs the *Mafia Life Blog*. "Pop culture is a reflection of what can become the most popular the fastest, and of what can sell the most. The Mafia and its members became the next cowboys versus indians or cops versus robbers. They became pop culture, because the notion of that style of organized crime became sellable to a popular audience.

"If you stay in the old country pretending the Mafia does not exist, quietly working in the shadows, you are not in the spotlight. Even getting caught occasionally doesn't reveal the inner workings of a bigger organization. I am sure opening the books to create five New York factions of the Mob increased the money they made. But it also increased the risk of the inner workings being revealed. That was most likely when the public learned that the Mafia truly did exist. Which eventually led to it's demise."

The Godfather and other movies in the genre brought the Mob's world out into the open. Where once they were only known and respected by those who were a part of the underworld, now they had regular citizens and even celebrities fawning over them. Criminal organizations generally don't like media attention, but as specific individuals from the Mob became household names—Al Capone, Lucky Luciano, John Gotti, Meyer Lansky—the public, media and law enforcement latched onto these mob poster boys and ran with it.

"Perhaps Capone created the poster boy monster for himself because he was so press-friendly and visible in public," Cipollini says. "Luciano was flashy, but basically an unknown name outside of New York until Thomas Dewey went after him. Gotti liked being a gangster, and that paired with his numerous acquittals pissed law enforcement off. He essentially made himself a poster boy. These guys had a following in the public, people rooting for the perceived underdog, the rebel, the one who tells the system to fuck itself, and the fan bases of these guys wasn't something to scoff at."

"For both Al Capone and John Gotti, the media attention meant their downfall," Amoruso says. "You have movies about their exploits, books, songs, even artists naming themselves after these two guys. Capone became the government's biggest target and had to be taken down one way or another. The same with Gotti. The government went after him with all they had. The Gotti name sells newspapers and attracts viewers to the evening news. And all that attention is good for the police, FBI, and prosecutors. Once the media starts writing about you, you will have the feds knocking on your door within a month."

HOW DO THE MOVIES COMPARE?

"It's no secret that some of the more contemporary mafia members were enamored by movies such as *The Godfather*," says Cipollini. "It's said that even Al Capone owned a copy of the original *Scarface* from 1932. Lucky Luciano met with several different producers in the 1950's and 60's to discuss making a movie about his own life. Just like everybody else in the world, mob guys are people too, and it should be no surprise that some of them wanted to emulate what they saw on screen."

But the real mobsters were more extreme than any movie could ever depict. Joe Pesci's character in Martin Scorsese's *Casino* had nothing on the real life version of Anthony "The Ant" Spilotro. Pesci actually needed to tone it down to get an R rating and allow the movie to be shown. Money is the driving force with these films usually and when they dramatize, sanitize, and elaborate on real life events something is always lost, but the story is told in an engaging way that captivates the audience.

"A lot of mobsters back in the day might have tried to live up to the guys they saw on the screen," McShane says. "Who wouldn't want to be a Corleone? The based on a true story movies stay pretty close to the real thing, although there's always a bit of artistic license. In real life, Henry Hill wasn't such a great witness against the Mob as the movie makes it seem. And when the Lufthansa case came to trial in 2015, audio tapes were introduced with other mobsters griping that *Goodfellas* gave Henry too much credit for the $6 million heist.

"The end of *Donnie Brasco* implies that Lefty Guns Ruggiero gets whacked for bringing the FBI agent inside the Bonnano family, which isn't true. He was convicted and jailed, and died of cancer in 1972. *Casino* provided a great look behind the Mob's infiltration of Las Vegas, with the skim and the families outside the city waiting for their cash. The Joe Pesci character, based on "The Ant" was very realistic. But no word on what he thought of Joe's performance, since the Ant and his brother, just as in the film, were beaten and buried in an Indiana cornfield."

Movies only have two hours to tell a story spanning several years, or even decades. Hollywood likes to add its own twist to story lines and characters. Three different real life characters could be turned into one for the movie. *Donnie Brasco* is a good example of a mob movie where reality was altered to make a better movie. In real life, Joe Pistone was nowhere near dismembering the bodies of the three captains, while in the movie we see him use a saw to go through a boot. The movie just changed the plot so Lefty and Brasco seemed like two soulmates surrounded by vicious sharks.

"The original *Scarface* film is still regarded as quite profound." Cipollini says. "It was timely, featured a charming, albeit sinister protagonist, more of an anti-hero really, and was unapologetic in displaying the violence, despite many script changes demanded by studio censors. That film in particular kickstarted a trend that continues today. But in my observation, to date, there has yet to be a movie version made that scores above sixty percent accurate. Hollywood historically has at best produced entertaining, albeit totally fucking inaccurate biopics—*Bugsy* is a good example.

"At the absolute worst, they've created what I call 'historical sacrilege', an outright abomination, such as *The Untouchables*, *Mobsters*, and the 1970's *Lucky Luciano*. Even some documentaries have mangled the stories. Here's the thing, truth is stranger than fiction, and in the case of organized crime history, this shit is crazier than any screenwriter could ever come up with. They don't need to 'create' bizarre and dramatic stuff for screen, if they just did their homework they'd see the real life shit that took place is out of this world and highly entertaining to boot."

THE STATE OF THE MAFIA TODAY

"Let's face it, all of the popular mobsters became popular because more people learned who they were," Chiarmonte says. "Through media coverage of getting caught, something they did or said was put in the newspaper, or they were turned into a character for pop culture to either root for against. Exposure of any kind in the Mafia business is a bad thing. It definitely hurt and hindered criminal activities. More people watching what you do means eventually getting caught. Guys like Gotti, who almost encouraged the spotlight, nearly doubled or tripled the eye balls on the Mob, which only fast fowarded the inevitable demise of the Mob."

After the Mafia was exposed as an entity in the Kefauver and McClellan hearings in the 1950's, TV and movie producers created a glorified version of the Mob for entertainment purposes. From the very moment the public learned the Mob was real, it was under major scrutiny. Scrutiny brought not only curiosity, but law enforcement attention. Years and years of mafia investigations led to the feds getting better tools and training to catch the bad guy. Time was not on the Mafia's side. Technology would only increase the governments chances of blowing the Mob up.

"I honestly think the Mafia never stood a chance once exposed," Chiarmonte says. "The US Government slowly worked ever advancing technology to their benefit. They slowly evolved litigation and laws to make it impossible for the Mob to do what it does best. DNA, The RICO act, and the way law enforcement organized itself against the Mob was the true cause of the murder of the Mob. Pop culture played its role in pushing it closer to the finish line, but they were doomed regardless of whether it made the mainstream or not. You cannot take on the US Government and win."

In the 1970's and even 1980's the chance of getting caught for a crime nobody witnessed was slim and rare. The notion that all you needed to do was not be seen and get rid of the body was powerful. That's how the Mafia flexed their muscles. People just vanished or turned up murdered with a canary in their mouth. Everybody knew that John Gotti made the guy who killed his son in a car accident disappear, but nobody could prove it. Some way or somehow that has been romanticized and glorified, but the truth of the matter remains that the feds took away the Mafia's power by turning them on themselves. Pop culture got them walking around like peacocks and then the feds knocked them off.

"I will always measure differences in the Mob's influence based on law enforcement ability," Chiarmonte says. "And back in the Mobs' heyday the laws were different. No RICO meant that getting caught came with a two, five, seven, or maybe ten year bid. So doing your time without snitching was easier. Guys from the 70's and 80's told cops to fuck off, and did their five years. But, with RICO a guy was looking at twenty to life. A lot of men honor told on their friends to get five years. And nowadays, if you fart at the scene of a crime, law enforcement most likely knows who farted."

With the Mafia being thrust into the forefront of out national consciousness they've become as much a part of the pop culture landscape as Madonna or Donald Trump. Their popularity has hastened their demise by bringing unwanted attention to their real life crime exploits. Life isn't a movie and mobsters, even though they think they are playing a gangster role, aren't actors. Because at the end of the day they're not walking off of a film set, they are swimming with the fishes or doing life in the slammer.

Vito Corleone has gone down in the annals of pop culture lore as the baddest Hollywood *mafioso* ever. Marlon Brando played the role sublimely, but he got a lot of his notes for the character by studying the mannerisms of mafia boss Giuseppe "Joe" Profaci, who led what is known today as the Colombo family.

DRESSED TO IMPRESS

The early bosses like Joe Profaci were sharp dressers in a classy kind of way and Vito Corleone emulated this in the film. Turning the *mafioso* into a man of honor.

BODY STYLE

Both the fictional don and the real one were heavy set and stoic men. Their size and girth gave them powerful images.

MANNERISMS

With an air of detachment and authority, Marlon Brando perfectly replicated how the mafia don carried himself. Heavy is the head that wears the crown.

THE HANDS

Surprisingly the actors hands matched the mafia bosses. Strong, powerful and well worn. Speaking of men who are not above physical labor or killing someone with their bare hands.

THE HAIRSTYLE

Slicked back, cut close to the head, thinning a little at the front, Brando goes for the conservative look with his hair, matching the mafia boss Joe Profaci, whose hair was thinning out rapidly.

POSTURE

With an upright posture the mafia boss was not afraid to stand out in a crowd. And among mob cutthroats this made him a leader of men, a posture that Don Vito emulates in *The Godfather*.

A SECRET SOCIETY IN THE PUBLIC EYE

The Mafia was introduced to America by Sicilian immigrants who brought the secret society with them to New York.

In the chronicles of gangster lore some mafioso seemed to forget that the Mafia was a secret society designed to enrich and empower the men pulling the strings rather than fodder for the gossip columns. But the New York media, in a lot of ways, changed things for the mob bosses by turning made men into newsmakers. Competing papers in the city were all looking for something splashy to cover and kept upping the ante and portraying mob bosses as criminal celebrities.

Crime stories have always been popular, but with television the Mafia in the media seemed to take on a life of its own and the organization that largely operated in the shadows of American society, ever since Prohibition, was put on blast. It was big drama for the public to witness these accused mob bigwigs, mostly Sicilian and Jewish immigrants or their first generation of offspring, being grilled by senators and chased by the FBI. The gangster, especially the *La Cosa Nostra* member, was romanticized and for some, the lines between good and bad were blurred.

THE ART OF IMITATING A GANGSTER

Is it art imitating life or vice versa? In the case of gangsters it goes both ways.

1932

Actor George Raft played in the 1932 version of *Scarface*. He was a childhood friend of New York City Irish mob legend Owney Madden. He worked as the gangster's driver and personal confident before he became an actor and went on to play many *mafioso* roles.

1971

In the 1971 film, *The Gang That Couldn't Shoot Straight*, actor Jerry Orbach played "Kid Sally Palumbo," a role loosely based on Crazy Joe Gallo from the Colombo crime Ffmily. Gallo took offense at the inept mobster that the Palumbo role portrayed. He felt it was demeaning and confronted Orbach. This led to a friendship with the actor and his wife that included their circle of of writer and actor friends like Joan Hackett, David Steinberg and Peter Stone.

1972

In *The Godfather*, actor Lenny Montana played the infamous mob enforcer Luca Brasi. The six-foot-six, 300 pound wrestler turned actor was in a sense playing himself. He acted as a bodyguard and enforcer for the Colombo crime family in the 1970's.

1980's

Frank Sinatra's ties to the mob have been well publicized. But one time Frank stood up John Gotti for a dinner before a performance at Carnegie Hall. Old Blue Eyes had promised a backstage dinner before the show but begged off due to sickness. Then Gotti saw him eating at the Savoy Grill and sent his enforcer to threaten Sinatra. The enforcer told Sinatra, "The next time you stand John up for a date my face will be the last one you see."

1990

In *Goodfellas*, actor Tony Darrow, real name Anthony "Tony" Borgese, was cast as Sonny Bunz, the nightclub owner. Tony was quoted in the *New York Post* saying how he grew up in Brooklyn, his dad was connected and he knew John Gotti and all those guys. Borgese pleaded guilty to extortion conspiracy and is expected to serve between 33 to 41 months in prison when he is sentenced.

1999

In *Analyze This*, actor Robert De Niro played the murderous gangster Paul Vitti. A role that he researched by hanging out with Gambino family *mafioso*, Anthony "Fat Andy" Ruggiano. De Niro wanted to sit down with the mafia killer and take notes for his Paul Vitti role.

When *The Sopranos* debuted on HBO in 1999 the man who played Paul "Paulie Walnuts" Gualtieri was real life mob associate Tony Sirico who had a rap sheet as long as his IMDB credits are now. A product of Bensonhurst, Brooklyn Tony has 28 arrests and two prison terms on his resume. He had the chops for the role.

OTHER WORKS BY SETH FERRANTI

Street Legends vol. 1

Street Legends vol. 2

Prison Stories

The Dope Game—Misadventures of Fat Cat & Pappy Mason

The Supreme Team: The Birth of Crack and Hip-Hop, Prince's Reign of Terror and the Supreme/50 Cent Beef Exposed

Washington DC Hitman - Wayne "Silk" Perry

Rayful Edmond: Washington DC's Most Notorious Drug Lord

The Ambassador of Chocolate City - Michael "Fray" Salters

Cocaine Tales: Vol 1: The Story of Brian "Waterhead Bo" Bennett

Cocaine Tales: Vol. 2: Iron City Drug Game Tales

Junior Black Mafia—Aaron Jones

Puerto Rican James Bond—George "Boy George" Rivera

Crack, Rap, and Murder: The Cocaine Dreams of Alpo and Rich Porter (Street Legends Book 6)

B-More Drug Lord—Anthony Jones

Street Kings of Miami—Boobie Boys

The New World of Islam—Muslim Gangsters

B-More Legend - Peanut King

Sex, Money, Murder—Peter "Pistol Pete" Rollock

The Short North Posse - Ohio Gangsters

American Gangster—Kenneth "Supreme" McGriff

The Black Godfather - Frank Matthews

Gorilla Convict: The Prison Writings of Seth Ferranti

ABOUT THE AUTHOR

When Seth Ferranti received a twenty-five year LSD kingpin conviction, after faking his suicide and landing on the US Marshals Top-15 Most Wanted list in 1993, he thought his life was over. As a first time, non-violent offender, the lengthy sentence attracted media attention from *The Washington Post, Rolling Stone, The Washington Times*, and others. But despair soon turned to drive as Seth embarked to rise above his past and focus on his future. Ferranti started penning prison and gangster stories for *VICE, Don Diva, FEDS, Hoopshype* and others from the cellblock. He went on to get three college degrees, start a publishing house Gorilla Convict, and write 22 books from behind the walls.

Released in 2015, Ferranti continued his writing career as a journalist penning pieces for *VICE, OZY, The Daily Beast, Dazed, MERRY JANE*, and features for *Penthouse* and *Real Crime Magazines*, among others. He also started writing and publishing comic books under his imprint GR1ND Studios and embarked on his true passion, filmmaking. Fresh out of prison, Ferranti wrote and directed a web-series, *Easter Bunny Assassin*, played the antagonist in an indie feature, *Dog Days*, and joined forces with Shawn Rech and Transitions Studios to make *WHITE BOY,* a feature documentary on Richard Wershe Jr. that is now airing on Netflix. Seth also starred in the season one finale of *VICE's "I Was A Teenage Felon"*. He currently has five films in production.

www.sethferranti.com

Subscribe to the Gorilla Convict
mailing list at www.gorillaconvict.com

www.ingramcontent.com/pod-product-compliance
Lightning Source LLC
Chambersburg PA
CBHW051922160426
43198CB00012B/2007